# FAMILY LAW STATUTES, TREATIES AND LEGISLATIVE MODELS

Selected and Edited by

WALTER WADLINGTON

James Madison Professor of Law
University of Virginia

Westbury, New York
THE FOUNDATION PRESS, INC.
1995

*TEXT IS PRINTED ON 10% POST
CONSUMER RECYCLED PAPER*

# FOREWORD

The burgeoning amount of family law material makes it necessary for teachers to choose selectively from among often lengthy statutes and legislative models that might be used effectively in their courses. The number of international treaties and conventions on family law has led to further choices. This Supplement was designed to augment the basic materials in various family law courses and seminars, as well as offerings in the field of children and the law. The material reflects the breadth of both national and international activity, the increasing complexity of legislation, and the growing federal involvement in family law matters in the United States.

The text is divided into four parts: Uniform Laws, Federal Laws, Treaties and Implementing Legislation, and State Laws. Some materials have been selectively edited, with ellipses or italicized notes indicating this. Comments to Uniform Laws have been omitted without specific indication.

I wish to express my appreciation to the National Conference of Commissioners on Uniform State Laws for their permission to reprint selected Uniform Laws and Comment.

Walter Wadlington

Charlottesville, Virginia
May 1, 1995

# TABLE OF CONTENTS

# TABLE OF CONTENTS

# PART I. UNIFORM LAWS

## UNIFORM ADOPTION ACT (1994)

*[Reprinted with permission from the National Council of Commissioners on Uniform State Laws.]*

### [ARTICLE] 1. GENERAL PROVISIONS

**§ 1-101. DEFINITIONS.** In this [Act]:

(1) "Adoptee" means an individual who is adopted or is to be adopted.

(2) "Adult" means an individual who has attained 18 years of age.

(3) "Agency" means a public or private entity, including the Department, that is authorized by the law of this State to place individuals for adoption.

(4) "Child" means a minor or adult son or daughter, by birth or adoption.

(5) "Court", with reference to a court of this State, means the [designate] court.

(6) "Department" means the [Department of Social Services, or Health Services, or Children's Services.]

(7) "Guardian" means an individual, other than a parent, appointed by a court under [applicable law] as general guardian or guardian of the person of a minor.

(8) "Legal custody" means the right and duty to exercise continuing general supervision of a minor as authorized by law.

(9) "Minor" means an individual who has not attained 18 years of age.

(10) "Parent" means an individual who is legally recognized as a mother or father or whose consent to the adoption of a minor is required under section 2-401(a)(1). The term does not include an individual whose parental relationship to a child has been terminated judicially or by operation of law.

(11) "Person" means an individual, corporation, limited liability company, business trust, estate, trust, partnership, association, agency, joint venture, government, governmental subdivision or instrumentality, public corporation, or any other legal or commercial entity.

(12) "Physical custody" means the physical care and supervision of a minor.

(13) "Place for adoption" means to selective a prospective adoptive parent for a minor and transfer physical custody of the minor to the prospective adoptive parent.

(14) "Relative" means a grandparent, great grandparent, sibling, first cousin, aunt, uncle, great-aunt, great-uncle, niece, or nephew of an individual by the whole or the half blood, affinity, or adoption. The term does not include an individual's stepparent.

(15) "Relinquishment" means the voluntary surrender to an agency by a minor's parent or guardian, for purposes of the minor's adoption, of the rights of the parent or guardian with respect to the minor, including legal and physical custody of the minor.

(16) "State" means a State of the United States, the District of Columbia, the Commonwealth of Puerto Rico, or any territory or insular possession subject to the jurisdiction of the United States.

(17) "Stepparent" means an individual who is the spouse or surviving spouse of a parent of a child but who is not a parent of the child.

§ 1-102.  WHO MAY ADOPT OR BE ADOPTED.  Subject to this [Act], any individual may adopt or be adopted by another individual for the purpose of creating the relationship of parent and child between them.

§ 1-103.  NAME OF ADOPTEE AFTER ADOPTION.  The name of an adoptee designated in a decree of adoption takes effect as specified in the decree.

§ 1-104.  LEGAL RELATIONSHIP BETWEEN ADOPTEE AND ADOPTIVE PARENT AFTER ADOPTION.  After a decree of adoption becomes final, each adoptive parent and the adoptee have the legal relationship of parent and child and have all the rights and duties of that relationship.

§ 1-105.  LEGAL RELATIONSHIP BETWEEN ADOPTEE AND FORMER PARENT AFTER ADOPTION.  Except as otherwise provided in section 4-102, after a decree of adoption becomes final:

(1) the legal relationship of parent and child between each of the adoptee's former parents and the adoptee terminates, except for a former parent's duty to pay arrearages for child support; and

(2) a prior court order for visitation or communication with an adoptee terminates.

§ 1-106.  OTHER RIGHTS OF ADOPTEE.  A decree of adoption does not affect any right or benefit vested in the adoptee before the decree becomes final.

§ 1-107.  PROCEEDINGS SUBJECT TO INDIAN CHILD WELFARE ACT.  A proceeding under this [Act] which pertains to an Indian child, as defined in the Indian Child Welfare Act, 25 U.S.C. §§ 1901 et seq., is subject to that Act.

**§ 1-108. RECOGNITION OF ADOPTION IN ANOTHER JURISDICTION.** A decree or order of adoption issued by a court of any other State which is entitled to full faith and credit in this State, or a decree or order of adoption entered by a court or administrative entity of another country acting pursuant to that country's law or to any convention or treaty on intercountry adoption law which the United States has ratified, has the same effect as a decree or order of this State. The rights and obligations of the parties as to matters within the jurisdiction of this State must be determined as though the decree or order were issued by a court of this State.

[ARTICLE] 2. ADOPTION OF MINORS
[PART] I. PLACEMENT OF MINOR FOR ADOPTION

**§ 2-101. WHO MAY PLACE MINOR FOR ADOPTION.**

(a) The only persons who may place a minor for adoption are:

(1) a parent having legal and physical custody of the minor, as provided in subsections (b) and (c);

(2) a guardian expressly authorized by the court to place the minor for adoption;

(3) an agency to which the minor has been relinquished for purposes of adoption; or

(4) an agency expressly authorized to place the minor for adoption by a court order terminating the relationship between the minor and the minor's parent or guardian.

(b) Except as provided in subsection (c), a parent having legal and physical custody of a minor may place the minor for adoption, even if the other parent has not executed a consent or relinquishment or the other parent's relationship to the minor has not been terminated.

(c) A parent having legal and physical custody of a minor may not place the minor for adoption if the other parent has legal custody or a right of visitation with the minor and the parent's whereabouts are known, unless the other parent agrees in writing to the placement or, before the placement, the parent sends notice by certified mail to the other parent's last known address that the parent intends to place the child for adoption.

(d) An agency authorized under this [Act] to place a minor for adoption may place the minor for adoption, even if only one parent has executed a relinquishment or has had his or her parental relationship to the minor terminated.

**§ 2-102. DIRECT PLACEMENT FOR ADOPTION BY PARENT OR GUARDIAN.**

(a) A parent or guardian authorized to place a minor directly for adoption may place the minor only with a prospective adoptive parent for whom a favorable preplacement evaluation has been prepared pursuant to sections 2-201 through 2-206 or for whom a preplacement evaluation is not required under section 2-201(b) or (c).

(b) A parent or guardian shall personally select a prospective adoptive parent for the direct placement of a minor. Subject to the direct limitations of [Article] 7, the parent or guardian may be assisted by another person, including a lawyer, health-care provider, or agency, in locating a prospective adoptive parent or transferring legal or physical custody of the minor to that individual.

(c) A prospective adoptive parent shall furnish a copy of the preplacement evaluation to the parent or guardian and may provide additional information requested by the parent or guardian. The evaluation and any additional information must be edited to exclude identifying information, except that information identifying a prospective adoptive parent need not be edited if that individual agrees to its disclosure. Subject to the limitations of [Article] 7, a prospective adoptive parent may be assisted by another person in locating a minor who is available for adoption.

(d) If a consent to a minor's adoption is not executed at the time the minor is placed for adoption, the parent or guardian who places the minor shall furnish to the prospective adoptive parent a signed writing stating that the transfer of physical custody is for the purposes of adoption and that the parent or guardian has been informed of the provisions of this [Act] relevant to placement for adoption, consent, relinquishment, and termination of parental rights. The writing must authorize the prospective adoptive parent to provide medical and other care and support for the minor pending the execution of the consent within a time specified in the writing, and the prospective adoptive parent shall acknowledge in a signed writing responsibility for the minor's medical and other care and support and for returning the minor to the custody of the parent or guardian if the consent is not executed within the time specified.

(e) A person who provides services with respect to direct placements for adoption shall furnish to an individual who inquires about the person's services a written statement of the person's services and a schedule of fees.

## § 2-103. PLACEMENT FOR ADOPTION BY AGENCY.

(a) An agency authorized to place a minor for adoption shall furnish to an individual who inquires about its services a written statement of its services, including the agency's procedure for selecting a prospective adoptive parent for a minor, and a schedule of fees.

(b) An agency that places a minor for adoption shall furnish to the prospective adoptive parent a written authorization to provide medical and other care and support for the minor pending entry of a decree of adoption, and the prospective adoptive parent shall acknowledge in a signed writing responsibility for the minor's medical and other care and support.

(c) Upon request by a parent who has relinquished a minor child pursuant to Part 4, the agency shall promptly inform the parent as to whether the minor has been placed for adoption, whether a petition for adoption has been granted, denied, or withdrawn, and, if the petition was not granted, whether another placement had been made.

## SECTION 2-104. PREFERENCES FOR PLACEMENT WHEN AGENCY PLACES MINOR.

(a) An agency may place a minor for adoption only with an individual for whom a favorable preplacement evaluation has been prepared pursuant to Sections 2-201 through 2-206. Placement must be made in the following order:

(1) if the agency has agreed to place the minor with a prospective adoptive parent selected by the parent or guardian, the individual selected by the parent or guardian;

(2) an individual selected by the agency in accordance with the best interest of the minor.

(b) In determining best interest under subsection (a)(2), the agency shall consider the following individuals in order of preference:

(1) an individual who has previously adopted a sibling of the minor and who makes a written request to adopt the minor;

(2) an individual with characteristics requested by a parent or guardian, if the agency agrees to comply with the request and locates the individual within a time agreed to by the parent or guardian and the agency;

(3) an individual who has had physical custody of the minor for six months or more within the preceding 24 months or for half of the minor's life, whichever is less, and makes a written request to adopt the minor;

(4) a relative with whom the minor has established a positive emotional relationship and who makes a written request to adopt the minor; and

(5) any other individual selected by the agency.

(c) Unless necessary to comply with a request under subsection (b)(2), an agency may not delay or deny a minor's placement for adoption solely on the basis of the minor's race, national origin, or ethnic background. A guardian ad litem of a minor or an individual with a favorable preplacement evaluation who makes a written request to an agency to adopt the minor may maintain an action or proceeding for equitable relief against an agency that violates this subsection.

(d) If practicable and in the best interest of minors who are siblings, an agency shall place siblings with the same prospective adoptive parent selected in accordance with subsections (a) through (c).

(e) If an agency places a minor pursuant to subsection (a)(2), an individual described in paragraph (b)(3) may commence an action or proceeding within 30 days after the placement to challenge the agency's placement. If the individual proves by a preponderance of the evidence that the minor has substantial emotional ties to the individual and that an adoptive placement of the minor with the individual would be in the best interest of the minor, the court shall place the minor with the individual.

**SECTION 2-105. RECRUITMENT OF ADOPTIVE PARENTS BY AGENCY.** An agency receiving public funds pursuant to Title IV-E of the federal Adoption Assistance and Child Welfare Act, 42 U.S.C. 670 et seq., or pursuant to the [State's adoption subsidy program], shall make a diligent search for and actively recruit prospective adoptive parents for minors in the agency's custody who are entitled to funding from those sources and who are difficult to place for adoption because of a special need as described in [the applicable law on minors with special needs]. The Department shall prescribe the procedure for recruiting prospective adoptive parents pursuant to this section.

**SECTION 2-106. DISCLOSURE OF INFORMATION ON BACKGROUND.**

(a) As early as practicable before a prospective adoptive parent accepts physical custody of a minor, a person placing the minor for adoption shall furnish to the prospective adoptive parent a written report containing all of the following information reasonably available from any person who has had legal or physical custody of the minor or who has provided medical, psychological, educational, or similar services to the minor:

(1) a current medical and psychological history of the minor, including an account of the minor's prenatal care, medical condition at birth, any drug or medication taken by the minor's mother during pregnancy, any subsequent medical, psychological, or psychiatric examination and diagnosis, any physical, sexual, or emotional abuse suffered by the minor, and a record of any immunizations and health care received while in foster or other care;

(2) relevant information concerning the medical and psychological history of the minor's genetic parents and relatives, including any known disease or hereditary predisposition to disease, any addiction to drugs or alcohol, the health of the minor's mother during her pregnancy, the health of each parent at the minor's birth; and

(3) relevant information concerning the social history of the minor and the minor's parents and relatives, including:

(i) the minor's enrollment and performance in school, results of educational testing, and any special educational needs;

(ii) the minor's racial, ethnic, and religious background, tribal affiliation, and a general description of the minor's parents;

(iii) an account of the minor's past and existing relationship with any individual with whom the minor has regularly lived or visited;

(iv) the level of educational and vocational achievement of the minor's parents and relatives and any noteworthy accomplishments;

(4) information concerning a criminal conviction of a parent for a felony, a judicial order terminating the parental rights of a parent, and a proceeding in which the parent was alleged to have abused, neglected, abandoned, or otherwise mistreated the minor, a sibling of the minor, or the other parent;

(5) information concerning a criminal conviction or delinquency adjudication of the minor; and

(6) information necessary to determine the minor's eligibility for state or federal benefits, including subsidies for adoption and other financial, medical, or similar assistance.

(b) Before a hearing on a petition for adoption, the person who placed a minor for adoption shall furnish to the prospective adoptive parent a supplemental written report containing information required by subsection (a) which was unavailable before the minor was placed for adoption, but becomes reasonably available to the person after the placement.

(c) The court may request that a respondent in a proceeding under Article 3, Part 5, supply the information required by this section.

(d) A report furnished under this section must indicate who prepared the report and, unless confidentiality has been waived, be edited to exclude the identity of any individual who furnished information or about whom information is reported.

(e) Information furnished under this section may not be used as evidence in any civil or criminal proceeding against an individual who is the subject of the information.

(f) The Department shall prescribe forms designed to obtain the specific information sought under this section and shall furnish the forms to a person who is authorized to place a minor for adoption or who provides services with respect to placements for adoption.

**SECTION 2-107. INTERSTATE PLACEMENT.** An adoption in this State of a minor brought into this State from another State by a prospective adoptive parent, or by a person who places the minor for adoption in this State, is governed by the laws of this State, including this [Act] and the Interstate Compact on the Placement of Children.

**SECTION 2-108. INTERCOUNTRY PLACEMENT.** An adoption in this State of a minor brought into this State from another country by a prospective adoptive parent, or by a person who places the minor for adoption in this State, is governed by this [Act], subject to any convention or treaty on intercountry adoption which the United States has ratified and any relevant federal law.

## [PART] 2. PREPLACEMENT EVALUATION

### SECTION 2-201. PREPLACEMENT EVALUATION REQUIRED.

(a) Except as otherwise provided in subsections (b) and (c), only an individual for whom a favorable written preplacement evaluation has been prepared may accept custody of a minor for purposes of adoption. An evaluation is favorable if it contains a finding that the individual is suited to be an adoptive parent, either in general or for a particular minor, and it is completed or brought current within the 18 months next preceding a placement of a minor with the individual for adoption.

(b) A court may waive the requirement of a preplacement evaluation for good cause shown, but an individual who is the subject of a waiver must be evaluated during the pendency of a proceeding for adoption.

(c) A preplacement evaluation is not required if a parent or guardian places a minor directly with a relative of the minor for purposes of adoption, but an evaluation of the relative is required during the pendency of a proceeding for adoption.

### SECTION 2-202. PREPLACEMENT EVALUATOR.

(a) A preplacement evaluation may be prepared only by an individual qualified by [a state-approved licensing, certifying, or other procedure] to make the evaluation.

(b) An agency from which an individual is seeking to adopt a minor may require the individual to be evaluated by its own qualified employee or independent contractor, even if the individual has received a favorable preplacement evaluation from another qualified evaluator.

### SECTION 2-203. TIMING AND CONTENT OF PREPLACEMENT EVALUATION.

(a) An individual requesting a preplacement evaluation need not have located a prospective minor adoptee when the request is made, and the individual may request more than one evaluation.

(b) A preplacement evaluation must be completed within 45 days after it is requested. An evaluator shall give priority to a request from an individual who has located a prospective adoptee.

(c) A preplacement evaluation must be based upon a personal interview and visit at the residence of the individual being evaluated, personal interviews with others who know the individual and may have information relevant to the evaluation, and the information required by subsection (d).

(d) A preplacement evaluation must contain the following information about the individual being evaluated:

(1) age and date of birth, nationality, racial or ethnic background, and any religious affiliation;

(2) marital status and family history, including the age and location of any child of the individual and the identity of and relationship to anyone else living in the individual's household;

(3) physical and mental health, and any history of abuse of alcohol or drugs;

(4) educational and employment history and any special skills;

(5) property and income, including outstanding financial obligations as indicated in a current credit report or financial statement furnished by the individual;

(6) any previous request for an evaluation or involvement in an adoptive placement and the outcome of the evaluation or placement;

(7) whether the individual has been subject to a restraining order for, or charged with, domestic violence, charged with a violation of [the State's child protection statute] listed on [the State's child abuse or neglect registry], and the disposition of the charges, or subject to a court order restricting the individual's right to custody or visitation with a child;

(8) whether the individual has been convicted of a crime other than a minor traffic violation;

(9) whether the individual has located a parent interested in placing a minor with the individual for adoption and, if so, a brief description of the parent and the minor; and

(10) any other fact or circumstance that may be relevant in determining whether the individual is suited to be an adoptive parent, including the quality of the environment in the home and the functioning of other children in the individual's household.

(e) An individual being evaluated must submit to fingerprinting and sign a release permitting the evaluator to obtain from an appropriate law enforcement agency any record indicating that the individual has been convicted of a crime other than a minor traffic violation.

(f) An individual being evaluated shall, at the request of the evaluator, sign any release necessary for the evaluator to obtain information required by subsection (d)

### SECTION 2-204. DETERMINING SUITABILITY TO BE ADOPTIVE PARENT.

(a) An evaluator shall assess the information required by Section 2-203 to determine whether it raises a specific concern that placement of any minor, or a particular minor, in the home of the individual would pose a significant risk of harm to the physical or psychological well-being of the minor.

(b) If an evaluator determines that the information assessed does not raise a specific concern, the evaluator shall find that the individual is suited to be an adoptive parent. The evaluator may comment about any factor that in the evaluator's opinion makes the individual suited in general or for a particular minor.

(c) If an evaluator determines that the information assessed does raise a specific concern, the evaluator, on the basis of the original or any further investigation, shall find that the individual is or is not suited to be an adoptive parent. The evaluator shall support the finding with a written explanation.

### SECTION 2-205. FILING AND COPIES OF PREPLACEMENT EVALUATION.

(a) If a preplacement evaluation contains a finding that an individual is suited to be an adoptive parent, the evaluator shall give the individual a signed copy of the evaluation. At the individual's request, the evaluator shall furnish a copy of the evaluation to a person authorized under this [Act] to place a minor for adoption and, unless the individual requests otherwise, edit the copy to exclude identifying information.

(b) If a preplacement evaluation contains a finding that an individual is not suited to be an adoptive parent of any minor, or a particular minor, the evaluator shall immediately give a signed copy of the evaluation to the individual and to the Department. The Department shall retain for 10 years the copy and a copy of any court order concerning the evaluation issued pursuant to Section 2-206 or 2-207.

(c) An evaluator shall retain for two years the original of a completed or incomplete preplacement evaluation and a list of every source for each item of information in the evaluation.

(d) An evaluator who conducted an evaluation in good faith is not subject to civil liability for anything contained in the evaluation.

### SECTION 2-206. REVIEW OF EVALUATION.

(a) Within 90 days after an individual receives a preplacement evaluation with a finding that he or she is not suited to be an adoptive parent, the individual may petition a court for review of the evaluation.

(b) If the court determines that the petitioner has failed to prove suitability by a preponderance of the evidence, it shall order that the petitioner not be permitted to adopt a minor and shall send a copy of the order to the Department to be retained with the copy of the original evaluation. If, at the time of the court's determination, the petitioner has custody of a minor for purposes of adoption, the court shall make an appropriate order for the care and custody of the minor.

(c) If the court determines that the petitioner has proved suitability, the court shall find the petitioner suitable to be an adoptive parent and the petitioner may commence or continue a proceeding for adoption of a minor. The court shall send a copy of its order to the Department to be retained with the copy of the original evaluation.

**SECTION 2-207. ACTION BY DEPARTMENT.** If, before a decree of adoption is issued, the Department learns from an evaluator or another person that a minor has been placed for adoption with an individual who is the subject of a preplacement evaluation on file with the Department containing a finding of unsuitability, the Department shall immediately review the evaluation and investigate the circumstances of the placement and may request that the individual return the minor to the custody of the person who placed the minor or to the Department. If the individual refuses to return the minor, the Department shall immediately commence an action or proceeding to remove the minor from the home of the individual pursuant to [the State's child protection statute] and, pending a hearing, the court shall make an appropriate order for the care and custody of the minor.

## [PART] 3. TRANSFER OF PHYSICAL CUSTODY OF MINOR BY HEALTH-CARE FACILITY FOR PURPOSES OF ADOPTION

**SECTION 2-301. "HEALTH-CARE FACILITY" DEFINED.** In this Part, "health-care facility" means a hospital, clinic, or other facility authorized by this State to provide services related to birth and neonatal care.

**SECTION 2-302. AUTHORIZATION TO TRANSFER PHYSICAL CUSTODY.**

(a) A health-care facility shall release a minor for the purpose of adoption to an individual or agency not otherwise legally entitled to the physical custody of the minor if, in the presence of an employee authorized by the health-care facility, the woman who gave birth to the minor signs an authorization of the transfer of physical custody.

(b) The attending practitioner or authorized employee in whose presence the authorization required under this section is signed shall attest the signing in writing.

**SECTION 2-303. REPORTS TO DEPARTMENT.**

(a) No later than 72 hours after a release pursuant to Section 2-302, a health-care facility that releases a minor for purposes of adoption shall transmit to the Department a copy of the authorization required by Section 2-302 and shall report:

(1) the name, address, and telephone number of the person who authorized the release;

(2) the name, address, and telephone number of the person to whom physical custody was transferred; and

(3) the date of the transfer.

(b) No later than 30 days after a release pursuant to Section 2-302, the person to whom physical custody of a minor was transferred shall report to the Department which, if any, of the following has occurred:

(1) the filing of a petition for adoption with the name and address of the petitioner;

(2) the acquisition of custody of the minor by an agency and the name and address of the agency;

(3) the return of the minor to a parent or other person having legal custody and the name and address of the parent or other person; or

(4) the transfer of physical custody of the minor to another individual and the name and address of the individual.

**SECTION 2-304. ACTION BY DEPARTMENT.**

(a) If the Department receives a report required under Section 2-303(a) from a health-care facility or attending practitioner, but does not receive the report required under Section 2-303(b) within 45 days after the transfer of a minor, the Department shall immediately investigate to determine the whereabouts of the minor.

(b) If none of the dispositions listed in Section 2303(b)(1) through (3) has occurred, or the minor has been transferred to an individual described in Section 2-303(b)(4) who has not filed a petition to adopt, the Department shall immediately take appropriate action to remove the minor from the individual to whom the minor has been transferred.

(c) The Department may also review and investigate compliance with the provisions of Sections 2-101 through 2-106 and may bring an action in the [    ] court to require compliance.

[PART] 4. CONSENT TO AND RELINQUISHMENT FOR ADOPTION

**SECTION 2-401. PERSONS WHOSE CONSENT REQUIRED.**

(a) Unless consent is not required or is dispensed with by Section 2-402, in a direct placement of a minor for adoption by a parent or guardian authorized under this [Act] to place the minor, a petition to adopt the minor may be granted only if consent to the adoption has been executed by:

(1) the woman who gave birth to the minor and the man, if any, who:

(i) is or has been married to the woman if the minor was born during the marriage or within 300 days after the marriage was terminated or a court issued a decree of separation;

(ii) attempted to marry the woman before the minor's birth by a marriage solemnized in apparent compliance with law, although the attempted marriage is or could be declared invalid, if the minor was born during the attempted marriage or within 300 days after the attempted marriage was terminated;

(iii) under applicable law, has been judicially determined to be the father of the minor, or has signed a document which has the effect of establishing his parentage of the minor, and:

(A) has provided, in accordance with his financial means, reasonable and consistent payments for the support of the minor and has visited or communicated with the minor; or

(B) after the minor's birth, but before the minor's placement for adoption, has married or attempted to marry the woman who gave birth to the minor by a marriage solemnized in apparent compliance with law, although the attempted marriage is or could be declared invalid; or

(iv) has received the minor into his home and openly held out the minor as his child;

(2) the minor's guardian if expressly authorized by a court to consent to the minor's adoption; or

(3) the current adoptive or other legally recognized mother and father of the minor.

(b) Unless consent is not required under Section 2402, in a placement of a minor for adoption by an agency authorized under this [Act] to place the minor, a petition to adopt the minor may be granted only if consent to the adoption has been executed by:

(1) the agency that placed the minor for adoption; and

(2) an individual described in subsection (a) who has not relinquished the minor.

(c) Unless the court dispenses with the minor's consent, a petition to adopt a minor who has attained 12 years of age may be granted only if, in addition to any consent required by subsections (a) and (b), the minor has executed an informed consent to the adoption.

**SECTION 2-402. PERSONS WHOSE CONSENT NOT REQUIRED.**

(a) Consent to an adoption of a minor is not required of:

(1) an individual who has relinquished the minor to an agency for purposes of adoption;

(2) an individual whose parental relationship to a minor has been terminated or determined not to exist

(3) a parent who has been judicially declared incompetent;

(4) a man who has not been married to the woman who gave birth to the minor and who, after the conception of the minor, executes a verified statement, denying paternity or disclaiming any interest in the minor and acknowledging that his statement shall be irrevocable when executed;

(5) the personal representative of a deceased parent's estate; or

(6) a parent or other person who has not executed a consent or a relinquishment and who fails to file an answer or an appearance in a proceeding for adoption or for termination of a parental relationship within the requisite time after service of notice of the proceeding.

(b) The court may dispense with the consent of:

(1) a guardian or an agency whose consent is otherwise required upon a finding that the consent is
being withheld contrary to the best interest of a minor adoptee; or

(2) a minor adoptee who has attained 12 years of age upon a finding that it is not in the best interest of the minor to require the consent.

**SECTION 2-403. INDIVIDUALS WHO MAY RELINQUISH MINOR.** A parent or guardian whose consent to the adoption of a minor is required by Section 2-401 may relinquish to an agency all of that individual's rights with respect to the minor, including legal and physical custody and the right to consent to the minor's adoption.

**SECTION 2-404. TIME FOR EXECUTION OF CONSENT OR RELINQUISHMENT.**

(a) A parent whose consent to the adoption of a minor is required by Section 2-401 may execute a consent or a relinquishment only after the minor is born. A parent who executes a consent or relinquishment may revoke the consent or relinquishment within 192 hours after the birth of the minor.

(b) A guardian may execute a consent to the adoption of a minor or a relinquishment at any time after being authorized by a court to do so.

(c) An agency that places a minor for adoption may execute its consent at any time at or before the hearing on the petition for adoption.

(d) A minor adoptee whose consent is required may execute a consent at any time at or before the hearing on the petition for adoption.

(e) Before executing a consent or relinquishment, a parent must have been informed of the meaning and consequences of adoption, the availability of personal and legal counseling, the procedure for releasing information about the health and other characteristics of the parent which may affect the physical or psychological well-being of the adoptee, and the procedure for the consensual release of the parent's identity to an adoptee, an adoptee's direct descendant, or an adoptive parent pursuant to Article 6. The parent must have had an opportunity to indicate in a signed document whether and under what circumstances the parent is or is not willing to release identifying information, and must have been informed of the procedure for changing the document at a later time.

### SECTION 2-405. PROCEDURE FOR EXECUTION OF CONSENT OR RELINQUISHMENT.

(a) A consent or relinquishment executed by a parent or guardian must be signed or confirmed in the presence of

(1) a judge of a court of record;

(2) an individual designated by a judge to take consents or relinquishments;

(3) an employee designated by an agency to take consents or relinquishments, but not an employee of an agency to which a minor is relinquished;

(4) a lawyer other than a lawyer who is representing an adoptive parent or the agency to which a minor is relinquished;

(5) a commissioned officer on active duty in the military service of the United States, if the individual executing the consent or relinquishment is in military service; or

(6) an officer of the foreign service or a consular officer of the United States in another country, if the individual executing the consent or relinquishment is in that country.

(b) A consent executed by a minor adoptee must be signed or confirmed in the presence of the court in the proceeding for adoption or in a manner the court directs.

(c) Minority of a parent does not affect competency to execute a consent or relinquishment, but a parent who is a minor must have had access to counseling and must have had the advice of a lawyer who is not representing an adoptive parent or the agency to which the parent's child is relinquished.

(d) An individual before whom a consent or relinquishment is signed or confirmed under subsection (a) shall certify in writing that he or she orally explained the contents and consequences of the consent or relinquishment, and to the best of his or her knowledge or belief, the individual executing the consent or relinquishment:

(1) read or was read the consent or relinquishment and understood it;

(2) signed the consent or relinquishment voluntarily;

(3) received or was offered a copy of the consent or relinquishment and the information described by Section 2404(e) and was afforded an opportunity to sign the document described in that section;

(4) was offered counseling services and information about adoption; and

(5) if the individual executing the consent or relinquishment is a parent who is a minor, was advised by a lawyer who is not representing an adoptive parent or the agency to which the parent's child is being relinquished, and, if an adult, was informed of the right to have a lawyer who is not representing an adoptive parent or an agency to which the parent's child is being relinquished.

(e) A prospective adoptive parent named or described in a consent to the adoption of a minor shall sign a statement indicating an intention to adopt the minor, acknowledging an obligation to return legal and physical custody of the minor to the minor's parent if the parent revokes the consent within the time specified in Section 2-404(a), and acknowledging responsibility for the minor's medical and other care and support if the consent is not revoked.

(f) An employee of an agency to which a minor child is being relinquished shall sign a statement indicating the agency's willingness to accept the relinquishment, acknowledging its obligation to return legal and physical custody of the child to the minor's parent if the parent revokes the relinquishment within the time indicated in Section 2-404(a), and acknowledging responsibility for the minor's medical and other care and support if the relinquishment is not revoked.

(g) An individual before whom a consent or a relinquishment is signed or confirmed shall certify that the statements required by subsections (e) and (f) were given to him or her.

(h) A consent by an agency to the adoption of a minor in the agency's legal custody must be executed by the executive head or another authorized employee and must be signed or confirmed under oath in the presence of an individual authorized to take acknowledgments.

(i) A consent or relinquishment executed and signed or confirmed in another State or in another country is valid if in accord with this [Act] or with the law and procedure of the State or country in which executed.

**SECTION 2-406. CONTENT OF CONSENT OR RELINQUISHMENT.**

(a) A consent or relinquishment required from a parent or guardian must be in writing and contain, in plain English or, if the native language of the parent or guardian is a language other than English, in that language:

(1) the date, place, and time of the execution of the consent or relinquishment;

(2) the name, date of birth, and current mailing address of the individual executing the consent or relinquishment;

(3) the date of birth and the name or pseudonym of the minor adoptee;

(4) if a consent, the name, address, and telephone and telecopier number of the lawyer representing the prospective adoptive parent with whom the individual executing the consent has placed or intends to place the minor for adoption;

(5) if a relinquishment, the name, address, and telephone and telecopier number of the agency to which the minor is being relinquished; and

(6) specific instructions for how a parent who executes a consent or relinquishment may revoke the consent or relinquishment or commence an action to set aside the consent or relinquishment.

(b) A consent must state that the parent or guardian executing the document is voluntarily and unequivocally consenting to the transfer of legal and physical custody to, and the adoption of the minor by, a specific adoptive parent whom the parent or guardian has selected.

(c) A relinquishment must state that the individual executing the relinquishment voluntarily consents to the permanent transfer of legal and physical custody of the minor to the agency for the purposes of adoption.

(d) A consent or relinquishment must state:

(1) an understanding that after the consent or relinquishment is signed or confirmed in substantial
compliance with Section 2-405, it is final and, except under a circumstance stated in Section 2-408 or 2-409, may not be revoked or set aside for any reason, including the failure of an adoptive parent to permit the individual executing the consent or relinquishment to visit or communicate with the minor adoptee;

(2) an understanding that the adoption will extinguish all parental rights and obligations the individual executing the consent or relinquishment has with respect to the minor adoptee, except for arrearages of child support, and will remain valid whether or not any agreement for visitation or communication with the minor adoptee is later performed;

(3) that the individual executing the consent or relinquishment has:

(i) received a copy of the consent or relinquishment;

(ii) received or been offered counseling services and information about adoption which explains the meaning and consequences of an adoption;

(iii) been advised, if a parent who is a minor, by a lawyer who is not representing an adoptive parent or the agency to which the minor is being relinquished, or, if an adult, has been informed of the right to have a lawyer who is not representing an adoptive parent or the agency;

(iv) received the information described in Section 2-404(e) and been afforded an opportunity to sign the document described in that section; and

(v) been advised of the obligation to provide the information required under Section 2-106;

(4) that the individual executing the consent or relinquishment has not received or been promised any money or anything of value for the consent or the relinquishment, except for payments authorized by Article 7;

(5) that the minor is not an Indian child as defined in the Indian Child Welfare Act, 25 U.S.C. 1901 et seq.;

(6) that the individual believes the adoption of the minor is in the minor's best interest

(7) if a consent, that the individual who is consenting waives further notice unless the adoption is contested, appealed, or denied.

(e) A relinquishment may provide that the individual who is relinquishing waives notice of any proceeding for adoption, or waives notice unless the adoption is contested, appealed, or denied.

(f) A consent or relinquishment may provide for its revocation if:

(1) another consent or relinquishment is not executed within a specified period;

(2) a court decides not to terminate another individual's parental relationship to the minor; or

(3) in a direct placement for adoption, a petition for adoption by a prospective adoptive parent, named or described in the consent, is denied or withdrawn.

## SECTION 2-407. CONSEQUENCES OF CONSENT OR RELINQUISHMENT.

(a) Except under a circumstance stated in Section 2408, a consent to the adoption of a minor which is executed by a parent or guardian in substantial compliance with Sections 2-405 and 2-406 is final and irrevocable, and:

(1) unless a court orders otherwise to protect the welfare of the minor, entitles the prospective adoptive parent named or described in the consent to the legal and physical custody of the minor and imposes on that individual responsibility for the medical and other care and support of the minor;

(2) terminates any duty of a parent who executed the consent with respect to the minor, except for arrearages of child support; and

(3) terminates any right of a parent or guardian who executed the consent to object to the minor's adoption by the prospective adoptive parent and any right to notice of the proceeding for adoption unless the adoption is contested,

appealed, or denied.

(b) Except under a circumstance stated in Section 2409, a relinquishment of a minor to an agency which is executed by a parent or guardian in substantial compliance with Sections 2-405 and 2-406 is final and irrevocable, and:

(1) unless a court orders otherwise to protect the welfare of the minor, entitles the agency to the legal custody of the minor until a decree of adoption becomes final;

(2) empowers the agency to place the minor for adoption, consent to the minor's adoption, and delegate to a prospective adoptive parent responsibility for the medical and other care and support of the minor;

(3) terminates any duty of the individual who executed the relinquishment with respect to the minor except for arrearages of child support; and

(4) terminates any right of the individual who executed the relinquishment to object to the minor's adoption and, unless otherwise provided in the relinquishment, any right to notice of the proceeding for adoption.

## SECTION 2-408. REVOCATION OF CONSENT.

(a) In a direct placement of a minor for adoption by a parent or guardian, a consent is revoked if:

(1) within 192 hours after the birth of the minor, a parent who executed the consent notifies in writing the prospective adoptive parent, or the adoptive parent's lawyer, that the parent revokes the consent, or the parent complies with any other instructions for revocation specified in the consent;

(2) the individual who executed the consent and the prospective adoptive parent named or described in the consent agree to its revocation.

(b) In a direct placement of a minor for adoption by a parent or guardian, the court shall set aside the consent if the individual who executed the consent establishes:

(1) by clear and convincing evidence, before a decree of adoption is issued, that the consent was obtained by fraud or duress;

(2) by a preponderance of the evidence that, without good cause shown, a petition to adopt was not filed within 60 days after the minor was placed for adoption; or

(3) by a preponderance of the evidence, that a condition permitting revocation has occurred, as expressly provided for in the consent pursuant to Section 2-406(f)(1) through (3).

(c) If the consent of an individual who had legal and physical custody of a minor when the minor was placed for adoption or the consent was executed is revoked under subsection (a)(1) or (2), the prospective adoptive parent shall immediately return the minor to the individual's custody and move to dismiss any proceeding for adoption or termination of the individual's parental relationship to the minor. If the minor is not returned immediately, the individual may petition the court named in the consent for appropriate relief. The court shall hear the petition expeditiously.

(d) If the consent of an individual who had legal and physical custody of a minor when the minor was placed for adoption or the consent was executed is set aside under subsection (b)(1), the court shall order the return of the minor to the custody of the individual and dismiss a pending proceeding for adoption.

(e) If the consent of an individual who had legal and physical custody of a minor when the minor was placed for adoption or the consent was executed is set aside under subsection (b)(2) or (3) and no ground exists under Article 3, Part 5, for terminating the parental relationship between the individual and the minor, the court shall dismiss a pending proceeding for adoption and order the return of the minor to the custody of the individual, unless the court finds that return will be detrimental to the minor.

(f) If the consent of an individual who did not have physical custody of a minor when the minor was placed for adoption or the consent was executed is revoked under subsection (a) or set aside under subsection (b) and no ground exists under Article 3, Part 5, for terminating the parental relationship between the individual and the minor, the court shall dismiss a pending proceeding for adoption and issue an order providing for the care and custody of the minor according to the best interest of the minor.

### SECTION 2-409. REVOCATION OF RELINQUISHMENT.

(a) A relinquishment is revoked if:

(1) within 192 hours after the birth of the minor, a parent who executed the relinquishment notifies in writing the agency to which the minor has been relinquished, that the parent revokes the relinquishment, or the parent complies with any other instructions for revocation specified in the relinquishment; or

(2) the individual who executed the relinquishment and the agency that accepted it agree to its revocation.

(b) The court shall set aside a relinquishment if the individual who executed the relinquishment establishes:

(1) by clear and convincing evidence, before a decree of adoption is issued, that the relinquishment was obtained by fraud or duress, or

(2) by a preponderance of the evidence, that a condition permitting revocation has occurred, as expressly provided for in the relinquishment pursuant to Section 2-406(f)(1) through (3).

(c) If a relinquishment by an individual who had legal and physical custody of a minor when the relinquishment was executed is revoked under subsection (a)(1) or (2), the agency shall immediately return the minor to the individual's custody and move to dismiss a proceeding for adoption. If the minor is not returned immediately, the individual may petition the court named in the relinquishment for appropriate relief. The court shall hear the petition expeditiously.

(d) If a relinquishment by an individual who had legal and physical custody of a minor when the relinquishment was executed is set aside under subsection (b)(1), the court shall dismiss any proceeding for adoption and order the return of the minor to the custody of the individual.

(e) If a relinquishment by an individual who had legal and physical custody of a minor when the relinquishment was executed is set aside under subsection (b)(2) and no ground exists under Article 3, Part 5, for terminating the parental relationship between the individual and the minor, the court shall dismiss a proceeding for adoption and order the return of the minor to the custody of the individual, unless the court finds that return will be detrimental to the minor.

(f) If a relinquishment by an individual who did not have physical custody of a minor when the relinquishment was executed is revoked under subsection (a) or set aside under subsection (b) and no ground exists under Article 3, Part 5, for terminating the parental relationship between the individual and the minor, the court shall dismiss a pending proceeding for adoption and shall issue an order providing for the care and custody of the minor according to the best interest of the minor.

## [ARTICLE] 3. GENERAL PROCEDURE FOR ADOPTION OF MINORS
### [PART] 1. JURISDICTION AND VENUE

### SECTION 3-101. JURISDICTION.

(a) Except as otherwise provided in subsections (b) and (c), a court of this State has jurisdiction over a proceeding for the adoption of a minor commenced under this [Act] if:

(1) immediately preceding commencement of the proceeding, the minor lived in this State with a parent, a guardian, a prospective adoptive parent, or another person acting as parent, for at least six consecutive months, excluding periods of temporary absence, or, in the case of a minor under six months of age, lived in this State from soon after birth with any of those individuals and there is available in this State substantial evidence concerning the minor's present or future care;

(2) immediately preceding commencement of the proceeding, the prospective adoptive parent lived in this State for at least six consecutive months, excluding periods of temporary absence, and there is available in this State substantial evidence concerning the minor's present or future care;

(3) the agency that placed the minor for adoption is located in this State and it is in the best interest of the minor that a court of this State assume jurisdiction because:

(i) the minor and the minor's parents, or the minor and the prospective adoptive parent, have a significant connection with this State; and

(ii) there is available in this State substantial evidence concerning the minor's present or future care;

(4) the minor and the prospective adoptive parent are physically present in this State and the minor has been abandoned or it is necessary in an emergency to protect the minor because the minor has been subjected to or threatened with mistreatment or abuse or is otherwise neglected; or

(5) it appears that no other State would have jurisdiction under prerequisites substantially in accordance with paragraphs (1) through (4), or another State has declined to exercise jurisdiction on the ground that this State is the more appropriate forum to hear a petition for adoption of the minor, and it is in the best interest of the minor that a court of this State assume jurisdiction.

(b) A court of this State may not exercise jurisdiction over a proceeding for adoption of a minor if at the time the petition for adoption is filed a proceeding concerning the custody or adoption of the minor is pending in a court of another State exercising jurisdiction substantially in conformity with [the Uniform Child Custody Jurisdiction Act] or this [Act], unless the proceeding is stayed by the court of the other State because this State is a more appropriate forum or for another reason.

(c) If a court of another State has issued a decree or order concerning the custody of a minor who may be the subject of a proceeding for adoption in this State, a court of this State may not exercise jurisdiction over a proceeding for adoption of the minor unless:

(1) the court of this State finds that the court of the State which issued the decree or order:

(i) does not have continuing jurisdiction to modify the decree or order under jurisdictional prerequisites substantially in accordance with [the Uniform Child Custody Jurisdiction Act] or has declined to assume jurisdiction to modify the decree or order; or

(ii) does not have jurisdiction over a proceeding for adoption substantially in conformity with subsection (a)(1) through (4) or has declined to assume jurisdiction over a proceeding for adoption; and

(2) the court of this State has jurisdiction under this section over the proceeding for adoption.

**SECTION 3-102. VENUE.** A petition for adoption of a minor may be filed in the court in the [county] in which a petitioner lives, the minor lives, or

(3) an office of an agency that placed the minor is located.

## [PART] 2. GENERAL PROCEDURAL PROVISIONS

### SECTION 3-201. APPOINTMENT OF LAWYER OR GUARDIAN AD LITEM.

(a) In a proceeding under this [Act] which may result in the termination of a parental relationship, the court shall appoint a lawyer for any indigent, minor, or incompetent individual who appears in the proceeding and whose parental relationship to a child may be terminated, unless the court finds that the minor or incompetent individual has sufficient financial means to hire a lawyer, or an indigent individual declines to be represented by a lawyer.

(b) The court shall appoint a guardian ad litem for a minor adoptee in a contested proceeding under this [Act] and may appoint a guardian ad litem for a minor adoptee in an uncontested proceeding.

### SECTION 3-202. NO RIGHT TO JURY. A proceeding under this [Act] for adoption or termination of a parental relationship must be heard by the court without a jury.

### SECTION 3-203. CONFIDENTIALITY OF PROCEEDINGS. Except for a proceeding pursuant to [Article] 7, a civil proceeding under this [Act] must be heard in closed court.

### SECTION 3-204. CUSTODY DURING PENDENCY OF PROCEEDING. In order to protect the welfare of the minor, the court shall make an interim order for custody of a minor adoptee according to the best interest of the minor in a contested proceeding under this [Act] for adoption or termination of a parental relationship and may make an interim order for custody in an uncontested proceeding.

### SECTION 3-205. REMOVAL OF ADOPTEE FROM STATE. Before a decree of adoption is issued, a petitioner may not remove a minor adoptee for more than 30 consecutive days from the State in which the petitioner resides without the permission of the court, if the minor was placed directly for adoption, or, if an agency placed the minor for adoption, the permission of the agency.

## [PART] 3. PETITION FOR ADOPTION OF MINOR

### SECTION 3-301. STANDING TO PETITION TO ADOPT.

(a) Except as otherwise provided in subsection (c), the only individuals who have standing to petition to adopt a minor under this Article are:

(1) an individual with whom a minor has been placed for adoption or who has been selected as a prospective adoptive parent by a person authorized under this [Act] to place the minor for adoption; or

(2) an individual with whom a minor has not been placed for adoption or who has not been selected or rejected as a prospective adoptive parent pursuant to Article 2, Parts 1 through 3, but who has had physical custody of the minor for at least six months immediately before seeking to file a petition for adoption and is allowed to file the petition by the court for good cause shown.

(b) The spouse of a petitioner must join in the petition unless legally separated from the petitioner or judicially declared mentally incompetent.

(c) A petition for adoption of a minor stepchild by a stepparent may be filed under Article 4 and a petition for adoption of an emancipated minor may be filed under Article 5.

**SECTION 3-302. TIME FOR FILING PETITION.** A prospective adoptive parent with standing under Section 3-301(a)(1) shall file a petition for adoption no later than 30 days after a minor is placed for adoption with that individual, unless the court allows a later filing.

**SECTION 3-303. CAPTION OF PETITION.** The caption of a petition for adoption of a minor must contain the name of or a pseudonym for the minor adoptee and may not contain the name of the petitioner.

**SECTION 3-304. CONTENT OF PETITION.**

(a) A petition for adoption of a minor must be signed and verified by the petitioner and contain the following information or state why any of the information omitted is not contained in the petition:

(1) the full name, age, and place and duration of residence of the petitioner;

(2) the current marital status of the petitioner, including the date and place of any marriage, the date of any legal separation or divorce, and the date of any judicial determination that a petitioner's spouse is incompetent;

(3) that the petitioner has facilities and resources to provide for the care and support of the minor;

(4) that a preplacement evaluation favorable to the petitioner has been completed or brought current within the 18 months next preceding the placement, or that a preplacement evaluation has been waived by a court for good cause shown or is not required under Section 2-201;

(5) the first name, sex, and the date, or approximate date, and place of birth of the minor adoptee, and a statement that the minor is or is not an Indian

child as defined in the Indian Child Welfare Act, 25 U.S.C. Sections 1901 et seq.;

(6) the circumstances under which the petitioner obtained physical custody of the minor, including the date of placement of the minor with the petitioner for adoption and the name of the agency or the name or relationship to the minor of the individual that placed the minor;

(7) the length of time the minor has been in the custody of the petitioner and, if the minor is not in the physical custody of the petitioner, the reason why the petitioner does not have custody and the date and manner in which the petitioner intends to obtain custody;

(8) a description and estimate of the value of any property of the minor;

(9) that any provision of law governing interstate or intercountry placement was complied with;

(10) the name or relationship to the minor of any individual who has executed a consent or relinquishment to the adoption or a disclaimer of paternal interest, and the name or relationship to the minor of any individual whose consent or relinquishment may be required, but whose parental relationship has not been terminated, and any fact or circumstance that may excuse the lack of consent;

(11) that a previous petition by the petitioner to adopt has or has not been made in any court, and its disposition; and

(12) a description of any previous court order or pending proceeding known to the petitioner concerning custody of or visitation with the minor and any other fact known to the petitioner and needed to establish the jurisdiction of the court.

(b) The petitioner shall request in the petition:

(1) that the petitioner be permitted to adopt the minor as the petitioner's child;

(2) that the court approve the full name by which the minor is to be known if the petition is granted; and

(3) any other relief sought by the petitioner.

### SECTION 3-305. REQUIRED DOCUMENTS.

(a) Before the hearing on the petition for adoption, the following must be filed in the proceeding:

(1) a certified copy of the birth certificate or other record of the date and place of birth of the minor adoptee;

(2) any consent, relinquishment, or disclaimer of paternal interest with respect to the minor that has been executed, and any written certifications required by Section 2-405(d) and (g) from the individual before whom a consent or relinquishment was executed;

(3) a certified copy of any court order terminating the rights and duties of the minor's parents or guardian;

(4) a certified copy of each parent's or former parent's marriage certificate, decree of divorce, annulment, or dissolution, or agreement or decree of legal separation, and a certified copy of any court order determining the parent's or former parent's incompetence;

(5) a certified copy of any existing court order or the petition in any pending proceeding concerning custody of or visitation with the minor;

(6) a copy of the preplacement evaluation and of the evaluation during the pendency of the proceeding for adoption;

(7) a copy of any report containing the information required by Section 2-106;

(8) a document signed pursuant to Section 2404(e);

(9) a certified copy of the petitioner's marriage certificate, decree of divorce, annulment, or dissolution, or agreement or decree of legal separation, and a certified copy of any court order determining the incompetence of the petitioner's spouse;

10) a copy of any agreement with a public agency to provide a subsidy for the benefit of a minor adoptee with a special need;

(11) if an agency placed the minor adoptee, a verified document from the agency stating:

(i) the circumstances under which it obtained custody of the minor for purposes of adoption

(ii) that it complied with any provision of law governing an interstate or intercountry placement of the minor;

(iii) the name or relationship to the minor of any individual whose consent is required, but who has not executed a consent or a relinquishment or whose parental relationship has not been terminated, and any fact or circumstance that may excuse the lack of consent or relinquishment; and

(iv) whether it has executed its consent to the proposed adoption and whether it waives notice of the proceeding; and

(12) the name and address, if known, of any person who is entitled to receive notice of the proceeding for adoption.

(b) If an item required by subsection (a) is not available, the person responsible for furnishing the item shall file an affidavit explaining its absence.

[PART] 4. NOTICE OF PENDENCY OF PROCEEDING

**SECTION 3-401.  SERVICE OF NOTICE.**

(a) Unless notice has been waived, notice of a proceeding for adoption of a minor must be served, within 20 days after a petition for adoption is filed, upon:

(1) an individual whose consent to the adoption is required under Section 2-401, but notice need not be served upon an individual whose parental relationship to the minor or whose status as a guardian has been terminated;

(2) an agency whose consent to the adoption is required under Section 2-401;

(3) an individual whom the petitioner knows is claiming to be or who is named as the father or possible father of the minor adoptee and whose paternity of the minor has not been judicially determined, but notice need not be served upon a man who has executed a verified statement, as described in Section 2-402(a)(4), denying paternity or disclaiming any interest in the minor;

(4) an individual other than the petitioner who has legal or physical custody of the minor adoptee or who has a right of visitation with the minor under an existing court order issued by a court in this or another State;

(5) the spouse of the petitioner if the spouse has not joined in the petition; and

(6) a grandparent of a minor adoptee if the grandparent's child is a deceased parent of the minor and before death, the deceased parent had not executed a consent or relinquishment or the deceased parent's parental relationship to the minor had not been terminated.

(b) The court shall require notice of a proceeding for adoption of a minor to be served upon any person the court finds, at any time during the proceeding, is:

(1) a person described in subsection (a) who has not been given notice;

(2) an individual who has revoked a consent or relinquishment pursuant to Section 2-408(a) or 2409(a) or is attempting to have a consent or relinquishment set aside pursuant to Section 2-408(b) or 2409(b); or

(3) a person who, on the basis of a previous relationship with the minor adoptee, a parent, an alleged parent, or the petitioner, can provide information that is relevant to the proposed adoption and that the court in its discretion wants to hear.

**SECTION 3-402. CONTENT OF NOTICE.** A notice required by Section 3-401 must use a pseudonym for a petitioner or any individual named in the petition for adoption who has not waived confidentiality and must contain:

(1) the caption of the petition;

(2) the address and telephone number of the court where the petition is pending;

(3) a concise summary of the relief requested in the petition;

(4) the name, mailing address, and telephone number of the petitioner or petitioner's lawyer;

(5) a conspicuous statement of the consequences of failure to respond to the notice of the proceeding for adoption and the method of responding; and

(6) any statement required by [other applicable law or rule].

### SECTION 3-403. MANNER AND EFFECT OF SERVICE.

(a) Personal service of the notice required by Section 3-401 must be made in a manner appropriate under [the rules of civil procedure for the service of process in a civil action in this State] unless the court otherwise directs.

(b) Except as otherwise provided in subsection (c), a person who fails to respond to the notice within 20 days after its service is not entitled to participate in or receive further notice of the proceeding for adoption.

(c) An individual who is a respondent in a petition to terminate the relationship of parent and child pursuant to Part S which is served upon the individual with the notice required by Section 3-401 is not entitled to participate in or receive further notice of the proceeding for adoption or for termination unless the individual responds to the notice as required by Section 3-504.

### SECTION 3-404. INVESTIGATION AND NOTICE TO UNKNOWN FATHER.

(a) If, at any time in a proceeding for adoption or for termination of a relationship of parent and child under Part 5, the court finds that an unknown father of a minor adoptee may not have received notice, the court shall determine whether he can be identified. The determination must be based on evidence that includes inquiry of appropriate persons in an effort to identify an unknown father for the purpose of providing notice.

(b) The inquiry required by subsection (a) must include whether:

(1) the woman who gave birth to the minor adoptee was married at the probable time of conception of the minor, or at a later time;

(2) the woman was cohabiting with a man at the probable time of conception of the minor;

(3) the woman has received payments or promises of support, other than from a governmental agency, with respect to the minor or because of her pregnancy;

(4) the woman has named any individual as the father on the birth certificate of the minor or in connection with applying for or receiving public assistance; and

(5) any individual has formally or informally acknowledged or claimed paternity of the minor in a jurisdiction in which the woman resided during or since her pregnancy, or in which the minor has resided or resides, at the time of the inquiry.

(c) If inquiry pursuant to subsection (b) identifies as the father of the minor an individual who has not received notice of the proceeding, the court shall require notice to be served upon him pursuant to Section 3-403, unless service is not possible because his whereabouts are unknown.

(d) If, after inquiry pursuant to subsection (b), the court finds that personal service cannot be made upon the father of the minor because his identity or whereabouts is unknown, the court shall order publication or public posting of the notice only if, on the basis of all information available, the court determines that publication or posting is likely to lead to receipt of notice by the father. If the court determines that publication or posting is not likely to lead to receipt of notice, the court may dispense with the publication or posting of a notice. (e) If, in an inquiry pursuant to this section, the woman who gave birth to the minor adoptee fails to disclose the identity of a possible father or reveal his whereabouts, she must be advised that the proceeding for adoption may be delayed or subject to challenge if a possible father is not given notice of the proceeding and that the lack of information about the father's medical and genetic history may be detrimental to the adoptee.

### SECTION 3-405. WAIVER OF NOTICE.

(a) Notice required under this [Act] may be waived before the court or in a consent, relinquishment, or other document signed by a person entitled to receive the notice.

(b) Except for the purpose of moving to revoke a consent or relinquishment on the ground that it was obtained by fraud or duress, a person who has waived notice may not appear in the proceeding for adoption.

### [PART] 5. PETITION TO TERMINATE
### RELATIONSHIP BETWEEN PARENT AND CHILD

A petition to terminate the relationship between a parent or an alleged parent and a minor child may be filed in a proceeding for adoption under this [Act] by:

(1) a parent or a guardian who has selected a prospective adoptive parent for a minor and who intends to place, or has placed, the minor with that individual;

(2) a parent whose spouse has filed a petition under Article 4 to adopt the parent's minor child;

(3) a prospective adoptive parent of the minor who has filed a petition to adopt under this Article or Article 4; or

(4) an agency that has selected a prospective adoptive parent for the minor and intends to place, or has placed, the minor with that individual.

## SECTION 3-502. TIME AND CONTENT OF PETITION.

(a) A petition under this Part may be filed at any time after a petition for adoption has been filed under this Article or Article 4 and before entry of a decree of adoption.

(b) A petition under this Part must be signed and verified by the petitioner, be filed with the court, and state:

(1) the name or pseudonym of the petitioner;

(2) the name of the minor;

(3) the name and last known address of the parent or alleged parent whose parental relationship to the minor is to be terminated;

(4) the facts and circumstances forming the basis for the petition and the grounds on which termination of a parental relationship is sought;

(5) if the petitioner is a prospective adoptive parent, that the petitioner intends to proceed with the petition to adopt the minor if the petition to terminate is granted; and

(6) if the petitioner is a parent, a guardian, or an agency, that the petitioner has selected the prospective adoptive parent who is the petitioner in the proceeding for adoption.

## SECTION 3-503. SERVICE OF PETITION AND NOTICE.

(a) A petition to terminate under this Part and a notice of hearing on the petition must be served upon the respondent, with notice of the proceeding for adoption, in the manner prescribed in Sections 3-403 and 3-404.

(b) The notice of the hearing must inform the respondent of the method for responding and that:

(1) the respondent has a right to be represented by a lawyer, and may be entitled to have a lawyer appointed by the court; and

(2) failure to respond within 20 days after service, and, in the case of an alleged father, failure to file a claim of paternity within 20 days after service, unless a claim of paternity is pending, will result in termination of the relationship of parent and child between the respondent and the minor, unless the proceeding for adoption is dismissed.

## SECTION 3-504. GROUNDS FOR TERMINATING RELATIONSHIP.

(a) If the respondent is served with a petition to terminate under this Part and the accompanying notice and does not respond, and, in the case of an alleged father, file a claim of paternity within 20 days after the service, unless a claim of paternity is pending, the court shall order the termination of any relationship of parent and child between the respondent and the minor unless the proceeding for adoption is dismissed.

(b) If, under Section 3-404, the court dispenses with service of the petition upon the respondent, the court shall order the termination of any relationship of parent and child between the respondent and the minor unless the proceeding for adoption is dismissed.

(c) If the respondent asserts parental rights, the court shall proceed with the hearing expeditiously and may order the termination of any relationship of parent and child between the respondent and the minor upon finding, upon clear and convincing evidence, that one of the following grounds exists, and, by a preponderance of the evidence, that termination is in the best interest of the minor:

(1) in the case of a minor who has not attained six months of age at the time the petition for adoption is filed, unless the respondent proves by a preponderance of the evidence a compelling reason for not complying with this paragraph, the respondent has failed to:

(i) pay reasonable prenatal, natal, and postnatal expenses in accordance with the respondent's financial means;

(ii) make reasonable and consistent payments, in accordance with the respondent's financial means, for the support of the minor;

(iii) visit regularly with the minor; and

(iv) manifest an ability and willingness to assume legal and physical custody of the minor, if, during this time, the minor was not in the physical custody of the other parent;

(2) in the case of a minor who has attained six months of age at the time a petition for adoption is filed, unless the respondent proves by a preponderance of the evidence a compelling reason for not complying with this paragraph, the respondent, for a period of at least six consecutive months immediately preceding the filing of the petition, has failed to:

(i) make reasonable and consistent payments, in accordance with the respondent's means, for the support of the minor;

(ii) communicate or visit regularly with the minor; and

(iii) manifest an ability and willingness to assume legal and physical custody of the minor, if, during this time, the minor was not in the physical custody of the other parent;

(3) the respondent has been convicted of a crime of violence or of violating a restraining or protective order, and the facts of the crime or violation and the respondent's behavior indicate that the respondent is unfit to maintain a relationship of parent and child with the minor;

(4) the respondent is a man who was not married to the minor's mother when the minor was conceived or born and is not the biological or adoptive father of the minor; or

(5) termination is justified on a ground specified in [the State's statute for involuntary termination of parental rights].

(d) If the respondent proves by a preponderance of the evidence that he or she had a compelling reason for not complying with the requirements of subsection (c)(1) or (2) and termination is not justified on a ground stated in subsection (c)(3) through (5), the court may terminate the respondent's parental relationship to a minor only upon a finding, upon clear and convincing evidence, that one of the following grounds exists and, by a preponderance of the evidence that termination is in the best interest of the minor:

(1) if the minor is not in the legal and physical custody of the other parent, the respondent is not able or willing promptly to assume legal and physical custody of the minor, and to pay for the minor's support, in accordance with the respondent's financial means;

(2) if the minor is in the legal and physical custody of the other parent and a stepparent, and the stepparent is the prospective adoptive parent, the respondent is not able or willing promptly to establish and maintain contact with the minor and to pay for the minor's support, in accordance with the respondent's financial means;

(3) placing the minor in the respondent's legal and physical custody would pose a risk of substantial harm to the physical or psychological well- being of the minor because the circumstances of the minor's conception, the respondent's behavior during the mother's pregnancy or since the minor's birth, or the respondent's behavior with respect to other minors, indicates that the respondent is unfit to maintain a relationship of parent and child with the minor; or

(4) failure to terminate would be detrimental to the minor.

(e) In determining whether to terminate under subsection (d)(4), the court shall consider any relevant factor, including the respondent's efforts to obtain or maintain legal and physical custody of the minor, the role of other persons in thwarting the respondent's efforts to assert parental rights, the respondent's ability to care for the minor, the age of the minor, the quality of any previous relationship between the respondent and the minor and between the respondent and any other minor children, the duration and suitability of the minor's present custodial environment, and the effect of a change of physical custody on the minor.

**SECTION 3-505. EFFECT OF ORDER GRANTING PETITION.** An order issued under this Part granting the petition:

(1) terminates the relationship of parent and child between the respondent and the minor, except for arrearages of child support;

(2) extinguishes any right the respondent had to withhold consent to a proposed adoption of the minor or to further notice of a proceeding for adoption; and

(3) is a final order for purposes of appeal.

## SECTION 3-506. EFFECT OF ORDER DENYING PETITION.

(a) If the court denies the petition to terminate a relationship of parent and child, the court shall dismiss the proceeding for adoption and shall determine the legal and physical custody of the minor according to the criteria stated in Section 3-704.

(b) An order issued under this Part denying a petition to terminate a relationship of parent and child is a final order for purposes of appeal.

## PART 6. EVALUATION OF ADOPTEE
## AND PROSPECTIVE ADOPTIVE PARENT

## SECTION 3-601. EVALUATION DURING PROCEEDING FOR ADOPTION.

(a) After a petition for adoption of a minor is filed, the court shall order that an evaluation be made by an individual qualified under Section 2-202.

(b) The court shall provide the evaluator with copies of the petition for adoption and of the items filed with the petition.

## SECTION 3-602. CONTENT OF EVALUATION.

(a) An evaluation must be based on a personal interview with the petitioner in the petitioner's residence and observation of the relationship between the minor adoptee and the petitioner.

(b) An evaluation must be in writing and contain:

(1) an account of any change in the petitioner's marital status or family history, physical or mental health, home environment, property, income, or financial obligations since the filing of the preplacement evaluation;

(2) all reasonably available information concerning the physical, mental, and emotional condition of the minor adoptee which is not included in any report on the minor's health, genetic, and social history filed in the proceeding for adoption;

(3) copies of any court order, judgment, decree, or pending legal proceeding affecting the minor adoptee, the petitioner, or any child of the petitioner;

(4) a list of the expenses, fees, or other charges incurred, paid, or to be paid, and anything of value exchanged or to be exchanged, in connection with the adoption;

(5) any behavior or characteristics of the petitioner which raise a specific concern, as described in Section 2-204(a), about the petitioner or the petitioner's home; and

(6) a finding by the evaluator concerning the suitability of the petitioner and the petitioner's home for the minor adoptee and a recommendation

concerning the granting of the petition for adoption.

## SECTION 3-603. TIME AND FILING OF EVALUATION.

(a) The evaluator shall complete a written evaluation and file it with the court within 60 days after receipt of the court's order for an evaluation, unless the court for good cause allows a later filing.

(b) If an evaluation produces a specific concern, as described in Section 2-204(a), the evaluation must be filed immediately, and must explain why the concern poses a risk of harm to the physical or psychological well-being of the minor.

(c) An evaluator shall give the petitioner a copy of an evaluation when filed with the court and for two years shall retain a copy and a list of every source for each item of information in the evaluation.

## [PART] 7. DISPOSITIONAL HEARING; DECREE OF ADOPTION

**SECTION 3-701. TIME FOR HEARING ON PETITION.** The court shall set a date and time for hearing the petition, which must be no sooner than 90 days and no later than 180 days after the petition for adoption has been filed, unless the court for good cause sets an earlier or later date and time.

**SECTION 3-702. DISCLOSURE OF FEES AND CHARGES.** At least ten days before the hearing:

(1) the petitioner shall file with the court a signed and verified accounting of any payment or disbursement of money or anything of value made or agreed to be made by or on behalf of the petitioner in connection with the adoption, or pursuant to Article 7. The accounting must include the date and amount of each payment or disbursement made, the name and address of each recipient, and the purpose of each payment or disbursement;

(2) the lawyer for the petitioner shall file with the court an affidavit itemizing any fee, compensation, or other thing of value received by, or agreed to be paid to, the lawyer incidental to the placement and adoption of the minor;

(3) the lawyer for each parent of the minor or for the guardian of the minor shall file with the court an affidavit itemizing any fee, compensation, or other thing of value received by, or agreed to be paid to, the lawyer incidental to the placement and adoption of the minor;

(4) if an agency placed the minor for adoption, the agency shall file with the court an affidavit itemizing any fee, compensation, or other thing of value received by the agency for, or incidental to, the placement and adoption of the minor; and

(5) if a guardian placed the minor for adoption, the guardian shall file with the court an affidavit itemizing any fee, compensation, or other thing of value received by the guardian for, or incidental to, the placement and adoption of the minor.

## SECTION 3-703. GRANTING PETITION FOR ADOPTION.

(a) A court shall grant a petition for adoption if it determines that the adoption will be in the best interest of the minor, and that:

(1) at least 90 days have elapsed since the filing of the petition for adoption unless the court for good cause shown waives this requirement;

(2) the adoptee has been in the physical custody of the petitioner for at least 90 days unless the court for good cause shown waives this requirement;

(3) notice of the proceeding for adoption has been served or dispensed with as to any person entitled to receive notice under Part 4;

(4) every necessary consent, relinquishment, waiver, disclaimer of paternal interest, or judicial order terminating parental rights, including an order issued under Part 5, has been obtained and filed with the court;

(5) any evaluation required by this [Act] has been filed with and considered by the court;

(6) the petitioner is a suitable adoptive parent for the minor;

(7) if applicable, any requirement of this [Act] governing an interstate or intercountry placement for adoption has been met;

(8) the Indian Child Welfare Act, 25 U.S.C. §§ 1901 et seq., is not applicable to the proceeding or, if applicable, its requirements have been met;

(9) an accounting and affidavit required by Section 3-702 has been reviewed by the court, and the court has denied, modified, or ordered reimbursement of any payment or disbursement that is not authorized by Article 7 or is unreasonable or unnecessary when compared with the expenses customarily incurred in connection with an adoption

(10) the petitioner has received each report required by Section 2-106; and

(11) any document signed pursuant to Section 2404(e) concerning the release of a former parent's identity to the adoptee after the adoptee attains 18 years of age has been filed with the court.

(b) Notwithstanding a finding by the court that an activity prohibited by Article 7 or another section of this [Act] has occurred, if the court makes the determinations required by subsection (a), the court shall grant the petition for adoption and report the violation to the appropriate authorities.

(c) Except as otherwise provided in Article 4, the court shall inform the petitioner and any other individual affected by an existing order for visitation or communication with the minor adoptee that the decree of adoption terminates any existing order for visitation or communication.

**SECTION 3-704. DENIAL OF PETITION FOR ADOPTION.** If a court denies a petition for adoption, it shall dismiss the proceeding and issue an appropriate order for the legal and physical custody of the minor. If the reason for the denial is that a consent or relinquishment is revoked or set aside pursuant to Section 2-408 or 2409, the court shall determine the minor's custody according to the criteria stated in those sections. If the petition for adoption is denied for any other reason, the court shall determine the minor's custody according to the best interest of the minor.

**SECTION 3-705. DECREE OF ADOPTION**.
        (a) A decree of adoption must state or contain:
                (1) the original name of the minor adoptee, if the adoption is by a stepparent or relative and, in all other adoptions, the original name or a pseudonym;
                (2) the name of the petitioner for adoption;
                (3) whether the petitioner is married or unmarried;
                (4) whether the petitioner is a stepparent of the adoptee;
                (5) the name by which the adoptee is to be known and when the name takes effect;
                (6) information to be incorporated into a new birth certificate to be issued by the State [Registrar of Vital Records], unless the petitioner or an adoptee who has attained 12 years of age requests that a new certificate not be issued;
                (7) the adoptee's date and place of birth, if known, or in the case of an adoptee born outside the United States, as determined pursuant to subsection (b);
                (8) the effect of the decree of adoption as stated in Sections 1-104 through 1-106; and
                (9) that the adoption is in the best interest of the adoptee.
        (b) In determining the date and place of birth of an adoptee born outside the United States, the court shall:
                (1) enter the date and place of birth as stated in the birth certificate from the country of origin, the United States Department of State's report of birth abroad, or the documents of the United States Immigration and Naturalization Service;
                (2) if the exact place of birth is unknown, enter the information that is known and designate a place of birth according to the best information known with respect to the country of origin;
                (3) if the exact date of birth is unknown, determine a date of birth

based upon medical evidence as to the probable age of the adoptee and other evidence the court considers appropriate; and

(4) if documents described in paragraph (1) are not available, determine the date and place of birth based upon evidence the court finds appropriate to consider.

(c) Unless a petitioner requests otherwise, the decree of adoption may not name a former parent of the adoptee.

(d) Except for a decree of adoption of a minor by a stepparent which is issued pursuant to Article 4, a decree of adoption of a minor must contain a statement that the adoption terminates any order for visitation or communication with the minor that was in effect before the decree is issued.

(e) A decree that substantially complies with the requirements of this section is not subject to challenge solely because one or more items required by this section are not contained in the decree.

**SECTION 3-706. FINALITY OF DECREE.** A decree of adoption is a final order for purposes of appeal when it is issued and becomes final for other purposes upon the expiration of the time for filing an appeal, if no appeal is filed, or upon the denial or dismissal of any appeal filed within the requisite time.

**SECTION 3-707. CHALLENGES TO DECREE.**

(a) An appeal from a decree of adoption or other appealable order issued under this [Act] must be heard expeditiously.

(b) A decree or order issued under this [Act] may not be vacated or annulled upon application of a person who waived notice, or who was properly served with notice pursuant to this [Act] and failed to respond or appear, file an answer, or file a claim of paternity within the time allowed.

(c) The validity of an adoption may not be challenged for failure to comply with an agreement for visitation or communication with an adoptee.

(d) A decree of adoption or other order issued under this [Act] is not subject to a challenge begun more than six months after the decree or order is issued. If a challenge is brought by an individual whose parental relationship to an adoptee is terminated by a decree or order under this [Act], the court shall deny the challenge, unless the court finds by clear and convincing evidence that the decree or order is not in the best interest of the adoptee.

[PART] 8. BIRTH CERTIFICATE

**SECTION 3-801. REPORT OF ADOPTION.**

(a) Within 30 days after a decree of adoption becomes final, the clerk of the court shall prepare a report of adoption on a form furnished by the [State

Registrar of Vital Records] and certify and send the report to the [Registrar]. The report must include:

(1) information in the court's record of the proceeding for adoption which is necessary to locate and identify the adoptee's birth certificate or, in the case of an adoptee born outside the United States, evidence the court finds appropriate to consider as to the adoptee's date and place of birth;

(2) information in the court's record of the proceeding for adoption which is necessary to issue a new birth certificate for the adoptee and a request that a new certificate be issued, unless the court, the adoptive parent, or an adoptee who has attained 12 years of age requests that a new certificate not be issued; and

(3) the file number of the decree of adoption and the date on which the decree became final.

(b) Within 30 days after a decree of adoption is amended or vacated, the clerk of the court shall prepare a report of that action on a form furnished by the [Registrar] and shall certify and send the report to the [Registrar]. The report must include information necessary to identify the original report of adoption, and shall also include information necessary to amend or withdraw any new birth certificate that was issued pursuant to the original report of adoption.

### SECTION 3-802. ISSUANCE OF NEW BIRTH CERTIFICATE.

(a) Except as otherwise provided in subsection (d), upon receipt of a report of adoption prepared pursuant to Section 3-801, a report of adoption prepared in accordance with the law of another State or country, a certified copy of a decree of adoption together with information necessary to identify the adoptee's original birth certificate and to issue a new certificate, or a report of an amended adoption, the [Registrar] shall:

(1) issue a new birth certificate for an adoptee born in this State and furnish a certified copy of the new certificate to the adoptive parent and to an adoptee who has attained 12 years of age;

(2) forward a certified copy of a report of adoption for an adoptee born in another State to the [Registrar] of the State of birth;

(3) issue a certificate of foreign birth for an adoptee adopted in this State and who was born outside the United States and was not a citizen of the United States at the time of birth, and furnish a certified copy of the certificate to the adoptive parent and to an adoptee who has attained 12 years of age;

(4) notify an adoptive parent of the procedure for obtaining a revised birth certificate through the United States Department of State for an adoptee born outside the United States who was a citizen of the United States at the time of birth; or

(5) in the case of an amended decree of adoption, issue an amended birth certificate according to the procedure in paragraph (1) or (3) or follow the

procedure in paragraph (2) or (4).

(b) Unless otherwise specified by the court, a new birth certificate issued pursuant to subsection (a)(1) or (3), or an amended certificate issued pursuant to subsection (a)(5) must include the date and place of birth of the adoptee, substitute the name of the adoptive parent for the name of the individual listed as the adoptee's parent on the original birth certificate, and contain any other information prescribed by [the State's vital records law or regulations].

(c) The [Registrar] shall substitute the new or amended birth certificate for the original birth certificate in the [Registrar's] files. The original certificate and all copies of the certificate in the files of the [Registrar] or any other custodian of vital records in the State must be sealed and are not subject to inspection until 99 years after the adoptee's date of birth, but may be inspected as provided in this [Act].

(d) If the court, the adoptive parent, or an adoptee who has attained 12 years of age requests that a new or amended birth certificate not be issued, the [Registrar] may not issue a new or amended certificate for an adoptee pursuant to subsection (a), but shall forward a certified copy of the report of adoption or of an amended decree of adoption for an adoptee who was born in another State to the appropriate office in the adoptee's State of birth.

{e) Upon receipt of a report that an adoption has been vacated, the [Registrar] shall:

(1) restore the original birth certificate for an individual born in this State to its place in the files, seal any new or amended birth certificate issued pursuant to subsection (a), and not allow inspection of a sealed certificate except upon court order or as otherwise provided in this [Act];

(2) forward the report with respect to an individual born in another State to the appropriate office in the State of birth; or

(3) notify the individual who is granted legal custody of a former adoptee after an adoption is vacated of the procedure for obtaining an original birth certificate through the United States Department of State for a former adoptee born outside the United States who was a citizen of the United States at the time of birth.

(f) Upon request by an individual who was listed as a parent on a child's original birth certificate and who furnishes appropriate proof of the individual's identity, the [Registrar] shall give the individual a noncertified copy of the original birth certificate.

## ARTICLE 4. ADOPTION OF MINOR STEPCHILD BY STEPPARENT

**SECTION 4-101. OTHER PROVISIONS APPLICABLE TO ADOPTION OF STEPCHILD.** Except as otherwise provided by this [article],

[Article] 3 applies to an adoption of a minor stepchild by a stepparent.

## SECTION 4-102. STANDING TO ADOPT MINOR STEPCHILD.

(a) A stepparent has standing under this Article to petition to adopt a minor stepchild who is the child of the stepparent's spouse if:

(1) the spouse has sole legal and physical custody of the child and the child has been in the physical custody of the spouse and the stepparent during the 60 days next preceding the filing of a petition for adoption;

(2) the spouse has joint legal custody of the child with the child's other parent and the child has resided primarily with the spouse and the stepparent during the 12 months next preceding the filing of the petition;

(3) the spouse is deceased or mentally incompetent, but before dying or being judicially declared mentally incompetent, had legal and physical custody of the child, and the child has resided primarily with the stepparent during the 12 months next preceding the filing of the petition; or

(4) an agency placed the minor stepchild with the stepparent pursuant to Section 2-104.

(b) For good cause shown, a court may allow an individual who does not meet the requirements of paragraphs (a)(1) through (4), but has the consent of the custodial parent of a minor to file a petition for adoption under this Article. A petition allowed under this subsection shall be treated as a petition for adoption by a stepparent.

(c) A petition for adoption by a stepparent may be joined with a petition under Article 3, Part 5, to terminate the parental relationship between the minor adoptee and the adoptee's parent who is not the stepparent's spouse.

## SECTION 4-103. LEGAL CONSEQUENCES OF ADOPTION OF STEPCHILD.

(a) Except as otherwise provided in subsections (b) and (c), the legal consequences of an adoption of a stepchild by a stepparent are the same as under Sections 1-103 through 1-106.

(b) An adoption by a stepparent does not affect:

(1) the relationship between the adoptee and the adoptee's parent who is the adoptive stepparent's spouse or deceased spouse;

(2) an existing court order for visitation or communication with a minor adoptee by an individual related to the adoptee through the parent who is the adoptive stepparent's spouse or deceased spouse;

(3) the right of the adoptee or a descendant of the adoptee to inheritance or intestate succession through or from the adoptee's former parent; or

(4) A court order or agreement for visitation or communication with a minor adoptee approved by the court pursuant to Section 4-113.

(c) Failure to comply with an agreement or order is not a ground for challenging the validity of the adoption.

**SECTION 4-104. CONSENT TO ADOPTION.** Unless consent is not required under Section 2-402, a petition to adopt a minor stepchild may be granted only if consent to the adoption has been executed by a stepchild who has attained 12 years of age; and

(1) the minor's parents as described in Section 2401 (a);

(2) the minor's guardian if expressly authorized by a court to consent to the minor's adoption; or

(3) an agency that placed the minor for adoption by the stepparent.

**SECTION 4-105. CONTENT OF CONSENT BY STEPPARENT'S SPOUSE.**

(a) A consent executed by a parent who is the stepparent's spouse must be signed or confirmed in the presence of an individual specified in Section 2-405, or an individual authorized to take acknowledgements.

(b) A consent under subsection (a) must be in writing, must contain the required statements described in Section 2-406(a)(1) through (3) and (d)(3) through (6), may contain the optional statements described in Section 2-406(f), and must state that:

(1) the parent executing the consent has legal and physical custody of the parent's minor child and voluntarily and unequivocally consents to the adoption of the minor by the stepparent;

(2) the adoption will not terminate the parental relationship between the parent executing the consent and the minor child; and

(3) the parent executing the consent understands and agrees that the adoption will terminate the parental relationship between the minor and the minor's other parent, and will terminate any existing court order for custody, visitation, or communication with the minor, but:

(i) the minor and any descendant of the minor will retain the opportunity to inherit from or through the other parent;

(ii) a court order for visitation or communication with the minor by an individual related to the minor through the parent executing the consent, or an agreement or order concerning another individual which is approved by the court pursuant to Section 4-113 survives the decree of adoption, but failure to comply with the terms of the order or agreement is not a ground for revoking or setting aside the consent or the adoption; and

(iii) the other parent remains liable for arrearages of child support, unless released from that obligation by the parent executing the consent and by a governmental entity providing public assistance to the minor.

(c) The consent may not waive further notice of the proceeding for adoption of the minor by the stepparent.

### SECTION 4-106. CONTENT OF CONSENT BY MINOR'S OTHER PARENT.

(a) A consent executed by a minor's parent who is not the stepparent's spouse must be signed or confirmed in the presence of an individual specified in Section 2-405.

(b) A consent under subsection (a) must be in writing, must contain the required statements described in Section 2-406(a)(1) through (3) and (d)(3) through (6), may contain the optional statements described in Section 2-406(f), and must state that:

(1) the parent executing the consent voluntarily and unequivocally consents to the adoption of the minor by the stepparent and the transfer to the stepparent's spouse and the adoptive stepparent of any right the parent executing the consent has to legal or physical custody of the minor;

(2) the parent executing the consent understands and agrees that the adoption will terminate his or her parental relationship to the minor and will terminate any existing court order for custody, visitation, or communication with the minor, but:

(i) the minor and any descendant of the minor will retain the opportunity to inherit from or through the parent executing the consent
(ii) a court order for visitation or communication with the minor by an individual related to the minor through the minor's other parent, or an agreement or order concerning another individual which is approved by the court pursuant to Section 4-113 survives the decree of adoption, but failure to comply with the terms of the order or agreement is not a ground for revoking or setting aside the consent or the adoption; and

(iii) the parent executing the consent remains liable for arrearages of child support, unless released from that obligation by the other parent and any guardian ad litem of the minor and by a governmental entity providing public assistance to the minor; and

(3) the parent executing the consent has provided the adoptive stepparent with the information required by Section 2-106.

(c) A consent under subsection (a) may waive notice of the proceeding for adoption of the minor by the stepparent, unless the adoption is contested, appealed, or denied.

### SECTION 4-107. CONTENT OF CONSENT BY OTHER PERSONS.

(a) A consent executed by the guardian of a minor stepchild or by an agency must be in writing and signed or confirmed in the presence of the court, or in a manner the court directs, and:

(1) must state the circumstances under which the guardian or agency obtained the authority to consent to the adoption of the minor by a stepparent;

(2) must contain the statements required by Sections 4-104 and 4-105, except for any that can be made only by a parent of the minor; and

(3) may waive notice of the proceeding for adoption, unless the adoption is contested, appealed, or denied.

(b) A consent executed by a minor stepchild in a proceeding for adoption by a stepparent must be signed or confirmed in the presence of the court or in a manner the court directs.

### SECTION 4-108. PETITION TO ADOPT.

(a) A petition by a stepparent to adopt a minor stepchild must be signed and verified by the petitioner and contain the following information or state why any of the information is not contained in the petition:

(1) the information required by Section 3-304(a) (1), (3), (5), and (8) through (12) and (b);

(2) the current marital status of the petitioner including the date and place of marriage, the name and date and place of birth of the petitioner's spouse, and, if the spouse is deceased, the date, place, and cause of death, and, if the spouse is incompetent, the date on which a court declared the spouse incompetent;

(3) the length of time the minor has been residing with the petitioner and the petitioner's spouse and, if the minor is not in the physical custody of the petitioner and the petitioner's spouse, the reason why they do not have custody and when they intend to obtain custody; and

(4) the length of time the petitioner's spouse or the petitioner has had legal custody of the minor and the circumstances under which legal custody was obtained.

### SECTION 4-109. REQUIRED DOCUMENTS.

(a) After a petition to adopt a minor stepchild is filed, the following must be filed in the proceeding:

(1) any item required by Section 3-305(a) which is relevant to an adoption by a stepparent; and

(2) a copy of any agreement to waive arrearages of child support.

(b) If any of the items required by subsection (a) is not available, the person responsible for furnishing the item shall file an affidavit explaining its absence.

**SECTION 4-110. NOTICE OF PENDENCY OF PROCEEDING.**

(a) Within 30 days after a petition to adopt a minor stepchild is filed, the petitioner shall serve notice of the proceeding upon:

(1) the petitioner's spouse;

(2) any other person whose consent to the adoption is required under this Article;

(3) any person described in Section 3-401 (a)(3), (4), and (6) and (b); and

(4) the parents of the minor's parent whose parental relationship will be terminated by the adoption unless the identity or the whereabouts of those parents are unknown.

**SECTION 4-111. EVALUATION OF STEPPARENT.**

(a) After a petition for adoption of a minor stepchild is filed, the court may order that an evaluation be made by an individual qualified under Section 2-202 to assist the court in determining whether the proposed adoption is in the best interest of the minor.

(b) The court shall provide an evaluator with copies of the petition for adoption and of the items filed with the petition.

(c) Unless otherwise directed by the court, an evaluator shall base the evaluation on a personal interview with the petitioner and the petitioner's spouse in the petitioner's residence, observation of the relationship between the minor and the petitioner, any personal interview of others who know the petitioner, and any information received pursuant to subsection (d).

(d) An evaluation under this section must be in writing and contain the following:

(1) the information required by Section 2-203(d) and (e);

(2) the information required by Section 3-602(b)(2) through (5); and

(3) the finding required by Section 3-602(b)(6).

(e) An evaluator shall complete an evaluation and file it with the court within 60 days after being asked for the evaluation under this section, unless the court allows a later filing.

(f) Section 3-603(b) and (c) apply to an evaluation under this section.

**SECTION 4-112. DISPOSITIONAL HEARING: DECREE OF ADOPTION.** Sections 3-701 through 3-707 apply to a proceeding for adoption of a minor stepchild by a stepparent, but the court may waive the requirements of Section 3-702.

## SECTION 4-113. VISITATION AGREEMENT AND ORDER.

(a) Upon the request of the petitioner in a proceeding for adoption of a minor stepchild, the court shall review a written agreement that permits another individual to visit or communicate with the minor after the decree of adoption becomes final, which must be signed by the individual, the petitioner, the petitioner's spouse, the minor if 12 years of age or older, and, if an agency placed the minor for adoption, an authorized employee of the agency.

(b) The court may enter an order approving the agreement only upon determining that the agreement is in the best interest of the minor adoptee. In making this determination, the court shall consider:

(1) the preference of the minor, if the minor is mature enough to express a preference;

(2) any special needs of the minor and how they would be affected by performance of the agreement;

(3) the length and quality of any existing relationship between the minor and the individual who would be entitled to visit or communicate, and the likely effect on the minor of allowing this relationship to continue;

(4) the specific terms of the agreement and the likelihood that the parties to the agreement will cooperate in performing its terms;

(5) the recommendation of the minor's guardian ad litem, lawyer, social worker, or other counselor; and

(6) any other factor relevant to the best interest of the minor.

(c) In addition to any agreement approved pursuant to subsections (a) and (b), the court may approve the continuation of an existing order or issue a new order permitting the minor adoptee's former parent, grandparent, or sibling to visit or communicate with the minor if:

(1) the grandparent is the parent of a deceased parent of the minor or the parent of the adoptee's parent whose parental relationship to the minor is terminated by the decree of adoption;

(2) the former parent, grandparent, or sibling requests that an existing order be permitted to survive the decree of adoption or that a new order be issued; and

(3) the court determines that the requested visitation or communication is in the best interest of the minor.

(d) In making a determination under subsection (c)(3), the court shall consider the factors listed in subsection (b) and any objections to the requested order by the adoptive stepparent and the stepparent's spouse.

(e) An order issued under this section may be enforced in a civil action only if the court finds that enforcement is in the best interest of a minor adoptee.

(f) An order issued under this section may not be modified unless the court finds that modification is in the best interest of a minor adoptee and:

(1) the individuals subject to the order request the modification; or

(2) exceptional circumstances arising since the order was issued justify the modification.

(g) Failure to comply with the terms of an order approved under this section or with any other agreement for visitation or communication is not a ground for revoking, setting aside, or otherwise challenging the validity of a consent, relinquishment, or adoption pertaining to a minor stepchild, and the validity of the consent, relinquishment, and adoption is not affected by any later action to enforce, modify, or set aside the order or agreement.

[ARTICLE] 5. ADOPTION OF ADULTS AND EMANCIPATED MINORS

### SECTION 5-101. WHO MAY ADOPT ADULT OR EMANCIPATED MINOR.

(a) An adult may adopt another adult or an emancipated minor pursuant to this Article, but:

(1) an adult may not adopt his or her spouse; and

(2) an incompetent individual of any age may be adopted only pursuant to Articles 2, 3, and 4.

(b) An individual who has adopted an adult or emancipated minor may not adopt another adult or emancipated minor within one year after the adoption unless the prospective adoptee is a sibling of the existing adoptee.

### SECTION 5-102. LEGAL CONSEQUENCES OF ADOPTION. The legal consequences of an adoption of an adult or emancipated minor are the same as under Sections 1-103 through 1-106, but the legal consequences of adoption of an adult stepchild by an adult stepparent are the same as under Section 4-103.

### SECTION 5-103. CONSENT TO ADOPTION.

(a) Consent to the adoption of an adult or emancipated minor is required only of:

(1) the adoptee;

(2) the prospective adoptive parent; and

(3) the spouse of the prospective adoptive parent, unless they are legally separated, or the court finds that the spouse is not capable of giving consent or is withholding consent contrary to the best interest of the adoptee and the prospective adoptive parent.

(b) The consent of the adoptee and the prospective adoptive parent must:

(1) be in writing and be signed or confirmed by each of them in the presence of the court or an individual authorized to take acknowledgments;

(2) state that they agree to assume toward each other the legal relationship of parent and child and to have all of the rights and be subject to all of the duties of that relationship; and

(3) state that they understand the consequences the adoption may have for any right of inheritance, property, or support each has.

(c) The consent of the spouse of the prospective adoptive parent:

(1) must be in writing and be signed or confirmed in the presence of the court or an individual authorized to take acknowledgments;

(2) must state that the spouse:

(i) consents to the proposed adoption; and (ii) understands the consequences the adoption
may have for any right of inheritance, property, or support the spouse has; and

(3) may waive notice of the adoption proceeding.

## SECTION 5-104. JURISDICTION AND VENUE.

(a) The court has jurisdiction over a proceeding for the adoption of an adult or emancipated minor under this Article if a petitioner lived in this State for at least 90 days immediately preceding the filing of a petition for adoption.

(b) A petition for adoption may be filed in the court in the [county] in which a petitioner lives.

## SECTION 5-105. PETITION FOR ADOPTION.

(a) A prospective adoptive parent and an adoptee under this Article must jointly file a petition for adoption.

(b) The petition must be signed and verified by each petitioner and state:

(1) the full name, age, and place and duration of residence of each petitioner;

(2) the current marital status of each petitioner, including the date and place of marriage, if married;

(3) the full name by which the adoptee is to be known if the petition is granted;

(4) the duration and nature of the relationship between the prospective adoptive parent and the adoptee;

(5) that the prospective adoptive parent and the adoptee desire to assume the legal relationship of parent and child and to have all of the rights and be subject to all of the duties of that relationship;

(6) that the adoptee understands that a consequence of the adoption will be to terminate the adoptee's relationship as the child of an existing parent, but if the adoptive parent is the adoptee's stepparent, the adoption will not affect the adoptee's relationship with a parent who is the stepparent's spouse, but will terminate the adoptee's relationship to the adoptee's other parent, except for the

right to inherit from or through that parent;

(7) the name and last known address of any other individual whose consent is required;

(8) the name, age, and last known address of any child of the prospective adoptive parent, including a child previously adopted by the prospective adoptive parent or his or her spouse, and the date and place of the adoption; and

(9) the name, age, and last known address of any living parent or child of the adoptee.

(c) The petitioners shall attach to the petition:

(1) a certified copy of the birth certificate or other evidence of the date and place of birth of the adoptee and the prospective adoptive parent, if available, and

(2) any required consent that has been executed.

### SECTION 5-106. NOTICE AND TIME OF HEARING.

(a) Within 30 days after a petition for adoption is filed, the petitioners shall serve notice of hearing the petition upon any individual whose consent to the adoption is required under Section 5-103, and who has not waived notice, by sending a copy of the petition and notice of hearing to the individual at the address stated in the petition, or according to the manner of service provided in Section 3-403.

(b) The court shall set a date and time for hearing the petition, which must be at least 30 days after the notice is served.

### SECTION 5-107. DISPOSITIONAL HEARING.

(a) Both petitioners shall appear in person at the hearing, unless an appearance is excused for good cause shown. In that event an appearance may be made for either or both of them by a lawyer authorized in writing to make the appearance, or a hearing may be conducted by telephone or other electronic medium.

(b) The court shall examine the petitioners, or the lawyer for a petitioner not present in person, and shall grant the petition for adoption if it determines that:

(1) at least 30 days have elapsed since the service of notice of hearing the petition for adoption;

(2) notice has been served, or dispensed with, as to any person whose consent is required under Section 5-103;

(3) every necessary consent, waiver, document, or judicial order has been obtained and filed with the court;

(4) the adoption is for the purpose of creating the relationship of parent and child between the petitioners and the petitioners understand the

consequences of the relationship; and

(5) there has been substantial compliance with this [Act] .

## SECTION 5-108. DECREE OF ADOPTION.

(a) A decree of adoption issued under this [article] must substantially conform to the relevant requirements of Section 3-705 and appeals from a decree, or challenges to it, are governed by Sections 3-706 and 3-707.

(b) The court shall send a copy of the decree to each individual named in the petition at the address stated in the petition.

(c) Within 30 days after a decree of adoption becomes final, the clerk of the court shall prepare a report of the adoption for the [State Registrar of Vital Records], and, if the petitioners have requested it, the report shall instruct the [Registrar] to issue a new birth certificate to the adoptee, as provided in Article 3, Part 8.

## [ARTICLE] 6. RECORDS OF ADOPTION PROCEEDING: RETENTION, CONFIDENTIALITY, AND ACCESS

**SECTION 6-101. RECORDS DEFINED.** Unless the context requires otherwise, for purposes of this Article, "records" includes all documents, exhibits, and data pertaining to an adoption.

## SECTION 6-102. RECORDS CONFIDENTIAL, COURT RECORDS SEALED.

(a) All records, whether on file with the court, or in the possession of an agency, the [Registrar of Vital Records or Statistics], a lawyer, or other provider of professional services in connection with an adoption, are confidential and may not be inspected except as provided in this [Act].

(b) During a proceeding for adoption, records are not open to inspection except as directed by the court.

(c) Within 30 days after a decree of adoption becomes final, the clerk of the court shall send to the [Registrar], in addition to the report of adoption required by Section 3-801, a certified copy of any document signed pursuant to Section 2-404(e) and filed in the proceeding for adoption.

(d) All records on file with the court must be retained permanently and sealed for 99 years after the date of the adoptee's birth. Sealed records and indices of the records are not open to inspection by any person except as provided in this [Act].

(e) Any additional information about an adoptee, the adoptee's former parents, and the adoptee's genetic history that is submitted to the court within the 99-year period, must be added to the sealed records of the court. Any additional information that is submitted to an agency, lawyer, or other professional provider of services within the 99-year period must be kept confidential.

## SECTION 6-103. RELEASE OF NONIDENTIFYING INFORMATION.

(a) An adoptive parent or guardian of an adoptee, an adoptee who has attained 18 years of age, an emancipated adoptee, a deceased adoptee's direct descendant who has attained 18 years of age, or the parent or guardian of a direct descendant who has not attained 18 years of age may request the court that granted the adoption or the agency that placed the adoptee for adoption, to furnish the nonidentifying information about the adoptee, the adoptee's former parents, and the adoptee's genetic history that has been retained by the court or agency, including the information required by Section 2-106.

(b) The court or agency shall furnish the individual who makes the request with a detailed summary of any relevant report or information that is included in the sealed records of the court or the confidential records of the agency. The summary must exclude identifying information concerning an individual who has not filed a waiver of confidentiality with the court or agency. The Department or the court shall prescribe forms and a procedure for summarizing any report or information released under this section.

(c) An individual who is denied access to nonidentifying information to which the individual is entitled under this Article or Section 2-106 may petition the court for relief.

(d) If a court receives a certified statement from a physician explaining in detail how a health condition may seriously affect the health of the adoptee or a direct descendant of the adoptee, the court shall make a diligent effort to notify an adoptee who has attained 18 years of age, an adoptive parent of an adoptee who has not attained 18 years of age, or a direct descendant of a deceased adoptee that the nonidentifying information is available and may be requested from the court.

(e) If a court receives a certified statement from a physician explaining in detail why a serious health condition of the adoptee or a direct descendant of the adoptee should be communicated to the adoptee's genetic parent or sibling to enable them to make an informed reproductive decision, the court shall make a diligent effort to notify those individuals that the nonidentifying information is available and may be requested from the court.

(f) If the [Registrar] receives a request or any additional information from an individual pursuant to this section, the [Registrar] shall give the individual the name and address of the court or agency having the records, and if the court or agency is in another State, shall assist the individual in locating the court or agency. The [Registrar] shall prescribe a reasonable procedure for verifying the identity, age, or other relevant characteristics of an individual who requests or furnishes information under this section.

### SECTION 6-104. DISCLOSURE OF IDENTIFYING INFORMATION.

(a) Except as otherwise provided in this Article, identifying information about an adoptee's former parent, an adoptee, or an adoptive parent which is contained in records, including original birth certificates, required by this [Act] to be confidential or sealed, may not be disclosed to any person.

(b) Identifying information about an adoptee's former parent must be disclosed by the [Registrar] to an adoptee who has attained 18 years of age, an adoptive parent of an adoptee who has not attained 18 years of age, a deceased adoptee's direct descendant who has attained 18 years of age, or the parent or guardian of a direct descendant who has not attained 18 years of age if one of these individuals requests the information and:

(1) the adoptee's former parent or, if the former parent is deceased or has been judicially declared incompetent, an adult descendant of the former parent authorizes the disclosure of his or her name, date of birth, or last known address, or other identifying information, either in a document signed pursuant to Section 2-404(e) and filed in the proceeding for adoption or in another signed document filed with the court, an agency, or the [Registrar]; or

(2) the adoptee's former parent authorizes the disclosure of the requested information only if the adoptee, adoptive parent, or direct descendant agrees to release similar identifying information about the adoptee, adoptive parent, or direct descendant and this individual authorizes the disclosure of the information in a signed document kept by the court, an agency, or the [Registrar].

(c) Identifying information about an adoptee or a deceased adoptee's direct descendant must be disclosed by the [Registrar] to an adoptee's former parent if that individual requests the information and:

(1) an adoptee who has attained 18 years of age, an adoptive parent of an adoptee who has not attained 18 years of age, a deceased adoptee's direct descendant who has attained 18 years of age, or the parent or guardian of a direct descendant who has not attained 18 years of age authorizes the disclosure of the requested information in the manner described in subsection (b)(2); or

(2) one of those individuals authorizes the disclosure of the requested information only if the adoptee's former parent agrees to release similar information about himself or herself, and the former parent authorizes the disclosure of the information in the manner described in subsection (b)(1).

(d) Identifying information about an adult sibling of an adoptee who has attained 18 years of age must be disclosed by the [Registrar] to an adoptee if:

(1) the sibling is also an adoptee; and

(2) both the sibling and the adoptee have consented to disclosure of the

information.

(e) Subsection (d) does not permit disclosure of a former parent's identity unless that parent has authorized disclosure under this [Act].

## SECTION 6-105. ACTION FOR DISCLOSURE OF INFORMATION.

(a) To obtain information not otherwise available under Section 6-103 or 6-104, an adoptee who has attained 18 years of age, an adoptee who has not attained 18 years of age and has the permission of an adoptive parent, an adoptive parent of an adoptee who has not attained 18 years of age, a deceased adoptee's direct descendant who has attained 18 years of age, the parent or guardian of a direct descendant who has not attained 18 years of age, or an adoptee's former parent may file a petition in the court to obtain information about another individual described in this section which is contained in records, including original birth certificates, required by this [Act] to be confidential or sealed. (b) In determining whether to grant a petition under this section, the court shall review the sealed records of the relevant proceeding for adoption and shall make specific findings concerning:

(1) the reason the information is sought;

(2) whether the individual about whom information is sought has filed a signed document described in Section 2-404(e) or 6-104 requesting that his or her identity not be disclosed, or has not filed any document;

(3) whether the individual about whom information is sought is alive;

(4) whether it is possible to satisfy the petitioner's request without disclosing the identity of another individual;

(5) the likely effect of disclosure on the adoptee, the adoptive parents, the adoptee's former parents, and other members of the adoptee's original and adoptive families; and

(6) the age, maturity, and expressed needs of the adoptee.

(c) The court may order the disclosure of the requested information only upon a determination that good cause exists for the release based on the findings required by subsection (b) and a conclusion that:

( 1 ) there is a compelling reason for disclosure of the information; and

(2) the benefit to the petitioner will be greater than the harm to any other individual of disclosing the information.

## SECTION 6-106. STATEWIDE REGISTRY. The [Registrar] shall:

(1) establish a statewide confidential registry for receiving, filing, and retaining documents requesting, authorizing, or not authorizing, the release of

identifying information;

(2) prescribe and distribute forms or documents on which an individual may request, authorize, or refuse to authorize the release of identifying information;

(3) devise a procedure for releasing identifying information in the [Registrar's] possession upon receipt of an appropriate request and authorization;

(4) cooperate with registries in other States to facilitate the matching of documents filed pursuant to this Article by individuals in different States; and

(5) announce and publicize to the general public the existence of the registry and the procedure for the consensual release of identifying information.

### SECTION 6-107. RELEASE OF ORIGINAL BIRTH CERTIFICATE.

(a) In addition to any copy of an adoptee's original birth certificate authorized for release by a court order issued pursuant to Section 6-105, the [Registrar] shall furnish a copy of the original birth certificate upon the request of an adoptee who has attained 18 years of age, the direct descendant of a deceased adoptee, or an adoptive parent of an adoptee who has not attained 18 years of age, if the individual who makes the request furnishes a consent to disclosure signed by each individual who was named as a parent on the adoptee's original birth certificate.

(b) When 99 years have elapsed after the date of birth of an adoptee whose original birth certificate is sealed under this [Act], the [Registrar] shall unseal the original certificate and file it with any new or amended certificate that has been issued. The unsealed certificates become public information in accordance with any statute or regulation applicable to the retention and disclosure of records by the [Registrar].

### SECTION 6-108. CERTIFICATE OF ADOPTION. Upon the request of an adoptive parent or an adoptee who has attained 18 years of age, the clerk of the court that entered a decree of adoption shall issue a certificate of adoption which states the date and place of adoption the date of birth of the adoptee, the name of each adoptive parent, and the name of the adoptee as provided in the decree.

### SECTION 6-109. DISCLOSURE AUTHORIZED IN COURSE OF EMPLOYMENT. This [article] does not preclude an employee or agent of a court, agency, or the [Registrar] from:

(1) inspecting permanent, confidential, or sealed records for the purpose of discharging any obligation under this [Act];

(2) disclosing the name of the court where a proceeding for adoption

occurred, or the name of an agency that placed an adoptee, to an individual described in Sections 6-103 through 6-105, who can verify his or her identity; or

(3) disclosing nonidentifying information contained in confidential or sealed records in accordance with any other applicable state or federal law.

**SECTION 6-110. FEE FOR SERVICES.** A court, an agency, or the [Registrar] may charge a reasonable fee for services, including copying services, it performs pursuant to this [article].

## [ARTICLE] 7. PROHIBITED AND PERMISSIBLE ACTIVITIES IN CONNECTION WITH ADOPTION

**SECTION 7-101. PROHIBITED ACTIVITIES IN PLACEMENT.**
(a) Except as provided in Article 2, Part 1:

(1) a person, other than a parent, guardian, or agency, as specified in Sections 2-101 through 2-103, may not place a minor for adoption or advertise in any public medium that the person knows of a minor who is available for adoption;

(2) a person, other than an agency or an individual with a favorable preplacement evaluation, as required by Sections 2-201 through 2-207, may not advertise in any public medium that the person is willing to accept a minor for adoption;

(3) an individual, other than a relative or stepparent of a minor, who does not have a favorable preplacement evaluation or a court-ordered waiver of the evaluation, or who has an unfavorable evaluation, may not obtain legal or physical custody of a minor for purposes of adoption; and

(4) a person may not place or assist in placing a minor for adoption with an individual, other than a relative or stepparent, unless the person knows that the individual has a favorable preplacement evaluation or a waiver pursuant to Section 2-201.

(b) A person who violates subsection (a) is liable for a [civil penalty] not to exceed [$5,000] for the first violation, and not to exceed [$10,000] for each succeeding violation in an action brought by the [appropriate official]. The court may enjoin from further violations any person who violates subsection (a) and shall refer the person to an appropriate licensing authority for disciplinary proceedings.

**SECTION 7-102. UNLAWFUL PAYMENTS RELATED TO ADOPTION.**
(a) Except as provided in Sections 7-103 and 7-104, a person may not pay or give or offer to pay or give to any other person, or request, receive, or accept

any money or anything of value, directly or indirectly, for:

(1) the placement of a minor for adoption;

(2) the consent of a parent, a guardian, or an agency to the adoption of a minor; or

(3) the relinquishment of a minor to an agency for the purpose of adoption.

(b) The following persons are liable for a [civil penalty] not to exceed [$5,000] for the first violation, and not to exceed [$10,000] for each succeeding violation in an action brought by the [appropriate official]:

(1) a person who knowingly violates subsection (a);

(2) a person who knowingly makes a false report to the court about a payment prohibited by this section or authorized by Section 7-103 or 7-104; and

(3) a parent or guardian who knowingly receives or accepts a payment authorized by Section 7-103 or 7104 with the intent not to consent to an adoption or to relinquish a minor for adoption.

(c) The court may enjoin from further violations any person described in subsection (b) and shall refer the person to an appropriate licensing authority for disciplinary proceedings.

## SECTION 7-103. LAWFUL PAYMENTS RELATED TO ADOPTION.

(a) Subject to the requirements of Sections 3-702 and 3-703 for an accounting and judicial approval of fees and charges related to an adoption, an adoptive parent, or a person acting on behalf of an adoptive parent, may pay for:

(1) the services of an agency in connection with an adoption;

(2) advertising and similar expenses incurred in locating a minor for adoption;

(3) medical, hospital, nursing, pharmaceutical, travel, or other similar expenses incurred by a mother or her minor child in connection with the birth or any illness of the minor;

(4) counseling services for a parent or a minor for a reasonable time before and after the minor's placement for adoption;

(5) living expenses of a mother for a reasonable time before the birth of her child and for no more than six weeks after the birth;

(6) expenses incurred in ascertaining the information required by Section 2-106;

(7) legal services, court costs, and travel or other administrative expenses connected with an adoption, including any legal services performed for a parent who consents to the adoption of a minor or relinquishes the minor to an agency;

(8) expenses incurred in obtaining a preplacement evaluation and

an evaluation during the proceeding for adoption; and

(9) any other service or expense the court finds is reasonable and necessary.

(b) A parent or a guardian, a person acting on the parent's or guardian's behalf, or a provider of a service listed in subsection (a), may receive or accept a payment authorized by subsection (a). The payment may not be made contingent on the placement of a minor for adoption, relinquishment of the minor, or consent to the adoption. If the adoption is not completed, a person who is authorized to make a specific payment by subsection (a) is not liable for that payment unless the person has agreed in a signed writing with a provider of a service to make the payment regardless of the outcome of the proceeding for adoption.

**SECTION 7-104. CHARGES BY AGENCY.** Subject to the requirements of Sections 3-702 and 3-703 for an accounting and judicial approval of fees and charges related to an adoption, an agency may charge or accept a fee or other compensation from a prospective adoptive parent for:

(1) medical, hospital, nursing, pharmaceutical, travel, or other similar expenses incurred by a mother or her minor child in connection with the birth or any illness of the minor;

(2) a percentage of the annual cost the agency incurs in locating and providing counseling services for minor adoptees, parents, and prospective parents;

(3) living expenses of a mother for a reasonable time before the birth of a child and for no more than six weeks after the birth;

(4) expenses incurred in ascertaining the information required by Section 2-106;

(5) legal services, court costs, and travel or other administrative expenses connected with an adoption, including the legal services performed for a parent who relinquishes a minor child to the agency;

(6) preparation of a preplacement evaluation and an evaluation during the proceeding for adoption; and

(7) any other service or expense the court finds is reasonable and necessary.

**SECTION 7-105. FAILURE TO DISCLOSE INFORMATION.**

(a) A person, other than a parent, who has a duty to furnish the nonidentifying information required by Section 2-106, or authorized for release under [Article] 6, and who intentionally refuses to provide the information is subject to a [civil penalty] not to exceed [S5,000] for the first violation, and not to exceed [$10,000] for each succeeding violation in an action brought by the [appropriate official]. The court may enjoin the person from further violations of the duty to furnish nonidentifying information.

(b) An employee or agent of an agency, the court, or the State [Registrar of Vital Records] who intentionally destroys any information or report compiled pursuant to Section 2-106, or authorized for release under Article 6, is guilty of a [misdemeanor] [punishable by a fine of not more than [$    ] or imprisonment for not more than [    ], or both].

(c) In addition to the penalties provided in subsections (a) and (b), an adoptive parent, an adoptee, or any person who is the subject of any information required by Section 2-106, or authorized for release under [Article] 6, may maintain an action for damages or equitable relief against a person, other than a parent who placed a minor for adoption, who fails to perform the duties required by Section 2-106 or [Article] 6.

(d) A prospective adoptive parent who knowingly fails to furnish information or knowingly furnishes false information to an evaluator preparing an evaluation pursuant to [Article] 2, [Part] 2 or [Article 3], [Part] 6, with the intent to deceive the evaluator, is guilty of a [misdemeanor] punishable by a fine of not more than [$    ] or imprisonment for not more than [    ], or both.

(e) An evaluator who prepares an evaluation pursuant to Article 2, Part 2 or [Article] 3, [Part] 6 and who knowingly omits or misrepresents information about the individual being evaluated with the intent to deceive a person authorized under this [Act] to place a minor for adoption is guilty of a [misdemeanor] [punishable by a fine of not more than [$    ] or imprisonment for not more than [    ], or both].

(f) A parent of a minor child who knowingly misidentifies the minor's other parent with an intent to deceive the other parent, an agency, or a prospective adoptive parent is subject to a [civil penalty] not to exceed [$5,000] in an action brought by the [appropriate official].

**SECTION    7-106.    UNAUTHORIZED    DISCLOSURE    OF INFORMATION.**

(a) Except as authorized in this [Act], a person who furnishes or retains a report or records pursuant to this [Act] may not disclose any identifying or nonidentifying information contained in the report or records.

(b) A person who knowingly gives or offers to give or who accepts or agrees to accept anything of value for an unauthorized disclosure of identifying information made confidential by this [Act] is guilty of a [misdemeanor] [punishable by a fine of not more than [$    ] or imprisonment for not more than [    ], or both,] for the first violation and of a [felony] [punishable by a fine of not more than [$    ] or imprisonment for not more than [    ], or both,] for each succeeding violation.

(c) A person who knowingly gives or offers to give or who accepts or agrees to accept anything of value for an unauthorized disclosure of nonidentifying information made confidential by this [Act] is subject to a [civil penalty] not to exceed [$5,000] for the first violation, and not to exceed [$10,000] for each succeeding violation in an action brought by the [appropriate official].

(d) A person who makes a disclosure, that the person knows is unauthorized, of identifying or nonidentifying information from a report or record made confidential by this [Act] is subject to a [civil penalty] not to exceed [$2,500] for the first violation, and not to exceed [$5,000] for each succeeding violation in an action brought by the [appropriate official].

(e) The court may enjoin from further violations any person who makes or obtains an unauthorized disclosure and shall refer the person to an appropriate licensing authority for disciplinary proceedings.

(f) In addition to the penalties provided in subsections (b) through (e), an individual who is the subject of any of the information contained in a report or records made confidential by this [Act] may maintain an action for damages or equitable relief against any person who makes or obtains, or is likely to make or obtain, an unauthorized disclosure of the information.

(g) Identifying information contained in a report or records required by this [Act] to be kept confidential or sealed may not be disclosed under any other law of this State.

**SECTION 7-107. ACTION BY DEPARTMENT.** The department may review and investigate compliance with this [Act] and may maintain an action in the [appropriate court] to compel compliance.

*[ED.—Sections 8-101 through 8-106, omitted here, deal with uniformity of application and construction, the short title of the Act, transitional provisions, repeals, the effective date of the Act and severability.]*

# UNIFORM CHILD CUSTODY JURISDICTION ACT (1968)
## 9 U.L.A. 115 (West 1988)

*[The Uniform Child Custody Jurisdiction Act was drafted by the National Conference of Commissioners on Uniform State Laws and it is reproduced with their permission. Only selected portions of the official Comments are included, and some citations in them have been omitted.]*

### Section 1. [Purposes of Act;  Construction of Provisions.]
(a) The general purposes of this Act are to:

(1) avoid jurisdictional competition and conflict with courts of other states in matters of child custody which have in the past resulted in the shifting of children from state to state with harmful effects on their well-being;

(2) promote cooperation with the courts of other states to the end that a custody decree is rendered in that state which can best decide the case in the interest of the child;

(3) assure that litigation concerning the custody of a child take place ordinarily in the state with which the child and his family have the closest connection and where significant evidence concerning his care, protection, training, and personal relationships is most readily available, and that courts of this state decline the exercise of jurisdiction when the child and his family have a closer connection with another state;

(4) discourage continuing controversies over child custody in the interest of greater stability of home environment and of secure family relationships for the child;

(5) deter abductions and other unilateral removals of children undertaken to obtain custody awards;

(6) avoid re-litigation of custody decisions of other states in this state insofar as feasible;

(7) facilitate the enforcement of custody decrees of other states;

(8) promote and expand the exchange of information and other forms of mutual assistance between the courts of this state and those of other states concerned with the same child;  and

(9) make uniform the law of those states which enact it.

(b) This Act shall be construed to promote the general purposes stated in this section.

### Section 2. [Definitions]  As used in this Act:
(1) "contestant" means a person, including a parent, who claims a

right to custody or visitation rights with respect to a child;

(2) "custody determination" means a court decision and court orders and instructions providing for the custody of a child, including visitation rights; it does not include a decision relating to child support or any other monetary obligation of any person;

(3) "custody proceeding" includes proceedings in which a custody determination is one of several issues, such as an action for divorce or separation, and includes child neglect and dependency proceedings;

(4) "decree" or "custody decree" means a custody determination contained in a judicial decree or order made in a custody proceeding, and includes an initial decree and a modification decree;

(5) "home state" means the state in which the child immediately preceding the time involved lived with his parents, a parent, or a person acting as parent, for at least 6 consecutive months, and in the case of a child less than 6 months old the state in which the child lived from birth with any of the persons mentioned. Periods of temporary absence of any of the named persons are counted as part of the 6-month or other period;

(6) "initial decree" means the first custody decree concerning a particular child;

(7) "modification decree" means a custody decree which modifies or replaces a prior decree, whether made by the court which rendered the prior decree or by another court;

(8) "physical custody" means actual possession and control of a child;

(9) "person acting as parent" means a person, other than a parent, who has physical custody of a child and who has either been awarded custody by a court or claims a right to custody; and

(10) "state" means any state, territory, or possession of the United States, the Commonwealth of Puerto Rico, and the District of Columbia.

## Section 3. [Jurisdiction]

(a) A court of this State which is competent to decide child custody matters has jurisdiction to make a child custody determination by initial or modification decree if:

(1) this State (i) is the home state of the child at the time of commencement of the proceeding, or (ii) had been the child's home state within 6 months before commencement of the proceeding and the child is absent from this State because of his removal or retention by a person claiming his custody or for other reasons, and a parent or person acting as parent continues to live in this State; or

(2) it is in the best interest of the child that a court of this State

assume jurisdiction because (i) the child and his parents, or the child and at least one contestant, have a significant connection with this State, and (ii) there is available in this State substantial evidence concerning the child's present or future care, protection, training, and personal relationships; or

       (3) the child is physically present in this State and (i) the child has been abandoned or (ii) it is necessary in an emergency to protect the child because he has been subjected to or threatened with mistreatment or abuse or is otherwise neglected [or dependent]; or

       (4) (i) it appears that no other state would have jurisdiction under prerequisites substantially in accordance with paragraphs (1), (2), or (3), or another state has declined to exercise jurisdiction on the ground that this State is the more appropriate forum to determine the custody of the child, and (ii) it is in the best interest of the child that this court assume jurisdiction.

       (b) Except under paragraphs (3) and (4) of subsection (a), physical presence in this State of the child, or of the child and one of the contestants, is not alone sufficient to confer jurisdiction on a court of this State to make a child custody determination.

       (c) Physical presence of the child, while desirable, is not a prerequisite for jurisdiction to determine his custody.

## COMMENT

       Paragraphs (1) and (2) of subsection (a) establish the two major bases for jurisdiction. In the first place, a court in the child's home state has jurisdiction, and secondly, if there is no home state or the child and his family have equal or stronger ties with another state, a court in that state has jurisdiction. If this alternative test produces concurrent jurisdiction in more than one state, the mechanisms provided in sections 6 and 7 are used to assure that only one state makes the custody decision.

       "Home state" is defined in section 2(5). A 6-month period has been selected in order to have a definite and certain test which is at the same time based on a reasonable assumption of fact. See Ratner, Child Custody in a Federal System, 62 Mich.L.Rev. 795, 818 (1964) who explains:

       "Most American children are integrated into an American community after living there six months; consequently this period of residence would seem to provide a reasonable criterion for identifying the established home."

       Subparagraph (ii) of paragraph (1) extends the home state rule for an additional six-month period in order to permit suit in the home state after the child's departure. The main objective is to protect a parent who has been left by his spouse taking the child along. The provision makes clear that the stay-at-home parent, if he acts promptly, may start proceedings in his own state if he desires, without the necessity of attempting to base jurisdiction on paragraph (2). This changes the law in those states which required presence of the child as a condition for jurisdiction and consequently forced the person left behind to follow the departed person to another state, perhaps to several states in succession. See also subsection (c).

Paragraph (2) comes into play either when the home state test cannot be met or as an alternative to that test. The first situation arises, for example, when a family has moved frequently and there is no state where the child has lived for 6 months prior to suit, or if the child has recently been removed from his home state and the person who was left behind has also moved away. See paragraph (1), last clause. A typical example of alternative jurisdiction is the case in which the stay-at-home parent chooses to follow the departed spouse to state 2 (where the child has lived for several months with the other parent) and starts proceedings there. Whether the departed parent also has access to a court in state 2, depends on the strength of the family ties in that state and on the applicability of the clean hands provision of section 8. If state 2, for example, was the state of the matrimonial home where the entire family lived for two years before moving to the "home state" for 6 months, and the wife returned to state 2 with the child with the consent of the husband, state 2 might well have jurisdiction upon petition of the wife. The same may be true if the wife returned to her parents in her former home state where the child had spent several months every year before. Compare Willmore v. Willmore, 273 Minn. 537, 143 N.W.2d 630 (1966), cert. denied 385 U.S. 898 (1966). While jurisdiction may exist in two states in these instances, it will not be *exercised* in both states. See sections 6 and 7.

Paragraph (2) of subsection (a) is supplemented by subsection (b) which is designed to discourage unilateral removal of children to other states and to guard generally against too liberal an interpretation of paragraph (2). Short-term presence in the state is not enough even though there may be an intent to stay longer, perhaps an intent to establish a technical "domicile" for divorce or other purposes.

Paragraph (2) perhaps more than any other provision of the Act requires that it be interpreted in the spirit of the legislative purposes expressed in section 1. The paragraph was phrased in general terms in order to be flexible enough to cover many fact situations too diverse to lend themselves to exact description. But its purpose is to limit jurisdiction rather than to proliferate it. The first clause of the paragraph is important: jurisdiction exists only if it is in the *child's* interest, not merely the interest or convenience of the feuding parties, to determine custody in a particular state. The interest of the child is served when the forum has optimum access to relevant evidence about the child and family. There must be maximum rather than minimum contact with the state. The submission of the parties to a forum, perhaps for purposes of divorce, is not sufficient without additional factors establishing closer ties with the state. Divorce jurisdiction does not necessarily include custody jurisdiction. See Clark, Domestic Relations 578 (1968).

Paragraph (3) of subsection (a) retains and reaffirms *parens patriae* jurisdiction, usually exercised by a juvenile court, which a state must assume when a child is in a situation requiring immediate protection. This jurisdiction exists when a child has been abandoned and in emergency cases of child neglect. Presence of the child in the state is the only prerequisite. This extraordinary jurisdiction is reserved for extraordinary circumstances. See Application of Lang, 9 App.Div.2d 401, 193 N.Y.S.2d 763 (1959). When there is child neglect without emergency or abandonment, jurisdiction cannot be based on this paragraph.

. . .

### Section 4. [Notice and Opportunity to be Heard]

Before making a decree under this Act, reasonable notice and opportunity to be heard shall be given to the contestants, any parent whose parental rights have not been previously terminated, and any person who has physical custody of the child. If any of these persons is outside this State, notice and opportunity to be heard shall be given pursuant to section 5.

### Section 5. [Notice to Persons Outside this State;   Submission to Jurisdiction]

(a) Notice required for the exercise of jurisdiction over a person outside this State shall be given in a manner reasonably calculated to give actual notice, and may be:

(1) by personal delivery outside this State in the manner prescribed for service of process within this State;

(2) in the manner prescribed by the law of the place in which the service is made for service of process in that place in an action in any of its courts of general jurisdiction;

(3) by any form of mail addressed to the person to be served and requesting a receipt;  or

(4) as directed by the court [including publication, if other means of notification are ineffective].

(b) Notice under this section shall be served, mailed, or delivered, [or last published] at least [10, 20] days before any hearing in this State.

(c) Proof of service outside this State may be made by affidavit of the individual who made the service, or in the manner prescribed by the law of this State, the order pursuant to which the service is made, or the law of the place in which the service is made. If service is made by mail, proof may be a receipt signed by the addressee or other evidence of delivery to the addressee.

(d) Notice is not required if a person submits to the jurisdiction of the court.

### Section 6. [Simultaneous Proceedings in Other States]

(a) A court of this State shall not exercise its jurisdiction under this Act if at the time of filing the petition a proceeding concerning the custody of the child was pending in a court of another state exercising jurisdiction substantially in conformity with this Act, unless the proceeding is stayed by the court of the other state because this State is a more appropriate forum or for other reasons.

(b) Before hearing the petition in a custody proceeding the court shall examine the pleadings and other information supplied by the parties under section 9 and shall consult the child custody registry established under section 16 concerning the pendency of proceedings with respect to the child in other states. If the court has reason to believe that proceedings may be pending in another state it shall direct an inquiry to the state court administrator or other appropriate official of the other state.

(c) If the court is informed during the course of the proceeding that a proceeding concerning the custody of the child was pending in another state before the court assumed jurisdiction it shall stay the proceeding and communicate with the court in which the other proceeding is pending to the end that the issue may be litigated in the more appropriate forum and that information be exchanged in accordance with sections 19 through 22. If a court of this state has made a custody decree before being informed of a pending proceeding in a court of another state it shall immediately inform that court of the fact. If the court is informed that a proceeding was commenced in another state after it assumed jurisdiction it shall likewise inform the other court to the end that the issues may be litigated in the more appropriate forum.

### Section 7. [Inconvenient Forum]

(a) A court which has jurisdiction under this Act to make an initial or modification decree may decline to exercise its jurisdiction any time before making a decree if it finds that it is an inconvenient forum to make a custody determination under the circumstances of the case and that a court of another state is a more appropriate forum.

(b) A finding of inconvenient forum may be made upon the court's own motion or upon motion of a party or a guardian ad litem or other representative of the child.

(c) In determining if it is an inconvenient forum, the court shall consider if it is in the interest of the child that another state assume jurisdiction. For this purpose it may take into account the following factors, among others:

(1) if another state is or recently was the child's home state;

(2) if another state has a closer connection with the child and his family or with the child and one or more of the contestants;

(3) if substantial evidence concerning the child's present or future care, protection, training, and personal relationships is more readily available in another state;

(4) if the parties have agreed on another forum which is no less appropriate; and

(5) if the exercise of jurisdiction by a court of this state would contravene any of the purposes stated in section 1.

(d) Before determining whether to decline or retain jurisdiction the court may communicate with a court of another state and exchange information pertinent to the assumption of jurisdiction by either court with a view to assuring that jurisdiction will be exercised by the more appropriate court and that a forum will be available to the parties.

(e) If the court finds that it is an inconvenient forum and that a court of another state is a more appropriate forum, it may dismiss the proceedings, or it may stay the proceedings upon condition that a custody proceeding be promptly commenced in another named state or upon any other conditions which may be just and proper, including the condition that a moving party stipulate his consent and submission to the jurisdiction of the other forum.

(f) The court may decline to exercise its jurisdiction under this Act if a custody determination is incidental to an action for divorce or another proceeding while retaining jurisdiction over the divorce or other proceeding.

(g) If it appears to the court that it is clearly an inappropriate forum it may require the party who commenced the proceedings to pay, in addition to the costs of the proceedings in this State, necessary travel and other expenses, including attorneys' fees, incurred by other parties or their witnesses. Payment is to be made to the clerk of the court for remittance to the proper party.

(h) Upon dismissal or stay of proceedings under this section the court shall inform the court found to be the more appropriate forum of this fact, or if the court which would have jurisdiction in the other state is not certainly known, shall transmit the information to the court administrator or other appropriate official for forwarding to the appropriate court.

(i) Any communication received from another state informing this State of a finding of inconvenient forum because a court of this State is the more appropriate forum shall be filed in the custody registry of the appropriate court. Upon assuming jurisdiction the court of this State shall inform the original court of this fact.

### Section 8. [Jurisdiction Declined by Reason of Conduct]

(a) If the petitioner for an initial decree has wrongfully taken the child from another state or has engaged in similar reprehensible conduct the court may decline to exercise jurisdiction if this is just and proper under the circumstances.

(b) Unless required in the interest of the child, the court shall not exercise its jurisdiction to modify a custody decree of another state if the petitioner, without consent of the person entitled to custody, has improperly removed the child from the physical custody of the person entitled to custody or has improperly retained the child after a visit or other temporary relinquishment of physical custody. If the petitioner has violated any other provision of a custody decree of another state the court may decline to exercise its jurisdiction if this is just and proper under the circumstances.

(c) In appropriate cases a court dismissing a petition under this section may charge the petitioner with necessary travel and other expenses, including attorneys' fees, incurred by other parties or their witnesses.

### COMMENT

This section incorporates the "clean hands doctrine," so named by Ehrenzweig, Interstate Recognition of Custody Decrees, 51 Mich.L.Rev. 345 (1953). Under this doctrine courts refuse to assume jurisdiction to re-examine an out-of-state custody decree when the petitioner has abducted the child or has engaged in some other objectionable scheme to gain or retain physical custody of the child in violation of the decree. But when adherence to this rule would lead to punishment of the parent at the expense of the wellbeing of the child, it is often not applied.

Subsection (a) extends the clean hands principle to cases in which a custody decree has not yet been rendered in any state. For example, if upon a de facto separation the wife returned to her own home with the children without objection by her husband and lived there for two years without hearing from him, and the husband without warning forcibly removes the children one night and brings them to another state, a court in that state although it has jurisdiction after 6 months may decline to hear the husband's custody petition. "Wrongfully" taking under this subsection does not mean that a "right" has been violated—both husband and wife as a rule have a right to custody until a court determination is made—but that one party's conduct is so objectionable that a court in the exercise of its inherent equity powers cannot in good conscience permit that party access to its jurisdiction.

Subsection (b) does not come into operation unless the court has power under section 14 to modify the custody decree of another state. It is a codification of the clean hands rule, except that it differentiates between (1) a taking or retention of the child and (2) other violations of custody decrees. In the case of illegal removal or retention refusal of jurisdiction is mandatory unless the harm done to the child by a denial of jurisdiction outweighs the parental misconduct. Compare Smith v. Smith and In Re Guardianship of Rodgers, supra; and see In re Walter, 228 Cal.App.2d 217, 39 Cal.Rptr. 243 (1964) where the court assumed jurisdiction after both parents had been guilty of misconduct. The qualifying word "improperly" is added to exclude cases in which a child is withheld because of illness or other emergency or in which there are other special justifying circumstances.

The most common violation of the second category is the removal of the child from the state by the parent who has the right to custody, thereby frustrating the exercise of visitation rights of the other parent. The second sentence of subsection (b) makes refusal of jurisdiction entirely discretionary in this situation because it depends on the circumstances whether noncompliance with the court order is serious enough to warrant the drastic sanction of denial of jurisdiction.

Subsection (c) adds a financial deterrent to child stealing and similar reprehensible conduct.

### Section 9. [Information under Oath to be Submitted to the Court]

(a) Every party in a custody proceeding in his first pleading or in an affidavit attached to that pleading shall give information under oath as to the child's present address, the places where the child has lived within the last 5 years, and the names and present addresses of the persons with whom the child has lived during that period. In this pleading or affidavit every party shall further declare under oath whether:

(1) he has participated (as a party, witness, or in any other capacity) in any other litigation concerning the custody of the same child in this or any other state;

(2) he has information of any custody proceeding concerning the child pending in a court of this or any other state; and

(3) he knows of any person not a party to the proceedings who has physical custody of the child or claims to have custody or visitation rights with respect to the child.

(b) If the declaration as to any of the above items is in the affirmative the declarant shall give additional information under oath as required by the court. The court may examine the parties under oath as to details of the information furnished and as to other matters pertinent to the court's jurisdiction and the disposition of the case.

(c) Each party has a continuing duty to inform the court of any custody proceeding concerning the child in this or any other state of which he obtained information during this proceeding.

### Section 10. [Additional Parties]

If the court learns from information furnished by the parties pursuant to section 9 or from other sources that a person not a party to the custody proceeding has physical custody of the child or claims to have custody or visitation rights with respect to the child, it shall order that person to be joined as a party and to be duly notified of the pendency of the proceeding and of his joinder as a party. If the person joined as a party is outside this State he shall be served with process or otherwise notified in accordance with section 5.

### Section 11. [Appearance of Parties and the Child]

[(a) The court may order any party to the proceeding who is in this State to appear personally before the court. If that party has physical custody of the child the court may order that he appear personally with the child.]

(b) If a party to the proceeding whose presence is desired by the court is outside this State with or without the child the court may order that the notice given under section 5 include a statement directing that party to appear personally with or without the child and declaring that failure to appear may result in a decision adverse to that party.

(c) If a party to the proceeding who is outside this State is directed to appear under subsection (b) or desires to appear personally before the court with or without the child, the court may require another party to pay to the clerk of the court travel and other necessary expenses of the party so appearing and of the child if this is just and proper under the circumstances.

### Section 12. [Binding Force and Res Judicata Effect of Custody Decree]

A custody decree rendered by a court of this State which had jurisdiction under section 3 binds all parties who have been served in this State or notified in accordance with section 5 or who have submitted to the jurisdiction of the court, and who have been given an opportunity to be heard. As to these parties the custody decree is conclusive as to all issues of law and fact decided and as to the custody determination made unless and until that determination is modified pursuant to law, including the provisions of this Act.

### Section 13. [Recognition of Out-of-State Custody Decrees]

The courts of this State shall recognize and enforce an initial or modification decree of a court of another state which had assumed jurisdiction under statutory provisions substantially in accordance with this Act or which was made under factual circumstances meeting the jurisdictional standards of the Act, so long as this decree has not been modified in accordance with jurisdictional standards substantially similar to those of this Act.

## COMMENT

This section and sections 14 and 15 are the key provisions which guarantee a great measure of security and stability of environment to the "interstate child" by discouraging relitigations in other states. See Section 1, and see Ratner, Child Custody in a Federal System, 62 Mich.L.Rev. 795, 828 (1964).

Although the full faith and credit clause may perhaps not require the recognition of out-of-state custody decrees, the states are free to recognize and enforce them. See Restatement of the Law Second, Conflict of Laws, Proposed Official Draft, section 109 (1967), and see the Prefatory Note, supra. This section declares as a matter of state law, that custody decrees of sister states will be recognized and enforced. Recognition and enforcement is mandatory if the state in which the prior decree was rendered 1) has adopted this Act, 2) has statutory jurisdictional requirements substantially like this Act, or 3) would have had jurisdiction under the facts of the case if this Act had been the law in the state. Compare Comment, Ford v. Ford: Full Faith and Credit to Child Custody Decrees? 73 Yale L.J. 134, 148 (1963).

"Jurisdiction" or "jurisdictional standards" under this section refers to the requirements of section 3 in the case of initial decrees and to the requirements of sections 3 and 14 in the case of modification decrees. The section leaves open the possibility of discretionary recognition of custody decrees of other states beyond the enumerated situations of mandatory acceptance. For the recognition of custody decrees of other nations, see section 23.

Recognition is accorded to a decree which is valid and binding under section 12. This means, for example, that a court in the state where the father resides will recognize and enforce a custody decree rendered in the home state where the child lives with the mother if the father was duly notified and given enough time to appear in the proceedings. Personal jurisdiction over the father is not required. See comment to section 12. This is in accord with a common interpretation of the inconclusive decision in May v. Anderson, 345 U.S. 528, 73 S.Ct. 840, 97 L.Ed. 1221 (1953). See Restatement of the Law Second, Conflict of Laws, Proposed Official Draft, section 79 and comment thereto, p. 298 (1967). Under this interpretation a state is permitted to recognize a custody decree of another state regardless of lack of personal jurisdiction, as long as due process requirements of notice and opportunity to be heard have been met. ... The Act emphasizes the need for the personal appearance of the contestants rather than any technical requirement for personal jurisdiction.

The mandate of this section could cause problems if the prior decree is a punitive or disciplinary measure. See Ehrenzweig, Inter-state Recognition of Custody Decrees, 51 Mich.L.Rev. 345, 370 (1953). If, for example, a court grants custody to the mother and after 5 years' of continuous life with the mother the child is awarded to the father by the same court for the sole reason that the mother who had moved to another state upon remarriage had not lived up to the visitation requirements of the decree, courts in other states may be reluctant to recognize the changed decree. Disciplinary decrees of this type can be avoided under this Act by enforcing the visitation provisions of the decree directly in another state. See Section 15. If the original plan for visitation does not fit the new conditions, a petition for modification of the visiting arrangements would be filed in a court which has jurisdiction, that is, in many cases the original court. See section 14.

### Section 14. [Modification of Custody Decree of Another State]

(a) If a court of another state has made a custody decree, a court of this State shall not modify that decree unless (1) it appears to the court of this State that the court which rendered the decree does not now have jurisdiction under jurisdictional prerequisites substantially in accordance with this Act or has declined to assume jurisdiction to modify the decree and (2) the court of this State has jurisdiction.

(b) If a court of this State is authorized under subsection (a) and section 8 to modify a custody decree of another state it shall give due consideration to the transcript of the record and other documents of all previous proceedings submitted to it in accordance with section 22.

### COMMENT

Courts which render a custody decree normally retain continuing jurisdiction to modify the decree under local law. Courts in other states have in the past often assumed jurisdiction to modify the out-of-state decree themselves without regard to the preexisting jurisdiction of the other state. See People ex rel. Halvey v. Halvey, 330 U.S. 610, 67 S.Ct. 903, 91 L.Ed. 1133 (1947). In order to achieve greater stability of custody arrangements and avoid forum shopping, subsection (a) declares that other states will defer to the continuing jurisdiction of the court of another state as long as that state has jurisdiction under the standards of this Act. In other words, all petitions for modification are to be addressed to the prior state if that state has sufficient contact with the case to satisfy section 3. The fact that the court had previously considered the case may be one factor favoring its continued jurisdiction. If, however, all the persons involved have moved away or the contact with the state has otherwise become slight, modification jurisdiction would shift elsewhere. Compare Ratner, Child Custody in a Federal System, 62 Mich.L.Rev. 795, 821–2 (1964).

For example, if custody was awarded to the father in state 1 where he continued to live with the children for two years and thereafter his wife kept the children in state 2 for 6½ months (3½ months beyond her visitation privileges) with or without permission of the husband, state 1 has preferred jurisdiction to modify the decree despite the fact that state 2 has in the meantime become the "home state" of the child. If, however, the father also moved away from state 1, that state loses modification jurisdiction interstate, whether or not its jurisdiction continues under local law. See Clark, Domestic Relations 322–23 (1968). Also, if the father in the same case continued to live in state 1, but let his wife keep the children for several years without asserting his custody rights and without visits of the children in state 1, modification jurisdiction of state 1 would cease. Compare Brengle v. Hurst, 408 S.W.2d 418 (Ky.1966). The situation would be different if the children had been abducted and their whereabouts could not be discovered by the legal custodian for several years. The abductor would be denied access to the court of another state under section 8(b) and state 1 would have modification jurisdiction in any event under section 3(a)(4). Compare Crocker v. Crocker, 122 Colo. 49, 219 P.2d 311 (1950).

The prior court has jurisdiction to modify under this section even though its original assumption of jurisdiction did not meet the standards of this Act, as long as it would have jurisdiction *now,* that is, at the time of the petition for modification.

If the state of the prior decree declines to assume jurisdiction to modify the decree, another state with jurisdiction under section 3 can proceed with the case. That is not so if the prior court dismissed the petition on its merits.

Respect for the continuing jurisdiction of another state under this section will serve the purposes of this Act only if the prior court will assume a corresponding obligation to make no changes in the existing custody arrangement which are not required for the good of the child. If the court overturns its own decree in order to discipline a mother or father, with whom the child had lived for years, for failure to comply with an order of the court, the objective of greater stability of custody decrees is not achieved. See Comment to section 13 last paragraph, and cases there cited. See also Sharpe v. Sharpe, 77 Ill.App. 295, 222 N.E.2d 340 (1966). Under section 15 of this Act an order of a court contained in a custody decree can be directly enforced in another state.

Under subsection (b) transcripts of prior proceedings if received under section 22 are to be considered by the modifying court. The purpose is to give the judge the opportunity to be as fully informed as possible before making a custody decision. "One court will seldom have so much of the story that another's inquiry is unimportant" says Paulsen, Appointment of a Guardian in the Conflict of Laws, 45 Iowa L.Rev. 212, 226 (1960). How much consideration is "due" this transcript, whether or under what conditions it is received in evidence, are matters of local, internal law which are not affected by this interstate act.

### Section 15. [Filing and Enforcement of Custody Decree of Another State]

(a) A certified copy of a custody decree of another state may be filed in the office of the clerk of any [District Court, Family Court] of this State. The clerk shall treat the decree in the same manner as a custody decree of the [District Court, Family Court] of this State. A custody decree so filed has the same effect and shall be enforced in like manner as a custody decree rendered by a court of this State.

(b) A person violating a custody decree of another state which makes it necessary to enforce the decree in this State may be required to pay necessary travel and other expenses, including attorneys' fees, incurred by the party entitled to the custody or his witnesses.

### Section 16. [Registry of Out-of-State Custody Decrees and Proceedings]

The clerk of each [District Court, Family Court] shall maintain a registry in which he shall enter the following:

(1) certified copies of custody decrees of other states received for filing;

(2) communications as to the pendency of custody proceedings in other states;

(3) communications concerning a finding of inconvenient forum by a court of another state; and

(4) other communications or documents concerning custody proceedings in another state which may affect the jurisdiction of a court of this State or the disposition to be made by it in a custody proceeding.

### Section 17. [Certified Copies of Custody Decree]

The Clerk of the [District Court, Family Court] of this State, at the request of the court of another state or at the request of any person who is affected by or has a legitimate interest in a custody decree, shall certify and forward a copy of the decree to that court or person.

### Section 18. [Taking Testimony in Another State]

In addition to other procedural devices available to a party, any party to the proceeding or a guardian ad litem or other representative of the child may adduce testimony of witnesses, including parties and the child, by deposition or otherwise, in another state. The court on its own motion may direct that the testimony of a person be taken in another state and may prescribe the manner in which and the terms upon which the testimony shall be taken.

## Section 19. [Hearings and Studies in Another State; Orders to Appear]

(a) A court of this State may request the appropriate court of another state to hold a hearing to adduce evidence, to order a party to produce or give evidence under other procedures of that state, or to have social studies made with respect to the custody of a child involved in proceedings pending in the court of this State; and to forward to the court of this State certified copies of the transcript of the record of the hearing, the evidence otherwise adduced, or any social studies prepared in compliance with the request. The cost of the services may be assessed against the parties or, if necessary, ordered paid by the [County, State].

(b) A court of this State may request the appropriate court of another state to order a party to custody proceedings pending in the court of this State to appear in the proceedings, and if that party has physical custody of the child, to appear with the child. The request may state that travel and other necessary expenses of the party and of the child whose appearance is desired will be assessed against another party or will otherwise be paid.

## Section 20. [Assistance to Courts of Other States]

(a) Upon request of the court of another state the courts of this State which are competent to hear custody matters may order a person in this State to appear at a hearing to adduce evidence or to produce or give evidence under other procedures available in this State [or may order social studies to be made for use in a custody proceeding in another state]. A certified copy of the transcript of the record of the hearing or the evidence otherwise adduced [and any social studies prepared] shall be forwarded by the clerk of the court to the requesting court.

(b) A person within this State may voluntarily give his testimony or statement in this State for use in a custody proceeding outside this state.

(c) Upon request of the court of another state a competent court of this State may order a person in this State to appear alone or with the child in a custody proceeding in another state. The court may condition compliance with the request upon assurance by the other state that state travel and other necessary expenses will be advanced or reimbursed.

## Section 21. [Preservation of Documents for Use in Other States]

In any custody proceeding in this State the court shall preserve the pleadings, orders and decrees, any record that has been made of its hearings, social studies, and other pertinent documents until the child reaches [18, 21] years of age. Upon appropriate request of the court of another state the court shall forward to the other court certified copies of any or all of such documents.

### Section 22. [Request for Court Records of Another State]

If a custody decree has been rendered in another state concerning a child involved in a custody proceeding pending in a court of this State, the court of this State upon taking jurisdiction of the case shall request of the court of the other state a certified copy of the transcript of any court record and other documents mentioned in section 21.

### Section 23. [International Application]

The general policies of this Act extend to the international area. The provisions of this Act relating to the recognition and enforcement of custody decrees of other states apply to custody decrees and decrees involving legal institutions similar in nature to custody institutions rendered by appropriate authorities of other nations if reasonable notice and opportunity to be heard were given to all affected persons.

### [Section 24. [Priority]

Upon the request of a party to a custody proceeding which raises a question of existence or exercise of jurisdiction under this Act the case shall be given calendar priority and handled expeditiously.]

*[Sections 25–28, dealing with the Act's short title, severability, repeal of other legislation, and time of taking effect, have been omitted.]*

# UNIFORM INTERSTATE FAMILY
# SUPPORT ACT (1992)
# 9A U.L.A. 127 (Supp. 1994)

*[Reproduced with the permission of the National Conference of Commissioners on Uniform State Laws. Only selected parts of the Commentary have been included.]*

## ARTICLE 1
## GENERAL PROVISIONS

### § 101. Definitions.

In this [Act]:

(1) "Child" means an individual, whether over or under the age of majority, who is or is alleged to be owed a duty of support by the individual's parent or who is or is alleged to be the beneficiary of a support order directed to the parent.

(2) "Child support order" means a support order for a child, including a child who has attained the age of majority under the law of the issuing state.

(3) "Duty of support" means an obligation imposed or imposable by law to provide support for a child, spouse, or former spouse, including an unsatisfied obligation to provide support.

(4) "Home state" means the state in which a child lived with a parent or a person acting as parent for at least six consecutive months immediately preceding the time of filing of a [petition] or comparable pleading for support and, if a child is less than six months old, the state in which the child lived from birth with any of them. A period of temporary absence of any of them is counted as part of the six-month or other period.

(5) "Income" includes earnings or other periodic entitlements to money from any source and any other property subject to withholding for support under the law of this State.

(6) "Income-withholding order" means an order or other legal process directed to an obligor's employer [or other debtor], as defined by [the income-withholding law of this State], to withhold support from the income of the obligor.

(7) "Initiating state" means a state in which a proceeding under this [Act] or a law substantially similar to this [Act], the Uniform Reciprocal Enforcement of Support Act, or the Revised Uniform Reciprocal Enforcement of Support Act is filed for forwarding to a responding state.

(8) "Initiating tribunal" means the authorized tribunal in an initiating state.

(9) "Issuing state" means the state in which a tribunal issues a support order or renders a judgment determining parentage.

(10) "Issuing tribunal" means the tribunal that issues a support order or renders a judgment determining parentage.

(11) "Law" includes decisional and statutory law and rules and regulations having the force of law.

(12) "Obligee" means:

(i) an individual to whom a duty of support is or is alleged to be owed or in whose favor a support order has been issued or a judgment determining parentage has been rendered;

(ii) a state or political subdivision to which the rights under a duty of support or support order have been assigned or which has independent claims based on financial assistance provided to an individual obligee; or

(iii) an individual seeking a judgment determining parentage of the individual's child.

(13) "Obligor" means an individual, or the estate of a decedent:

(i) who owes or is alleged to owe a duty of support;

(ii) who is alleged but has not been adjudicated to be a parent of a child; or

(iii) who is liable under a support order.

(14) "Register" means to [record; file] a support order or judgment determining parentage in the [appropriate location for the recording or filing of foreign judgments generally or foreign support orders specifically].

(15) "Registering tribunal" means a tribunal in which a support order is registered.

(16) "Responding state" means a state to which a proceeding is forwarded under this [Act] or a law substantially similar to this [Act], the Uniform Reciprocal Enforcement of Support Act, or the Revised Uniform Reciprocal Enforcement of Support Act.

(17) "Responding tribunal" means the authorized tribunal in a responding state.

(18) "Spousal-support order" means a support order for a spouse or former spouse of the obligor.

(19) "State" means a state of the United States, the District of Columbia, the Commonwealth of Puerto Rico, or any territory or insular possession subject to the jurisdiction of the United States. The term "state" includes an Indian tribe and includes a foreign jurisdiction that has established procedures for issuance and enforcement of support orders which are substantially similar to the procedures under this [Act].

(20) "Support enforcement agency" means a public official or agency authorized to seek:

(i) enforcement of support orders or laws relating to the duty of support;

(ii) establishment or modification of child support;

(iii) determination of parentage; or

(iv) to locate obligors or their assets.

(21) "Support order" means a judgment, decree, or order, whether temporary, final, or subject to modification, for the benefit of a child, a spouse, or a former spouse, which provides for monetary support, health care, arrearages, or reimbursement, and may include related costs and fees, interest, income withholding, attorney's fees, and other relief.

(22) "Tribunal" means a court, administrative agency, or quasi-judicial entity authorized to establish, enforce, or modify support orders or to determine parentage.

## COMMENT

Several additional terms are defined in this section as compared to the parallel RURESA § 2, which has fourteen entries. Many crucial definitions continue to be left to local law. For example, the definitions of "child" and "child support order" provided by Subsections (1) and (2) refer to "the age of majority" without further elaboration. The exact age at which a child becomes an adult for different purposes is a matter for the law of each state, as is the age at which a parent's duty to furnish child support terminates. Similarly, a wide variety of other terms of art are implicitly left to state law. For example, Subsection (21) refers inter alia to "health care, arrearages, or reimbursement...." All of these terms are subject to individualized definitions on a state-by-state basis.

Subsection (3) defines "duty of support" to mean the legal obligation to provide support before it has been reduced to judgment. It is broadly defined to include both prospective and retrospective obligations, to the extent they are imposed by the relevant state law.

In order to resolve certain conflicts in the exercise of jurisdiction, for limited purposes Subsection (4) borrows the concept of the "home state" of a child from the Uniform Child Custody Jurisdiction Act, versions of which have been adopted in all 50 states, and from the federal Parental Kidnapping Prevention Act, 42 U.S.C. § 1738A.

Subsection (6) is written broadly so that states that direct income withholding by an obligor's employer based on "other legal process," as distinguished from an order of a tribunal, may have that "legal process" recognized as an "income-withholding order." Federal law requires that each state provide for income withholding "without the necessity of any application therefor ... or for any further action ... by the court or other entity which issued such order." 42 U.S.C. 666(b)(2). States have complied with this directive in a variety of ways.

For example, New York provides a method for obtaining income withholding of court-ordered support by authorizing an attorney, clerk of court, sheriff or agent of the child support enforcement agency to serve upon the defaulting obligor's employer an "income execution for support enforcement." New York McKinney's C.P.L.R. 5241. This "other legal process" reportedly is the standard method for obtaining income withholding in that state, while the statutory provision for an income withholding order, C.P.L.R. 5242, is rarely used by either the courts or the litigants.

Subsections (7) and (8) define "initiating state" and "initiating tribunal" similarly to RURESA § 2(d). It is important to note, however, that this Act permits the direct filing of an interstate action in the responding state without an initial filing in an initiating tribunal. Thus, a petitioner in one state could seek to establish a support order in a second state by either filing in the second state's tribunal or seeking the assistance of the support enforcement agency in the second state.

The term "obligee" in Subsection (12) is defined in a broad manner similar to RURESA § 2(f), which is consistent with common usage. In instances of spousal support, the person owed the duty of support and the person receiving the payments are almost always the same. Use of the term is more complicated in the context of a child support order. The child is the person to whom the duty of support is owed and therefore can be viewed as the ultimate obligee. However, "obligee" usually refers to the individual receiving the payments. While this is most commonly the custodial parent or other legal custodian, the "obligee" may be a support enforcement agency which has been assigned the right to receive support payments in order to recoup AFDC (Aid to Families with Dependent Children, 42 U.S.C.§ 601 et seq.). Even in the absence of such an assignment, a state may have an independent statutory claim for reimbursement for general assistance provided to a spouse, a former spouse, or a child of an obligor. The Act also uses "obligee" to identify an individual who is asserting a claim for support, not just for a person whose right to support is unquestioned, presumed, or has been established in a legal action. Subsection (13) provides the correlative definition of an "obligor," which includes an individual who is alleged to owe a duty of support as well as a person whose obligation has previously been determined.

Note that the definitions of "responding state" and "responding tribunal" in Subsections (16) and (17) accommodate the direct filing of a petition under this Act without the intervention of an initiating tribunal. Both definitions acknowledge the possibility that there might be a responding state or tribunal in a situation where there is no initiating state or tribunal.

Subsection (19) withdraws the requirement of reciprocity demanded by RURESA and URESA. A state need not enact UIFSA in order for support orders issued by its tribunal to be enforced by other states. Public policy favoring such enforcement is sufficiently strong to warrant waiving any quid pro quo among the states. This policy extends to foreign jurisdictions, as well, which is intended to facilitate establishment and enforcement of orders from those jurisdictions. Specifically, if a support order from a Canadian province or Mexican state conforms to the principles of UIFSA, that order should be honored when it crosses the border in a spirit of comity.

Subsection (20), "Support Enforcement Agency," includes the state IV-D agency (Part IV-D, Social Security Act, 42 U.S.C. § 651 et seq.), and other state or local governmental entities charged with establishing or enforcing support.

Subsection (22) introduces a completely new term, "tribunal," which replaces the term "court" used in RURESA. With the advent of the federal IV-D program, a number of states have delegated various aspects of child support establishment and enforcement to quasi-judicial bodies and administrative agencies. UIFSA adopts the term "tribunal" to account for the breadth of state variations in dealing with support orders.

Throughout the Act the term refers to a tribunal of the enacting state unless expressly noted otherwise. To avoid confusion, however, when actions of tribunals of the enacting state and another state are contrasted in the same section or subsection, the phrases "tribunal of this State" and "tribunal of another state" are used for the sake of clarity.

## ARTICLE 2
## JURISDICTION

### § 201. Bases for Jurisdiction over Nonresident.

In a proceeding to establish, enforce, or modify a support order or to determine parentage, a tribunal of this State may exercise personal jurisdiction over a nonresident individual [or the individual's guardian or conservator] if:

(1) the individual is personally served with [citation, summons, notice] within this State;

(2) the individual submits to the jurisdiction of this State by consent, by entering a general appearance, or by filing a responsive document having the effect of waiving any contest to personal jurisdiction;

(3) the individual resided with the child in this State;

(4) the individual resided in this State and provided prenatal expenses or support for the child;

(5) the child resides in this State as a result of the acts or directives of the individual;

(6) the individual engaged in sexual intercourse in this State and the child may have been conceived by that act of intercourse;

[ (7) the individual asserted parentage in the [putative father registry] maintained in this State by the [appropriate agency];] or

(8) there is any other basis consistent with the constitutions of this State and the United States for the exercise of personal jurisdiction.

## § 202. Procedure When Exercising Jurisdiction over Nonresident.

A tribunal of this State exercising personal jurisdiction over a nonresident under Section 201 may apply Section 316 (Special Rules of Evidence and Procedure) to receive evidence from another state, and Section 318 (Assistance with Discovery) to obtain discovery through a tribunal of another state. In all other respects, Articles 3 through 7 do not apply and the tribunal shall apply the procedural and substantive law of this State, including the rules on choice of law other than those established by this [Act].

## § 203. Initiating and Responding Tribunal of this State.

Under this [Act], a tribunal of this State may serve as an initiating tribunal to forward proceedings to another state and as a responding tribunal for proceedings initiated in another state.

## § 204. Simultaneous Proceedings in another State.

(a) A tribunal of this State may exercise jurisdiction to establish a support order if the [petition] or comparable pleading is filed after a [petition] or comparable pleading is filed in another state only if:

(1) the [petition] or comparable pleading in this State is filed before the expiration of the time allowed in the other state for filing a responsive pleading challenging the exercise of jurisdiction by the other state;

(2) the contesting party timely challenges the exercise of jurisdiction in the other state; and

(3) if relevant, this State is the home state of the child.

(b) A tribunal of this State may not exercise jurisdiction to establish a support order if the [petition] or comparable pleading is filed before a [petition] or comparable pleading is filed in another state if:

(1) the [petition] or comparable pleading in the other state is filed before the expiration of the time allowed in this State for filing a responsive pleading challenging the exercise of jurisdiction by this State;

(2) the contesting party timely challenges the exercise of jurisdiction in this State; and

(3) if relevant, the other state is the home state of the child.

## § 205. Continuing, Exclusive Jurisdiction.

(a) A tribunal of this State issuing a support order consistent with the law of this State has continuing, exclusive jurisdiction over a child support order:

(1) as long as this State remains the residence of the obligor, the individual obligee, or the child for whose benefit the support order is issued; or

(2) until each individual party has filed written consent with the tribunal of this State for a tribunal of another state to modify the order and assume continuing, exclusive jurisdiction.

(b) A tribunal of this State issuing a child support order consistent with the law of this State may not exercise its continuing jurisdiction to modify the order if the order has been modified by a tribunal of another state pursuant to a law substantially similar to this [Act].

(c) If a child support order of this State is modified by a tribunal of another state pursuant to a law substantially similar to this [Act], a tribunal of this State loses its continuing, exclusive jurisdiction with regard to prospective enforcement of the order issued in this State, and may only:

(1) enforce the order that was modified as to amounts accruing before the modification;

(2) enforce nonmodifiable aspects of that order; and

(3) provide other appropriate relief for violations of that order which occurred before the effective date of the modification.

(d) A tribunal of this State shall recognize the continuing, exclusive jurisdiction of a tribunal of another state which has issued a child support order pursuant to a law substantially similar to this [Act].

(e) A temporary support order issued ex parte or pending resolution of a jurisdictional conflict does not create continuing, exclusive jurisdiction in the issuing tribunal.

(f) A tribunal of this State issuing a support order consistent with the law of this State has continuing, exclusive jurisdiction over a spousal support order throughout the existence of the support obligation. A tribunal of this State may not modify a spousal support order issued by a tribunal of another state having continuing, exclusive jurisdiction over that order under the law of that state.

## COMMENT

This section is perhaps the most crucial provision in UIFSA. It establishes the principle that the issuing tribunal retains continuing, exclusive jurisdiction over the support order except in very narrowly defined circumstances. If all parties and the child reside elsewhere, the issuing state loses its continuing, exclusive jurisdiction--which in practical terms means the issuing tribunal loses its authority to modify its order. The issuing state no longer has a nexus with the parties or child and, furthermore, the issuing tribunal has no current information about the circumstances of anyone involved. Note, however, that the one-order of the issuing tribunal remains valid and enforceable. That order is in effect not only in the issuing state and those states in which the order has been registered, but also may be enforced in additional states in which the one-order is registered for enforcement after the issuing state loses its power to modify the original order, see Sections 601-604 (Registration and Enforcement of Support Order), infra. The one-order remains in effect until it is properly modified in accordance with the narrow terms of the Act, see Sections 609-612 (Registration and Modification of Child Support Order), infra.

Child support orders may be modified under certain, specific conditions: (1) on the agreement of both parties; or, (2) if all the relevant persons, that is, the obligor, the individual obligee, and the child, have permanently left the issuing state. Note that while Subsection (b)(2) identifies the method for the release of continuing, exclusive jurisdiction by the issuing tribunal, it does not confer jurisdiction to modify on another tribunal. Modification requires that a tribunal have personal jurisdiction over both parties, as provided in Article 6, Part C. It should also be noted that nothing in this section is intended to deprive a court which has lost continuing, exclusive jurisdiction of the power to enforce arrearages which have accrued during the existence of a valid order.

With regard to spousal support, the issuing tribunal retains continuing, exclusive jurisdiction over an order of spousal support throughout the entire existence of the support obligation. The prohibition against a modification of an existing spousal support order of another state imposed by Sections 205 and 206 marks a radical departure from RURESA, which treats spousal and child support orders identically. Under UIFSA, modification of spousal support is permitted in the interstate context only if an action is initiated outside of, and modified by the original issuing state. While UIFSA revises RURESA in this regard, in fact this will have a minimal effect on actual practice. Interstate modification of spousal support has been relatively rare under RURESA. Moreover, the prohibition of modification of spousal support is consistent with the basic principle that a tribunal should apply local law if at all possible to insure efficient handling of cases and to minimize choice of law problems. Avoiding conflict of law problems is almost impossible if spousal support orders are subject to modification in a second state. For example, there is wide variation among state laws on the effect on a spousal support order following the obligee's remarriage or nonmarital cohabitation with another person.

The distinction between spousal and child support is further justified because the standards for modification of child support and spousal support are so different. In most jurisdictions a dramatic improvement in the obligor's economic circumstances will have little or no relevance in an action seeking an upward modification of spousal support, while a similar change in an obligor's situation typically is a primary basis for an increase in child support. This disparity is founded on a policy choice that post-divorce success should benefit the obligor's child, but not an ex-spouse.

## § 206. Enforcement and Modification of Support Order by Tribunal Having Continuing Jurisdiction.

(a) A tribunal of this State may serve as an initiating tribunal to request a tribunal of another state to enforce or modify a support order issued in that state.

(b) A tribunal of this State having continuing, exclusive jurisdiction over a support order may act as a responding tribunal to enforce or modify the order. If a party subject to the continuing, exclusive jurisdiction of the tribunal no longer resides in the issuing state, in subsequent proceedings the tribunal may apply Section 316 (Special Rules of Evidence and Procedure) to receive evidence from another state and Section 318 (Assistance with Discovery) to obtain discovery through a tribunal of another state.

(c) A tribunal of this State which lacks continuing, exclusive jurisdiction over a spousal support order may not serve as a responding tribunal to modify a spousal support order of another state.

## § 207. Recognition of Child Support Orders.

(a) If a proceeding is brought under this [Act], and one or more child support orders have been issued in this or another state with regard to an obligor and a child, a tribunal of this State shall apply the following rules in determining which order to recognize for purposes of continuing, exclusive jurisdiction:

(1) If only one tribunal has issued a child support order, the order of that tribunal must be recognized.

(2) If two or more tribunals have issued child support orders for the same obligor and child, and only one of the tribunals would have continuing, exclusive jurisdiction under this [Act], the order of that tribunal must be recognized.

(3) If two or more tribunals have issued child support orders for the same obligor and child, and more than one of the tribunals would have continuing, exclusive jurisdiction under this [Act], an order issued by a tribunal in the current home state of the child must be recognized, but if an order has not been issued in the current home state of the child, the order most recently issued must be recognized.

(4) If two or more tribunals have issued child support orders for the same obligor and child, and none of the tribunals would have continuing, exclusive jurisdiction under this [Act], the tribunal of this State may issue a child support order, which must be recognized.

(b) The tribunal that has issued an order recognized under subsection (a) is the tribunal having continuing, exclusive jurisdiction.

COMMENT

This section establishes a priority scheme for recognition and enforcement of existing multiple orders regarding the same obligor, obligee or obligees, and the same child. Even assuming universal enactment of UIFSA, many years will pass before its one-order system will be completely in place. Part C is designed to span the gulf between the one-order system and the multiple order system in place under RURESA. If only one order has been issued, it is to be treated as if it had been issued under UIFSA if it was issued under a statute which is consistent with the principles of UIFSA. But, multiple orders issued under RURESA number in the tens of thousands; it can be reasonably anticipated that those orders, covering the same parties and child, will continue in effect far into the future.

Assuming multiple orders exist, none of which can be distinguished as being in conflict with the principles of UIFSA, an order issued by a tribunal of the child's home state is given the higher priority. If more than one of these orders exists, priority is given to the order most recently issued. If none of the priorities apply, the forum tribunal is directed to issue a new order. Note, however, that multiple orders issued by different states may be entitled to full faith and credit. While this section cannot and does not attempt to interfere with that constitutional directive with regard to accrued arrearages, it may and does establish a system for prospective enforcement of competing orders.

### § 208. Multiple Child Support Orders for Two or More Obligees.

In responding to multiple registrations or [petitions] for enforcement of two or more child support orders in effect at the same time with regard to the same obligor and different individual obligees, at least one of which was issued by a tribunal of another state, a tribunal of this State shall enforce those orders in the same manner as if the multiple orders had been issued by a tribunal of this State.

COMMENT

Multiple orders may involve two or more families of the same obligor. Although all such orders are entitled to future enforcement, practical difficulties are often presented. For example, full enforcement of all orders may exceed the maximum allowed for income withholding, i.e., the federal statute, 42 U.S.C. 666(b)(1), requires that states cap the maximum to be withheld in accordance with the federal consumer credit code limitations on wage garnishment, 15 U.S.C. 1673(b). In order to allocate resources between competing families, the Act refers to state law. The basic principle is that one or more foreign orders for the support of the obligor's families are of equal dignity and should be treated as if all of the multiple orders had been issued by a tribunal of the forum state.

## § 209. Credit for Payments.

Amounts collected and credited for a particular period pursuant to a support order issued by a tribunal of another state must be credited against the amounts accruing or accrued for the same period under a support order issued by the tribunal of this State.

## ARTICLE 3
## CIVIL PROVISIONS OF GENERAL APPLICATION

## § 301. Proceedings under this [Act].

(a) Except as otherwise provided in this [Act], this article applies to all proceedings under this [Act].

(b) This [Act] provides for the following proceedings:

(1) establishment of an order for spousal support or child support pursuant to Article 4;

(2) enforcement of a support order and income-withholding order of another state without registration pursuant to Article 5;

(3) registration of an order for spousal support or child support of another state for enforcement pursuant to Article 6;

(4) modification of an order for child support or spousal support issued by a tribunal of this State pursuant to Article 2, Part B;

(5) registration of an order for child support of another state for modification pursuant to Article 6;

(6) determination of parentage pursuant to Article 7; and

(7) assertion of jurisdiction over nonresidents pursuant to Article 2, Part A.

(c) An individual [petitioner] or a support enforcement agency may commence a proceeding authorized under this [Act] by filing a [petition] in an initiating tribunal for forwarding to a responding tribunal or by filing a [petition] or a comparable pleading directly in a tribunal of another state which has or can obtain personal jurisdiction over the [respondent].

## § 302. Action by Minor Parent.

A minor parent may maintain a proceeding on behalf of or for the benefit of the minor's child.

## § 303. Application of Law of this State.

Except as otherwise provided by this [Act], a responding tribunal of this State:

(1) shall apply the procedural and substantive law

choice of law, including the rules on choice of law, generally applicable to similar proceedings originating in this State and may exercise all powers and provide all remedies available in those proceedings;  and

(2) shall determine the duty of support and the amount payable in accordance with the law and support guidelines of this State.

## § 304. Duties of Initiating Tribunal.

Upon the filing of a [petition] authorized by this [Act] tribunal of this State shall forward three copies of the [petition] and its accompanying documents:
(1) to the responding tribunal or appropriate support enforcement agency in t he responding state;  or
(2) if the identity of the responding tribunal is unknown information agency of the responding state with a request that they be forwarded to the appropriate tribunal and that receipt be acknowledged.

## § 305. Duties and Powers of Responding Tribunal.

(a) When a responding tribunal of this State receives a [petition] or comparable pleading from an initiating tribunal or directly pursuant to Section 301(c) (Proceedings Under this [Act] ), it shall cause the pleading to be filed and notify the [petitioner] by first class mail where and when it was filed.

(b) A responding tribunal of this State, to the extent otherwise authorized by law,  may do one or more of the following:

(1) issue or enforce a support order a judgment to determine parentage;

(2) order an obligor to comply with a support order and the manner of compliance;

(3) order income withholding;

(4) determine the amount of any arrearages

(5) enforce orders by civil or criminal contempt

(6) set aside property for satisfaction of the support order;

(7) place liens and order execution on the obligor's property;

(8) order an obligor to keep the tribunal informed of the obligor's current residential address telephone number at the place of employment;

(9) issue a [bench warrant;  capias] for an obligor who has failed after proper notice to appear at a hearing ordered by the tribunal and enter the  [bench warrant;  capias] in any local and state computer systems for criminal warrants;

(10) order the obligor to seek appropriate employment by specified methods;

(11) award reasonable attorney's fees and other fees and costs;  and

(12) grant any other available remedy.

(c) A responding tribunal of this State shall include in a support order issued under this [Act], or in the documents accompanying the order, the calculations on which the support order is based.

(d) A responding tribunal of this State may not condition the payment of a support order issued under this [Act] upon compliance by a party with provisions for visitation.

(e) If a responding tribunal of this State issues an order under this [Act] the tribunal shall send a copy of the order by first class mail to the [petitioner] and the [respondent] and to the initiating tribunal, if any.

## § 306. Inappropriate Tribunal.

If a [petition] or comparable pleading is received by an inappropriate tribunal of this State documents to an appropriate tribunal in this State or another state and notify the [petitioner] by first class mail where and when the pleading was sent.

## § 307. Duties of Support Enforcement Agency.

(a) A support enforcement agency of this State services to a [petitioner] in a proceeding under this [Act].

(b) A support enforcement agency that is providing services to the [petitioner] as appropriate shall:

(1) take all steps necessary to enable an appropriate tribunal in this State or another state to obtain jurisdiction over the [respondent];

(2) request an appropriate tribunal to set a date, time, and place for a hearing;

(3) make a reasonable effort to obtain all relevant information as to income and property of the parties;

(4) within [two] days, exclusive of Saturdays, Sundays and legal holidays, after receipt of a written notice from an initiating, responding or registering tribunal, send a copy of the communication by first class mail to the [petitioner]; and

(5) within [two] days, exclusive of Saturdays, Sundays and legal holidays, after receipt of a written communication from the [respondent] or the [respondent's] attorney, send a copy of the communication to the [petitioner]; and

(6) notify the [petitioner] if jurisdiction over the [respondent] cannot be obtained.

(c) This [Act] does not create or negate a relationship of attorney and client or other fiduciary relationship between a support enforcement agency or the attorney for the agency and the individual being assisted by the agency.

## § 308. Duty of [Attorney General].

If the [Attorney General] determines that the support enforcement agency is neglecting or refusing to provide services to an individual, the [Attorney General] may order the agency to perform its duties under this [Act] or may provide those services directly to the individual.

## § 309. Private Counsel.

An individual may employ private counsel to represent the individual in proceedings authorized by this [Act].

## § 310. Duties of [State Information Agency].

(a) The [Attorney General's Office, State Attorney's Office, State Central Registry or other information agency] is the state information agency under this [Act].

(b) The state information agency shall:

(1) compile and maintain a current list, including addresses, of the tribunals in this State which have jurisdiction under this [Act] and any support enforcement agencies in this State and transmit a copy to the state information agency of every other state;

(2) maintain a register of tribunals and support enforcement agencies received from other states;

(3) forward to the appropriate tribunal in the place in this State in which the individual obligee or the obligor resides, or in which the obligor's property is believed to be located, all documents concerning a proceeding under this [Act] received from an initiating tribunal or the state information agency of the initiating state; and

(4) obtain information concerning the location of the obligor and the obligor's property within this State not exempt from execution, by such means a postal verification and federal or state locator services, examination of telephone directories, requests for the obligor's address from employers, and examination of governmental records, including, to the extent not prohibited by law, those relating to real property, vital statistics, law enforcement, taxation, motor vehicles, driver's licenses, and social security.

## § 311. Pleadings and Accompanying Documents.

(a) A [petitioner] seeking to establish or modify a support order or to determine parentage in a proceeding under this [Act] must verify the [petition]. Unless otherwise ordered under Section 312 (Nondisclosure of Information in Exceptional Circumstances), the [petition] or accompanying documents must provide, so far as known, the name, sex, residential address, social security number, and date of birth of each child for whom support is sought. The [petition] must be accompanied by a certified copy of any support order in effect. The [petition] may include any other information that may assist in locating or identifying the [respondent.]

(b) The [petition] must specify the relief sought. The [petition] and accompanying documents must conform substantially with the requirements imposed by the forms mandated by federal law for use in cases filed by a support enforcement agency.

## § 312. Nondisclosure of Information in Exceptional Circumstances.

Upon a finding, which may be made ex parte, that the health, safety, or liberty of a party or child would be unreasonably put at risk by the disclosure of identifying information, or if an existing order so provides, a tribunal shall order that the address of the child or party or other identifying information not be disclosed in a pleading or other document filed in a proceeding under this [Act].

## § 313. Costs and Fees.

(a) The [petitioner] may not be required to pay a filing fee or other costs.

(b) If an obligee prevails, a responding tribunal may assess against an obligor filing fees, reasonable attorney's fees, other costs, and necessary travel and other reasonable expenses incurred by the obligee and the obligee's witnesses. The tribunal may not assess fees, costs, or expenses against the obligee or the support enforcement agency of either the initiating or the responding state, except as provided by other law. Attorney's fees may be taxed as costs, and may be ordered paid directly to the attorney, who may enforce the order in the attorney's own name. Payment of support owed to the obligee has priority over fees, costs and expenses.

(c) The tribunal shall order the payment of costs and reasonable attorney's fees if it determines that a hearing was requested primarily for delay. In a proceeding under Article 6 (Enforcement and Modification of Support Order After Registration), a hearing is presumed to have been requested primarily for delay if a registered support order is confirmed or enforced without change.

## § 314. Limited Immunity of [Petitioner].

(a) Participation by a [petitioner] in a proceeding before a responding tribunal, whether in person, by private attorney, or through services provided by the support enforcement agency, does not confer personal jurisdiction over the [petitioner] in another proceeding.

(b) A [petitioner] is not amenable to service of civil process while physically present in this State to participate in a proceeding under this [Act].

(c) The immunity granted by this section does not extend to civil litigation based on acts unrelated to a proceeding under this [Act] committed by a party while present in this State to participate in the proceeding.

## § 315. Nonparentage as Defense.

A party whose parentage of a child has been previously determined by or pursuant to law may not plead nonparentage as a defense to a proceeding under this [Act].

## § 316. Special Rules of Evidence and Procedure.

(a) The physical presence of the [petitioner] in a responding tribunal of this State is not required for the establishment, enforcement, or modification of a support order or the rendition of a judgment determining parentage.

(b) A verified [petition], affidavit, document substantially complying with federally mandated forms, and a document incorporated by reference in any of them, not excluded under the hearsay rule if given in person, is admissible in evidence if given under oath by a party or witness residing in another state.

(c) A copy of the record of child support payments certified as a true copy of the original by the custodian of the record may be forwarded to a responding tribunal. The copy is evidence of facts asserted in it, and is admissible to show whether payments were made.

(d) Copies of bills for testing for parentage, and for prenatal and postnatal health care of the mother and child, furnished to the adverse party at least [ten] days before trial, are admissible in evidence to prove the amount of the charges billed and that the charges were reasonable, necessary, and customary.

(e) Documentary evidence transmitted from another state to a tribunal of this State by telephone, telecopier, or other means that do not provide an original writing may not be excluded from evidence on an objection based on the means of transmission.

(f) In a proceeding under this [Act], a tribunal of this State may permit a party or witness residing in another state to be deposed or to testify by telephone, audiovisual means, or other electronic means at a designated tribunal or other location in that state. A tribunal of this State shall cooperate with tribunals of other states in designating an appropriate location for the deposition or testimony.

(g) If a party called to testify at a civil hearing refuses to answer on the ground that the testimony may be self-incriminating, the trier of fact may draw an adverse inference from the refusal.

(h) A privilege against disclosure of communications between spouses does not apply in a proceeding under this [Act].

(i) The defense of immunity based on the relationship of husband and wife or parent and child does not apply in a proceeding under this [Act].

## § 317. Communications Between Tribunals.

A tribunal of this State may communicate with a tribunal of another state in writing, or by telephone or other means, to obtain information concerning the laws of that state, the legal effect of a judgment, decree, or order of that tribunal, and the status of a proceeding in the other state. A tribunal of this State may furnish similar information by similar means to a tribunal of another state.

## § 318. Assistance with Discovery.

A tribunal of this State may:

(1) request a tribunal of another state to assist in obtaining discovery; and

(2) upon request, compel a person over whom it has jurisdiction to respond to a discovery order issued by a tribunal of another state.

## § 319. Receipt and Disbursement of Payments.

A support enforcement agency or tribunal of this State shall disburse promptly any amounts received pursuant to a support order, as directed by the order. The agency or tribunal shall furnish to a requesting party or tribunal of another state a certified statement by the custodian of the record of the amounts and dates of all payments received.

ARTICLE 4
ESTABLISHMENT OF SUPPORT ORDER

## § 401. [Petition] to Establish Support Order.

(a) If a support order entitled to recognition under this [Act] has not been issued, a responding tribunal of this State may issue a support order if:

(1) the individual seeking the order resides in another state; or

(2) the support enforcement agency seeking the order is located in another state.

(b) The tribunal may issue a temporary child support order if:

(1) the [respondent] has signed a verified statement acknowledging parentage;

(2) the [respondent] has been determined by or pursuant to law to be the parent; or

(3) there is other clear and convincing evidence that the [respondent] is the child's parent.

(c) Upon finding, after notice and opportunity to be heard, that an obligor owes a duty of support, the tribunal shall issue a support order directed to the

obligor and may issue other orders pursuant to Section 305 (Duties and Powers of Responding Tribunal).

## ARTICLE 5
## DIRECT ENFORCEMENT OF ORDER OF ANOTHER
## STATE WITHOUT REGISTRATION

### § 501. Recognition of Income-Withholding Order of Another State.

(a) An income-withholding order issued in another state may be sent by first class mail to the person or entity defined as the obligor's employer under [the income-withholding law of this State] without first filing a [petition] or comparable pleading or registering the order with a tribunal of this State. Upon receipt of the order, the employer shall:

(1) treat an income-withholding order issued in another state which appears regular on its face as if it had been issued by a tribunal of this State;

(2) immediately provide a copy of the order to the obligor; and

(3) distribute the funds as directed in the withholding order.

(b) An obligor may contest the validity or enforcement of an income-withholding order issued in another state in the same manner as if the order had been issued by a tribunal of this State. Section 604 (Choice of Law) applies to the contest. The obligor shall give notice of the contest to any support enforcement agency providing services to the obligee and to:

(1) the person or agency designated to receive payments in the income-withholding order; or

(2) if no person or agency is designated, the obligee.

### § 502. Administrative Enforcement of Orders.

(a) A party seeking to enforce a support order or an income-withholding order, or both, issued by a tribunal of another state may send the documents required for registering the order to a support enforcement agency of this State.

(b) Upon receipt of the documents, the support enforcement agency, without initially seeking to register the order, shall consider and, if appropriate, use any administrative procedure authorized by the law of this State to enforce a support order or an income-withholding order, or both. If the obligor does not contest administrative enforcement, the order need not be registered. If the obligor contests the validity or administrative enforcement of the order, the support enforcement agency shall register the order pursuant to this [Act].

## ARTICLE 6
## ENFORCEMENT AND MODIFICATION OF SUPPORT ORDER
## AFTER REGISTRATION

## PART A
## REGISTRATION AND ENFORCEMENT OF SUPPORT ORDER

## § 601. Registration of Order for Enforcement.

A support order or an income-withholding order issued by a tribunal of another state may be registered in this State for enforcement.

## § 602. Procedure to Register Order for Enforcement.

(a) A support order or income-withholding order of another state may be registered in this State by sending the following documents and information to the [appropriate tribunal] in this State:

(1) a letter of transmittal to the tribunal requesting registration and enforcement;

(2) two copies, including one certified copy, of all orders to be registered, including any modification of an order;

(3) a sworn statement by the party seeking registration or a certified statement by the custodian of the records showing the amount of any arrearage;

(4) the name of the obligor and, if known:

(i) the obligor's address and social security number;

(ii) the name and address of the obligor's employer and any other source of income of the obligor; and

(iii) a description and the location of property of the obligor in this State not exempt from execution; and

(5) the name and address of the obligee and, if applicable, the agency or person to whom support payments are to be remitted.

(b) On receipt of a request for registration, the registering tribunal shall cause the order to be filed as a foreign judgment, together with one copy of the documents and information, regardless of their form.

(c) A [petition] or comparable pleading seeking a remedy that must be affirmatively sought under other law of this State may be filed at the same time as the request for registration or later. The pleading must specify the grounds for the remedy sought.

## § 603. Effect of Registration for Enforcement.

(a) A support order or income-withholding order issued in another state is registered when the order is filed in the registering tribunal of this State.

(b) A registered order issued in another state is enforceable in the same manner and is subject to the same procedures as an order issued by a tribunal of this State.

(c) Except as otherwise provided in this article, a tribunal of this State shall recognize and enforce, but may not modify, a registered order if the issuing tribunal had jurisdiction.

## § 604. Choice of Law.

(a) The law of the issuing state governs the nature, extent, amount, and duration of current payments and other obligations of support and the payment of arrearages under the order.

(b) In a proceeding for arrearages, the statute of limitation under the laws of this State or of the issuing state, whichever is longer, applies.

## § 605. Notice of Registration of Order.

(a) When a support order or income-withholding order issued in another state is registered, the registering tribunal shall notify the nonregistering party. Notice must be given by first class, certified, or registered mail or by any means of personal service authorized by the law of this State. The notice must be accompanied by a copy of the registered order and the documents and relevant information accompanying the order.

(b) The notice must inform the nonregistering party:

(1) that a registered order is enforceable as of the date of registration in the same manner as an order issued by a tribunal of this State;

(2) that a hearing to contest the validity or enforcement of the registered order must be requested within [20] days after the date of mailing or personal service of the notice;

(3) that failure to contest the validity or enforcement of the registered order in a timely manner will result in confirmation of the order and enforcement of the order and the alleged arrearages and precludes further contest of that order with respect to any matter that could have been asserted;   and

(4) of the amount of any alleged arrearages.

(c) Upon registration of an income-withholding order for enforcement, the registering tribunal shall notify the obligor's employer pursuant to [the income-withholding law of this State].

## § 606. Procedure to Contest Validity or Enforcement of Registered Order.

(a) A nonregistering party seeking to contest the validity or enforcement of a registered order in this State shall request a hearing within [20] days after the date of mailing or personal service of notice of the registration. The nonregistering party may seek to vacate the registration, to assert any defense to an allegation of noncompliance with the registered order, or to contest the remedies being sought or the amount of any alleged arrearages pursuant to Section 607 (Contest of Registration or Enforcement).

(b) If the nonregistering party fails to contest the validity or enforcement of the registered order in a timely manner, the order is confirmed by operation of law.

(c) If a nonregistering party requests a hearing to contest the validity or enforcement of the registered order, the registering tribunal shall schedule the matter for hearing and give notice to the parties by first class mail of the date, time, and place of the hearing.

## § 607. Contest of Registration or Enforcement.

(a) A party contesting the validity or enforcement of a registered order or seeking to vacate the registration has the burden of proving one or more of the following defenses:

(1) the issuing tribunal lacked personal jurisdiction over the contesting party;

(2) the order was obtained by fraud;

(3) the order has been vacated, suspended, or modified by a later order;

(4) the issuing tribunal has stayed the order pending appeal;

(5) there is a defense under the law of this State to the remedy sought;

(6) full or partial payment has been made;  or

(7) the statute of limitation under Section 604 (Choice of Law) precludes enforcement of some or all of the arrearages.

(b) If a party presents evidence establishing a full or partial defense under subsection (a), a tribunal may stay enforcement of the registered order, continue the proceeding to permit production of additional relevant evidence, and issue other appropriate orders. An uncontested portion of the registered order may be enforced by all remedies available under the law of this State.

(c) If the contesting party does not establish a defense under subsection (a) to the validity or enforcement of the order, the registering tribunal shall issue an order confirming the order.

## § 608. Confirmed Order.

Confirmation of a registered order, whether by operation of law or after notice and hearing, precludes further contest of the order with respect to any matter that could have been asserted at the time of registration.

## § 609. Procedure to Register Child Support Order of Another State for Modification.

A party or support enforcement agency seeking to modify, or to modify and enforce, a child support order issued in another state shall register that order in this State in the same manner provided in Part A of this article if the order has not been registered. A [petition] for modification may be filed at the same time as a request for registration, or later. The pleading must specify the grounds for modification.

### § 610. Effect of Registration for Modification.

A tribunal of this State may enforce a child support order of another state registered for purposes of modification, in the same manner as if the order had been issued by a tribunal of this State, but the registered order may be modified only if the requirements of Section 611 (Modification of Child Support Order of Another State) have been met.

### § 611. Modification of Child Support Order of Another State.

(a) After a child support order issued in another state has been registered in this State, the responding tribunal of this State may modify that order only if, after notice and hearing, it finds that:

(1) the following requirements are met:

(i) the child, the individual obligee, and the obligor do not reside in the issuing state;

(ii) a [petitioner] who is a nonresident of this State seeks modification; and

(iii) the [respondent] is subject to the personal jurisdiction of the tribunal of this State;  or

(2) an individual party or the child is subject to the personal jurisdiction of the tribunal and all of the individual parties have filed a written consent in the issuing tribunal providing that a tribunal of this State may modify the support order and assume continuing, exclusive jurisdiction over the order.

(b) Modification of a registered child support order is subject to the same requirements, procedures, and defenses that apply to the modification of an order issued by a tribunal of this State and the order may be enforced and satisfied in the same manner.

(c) A tribunal of this State may not modify any aspect of a child support order that may not be modified under the law of the issuing state.

(d) On issuance of an order modifying a child support order issued in another state, a tribunal of this State becomes the tribunal of continuing, exclusive jurisdiction.

(e) Within [30] days after issuance of a modified child support order, the party obtaining the modification shall file a certified copy of the order with the issuing tribunal which had continuing, exclusive jurisdiction over the earlier order, and in each tribunal in which the party knows that earlier order has been registered.

### § 612. Recognition of Order Modified in Another State.

A tribunal of this State shall recognize a modification of its earlier child support order by a tribunal of another state which assumed jurisdiction pursuant to a law substantially similar to this [Act] and, upon request, except as otherwise provided in this [Act], shall:

(1) enforce the order that was modified only as to amounts accruing before the modification;

(2) enforce only nonmodifiable aspects of that order;

(3) provide other appropriate relief only for violations of that order which occurred before the effective date of the modification; and

(4) recognize the modifying order of the other state, upon registration, for the purpose of enforcement.

## ARTICLE 7
## DETERMINATION OF PARENTAGE

### § 701. Proceeding to Determine Parentage.

(a) A tribunal of this State may serve as an initiating or responding tribunal in a proceeding brought under this [Act] or a law substantially similar to this [Act], the Uniform Reciprocal Enforcement of Support Act, or the Revised Uniform Reciprocal Enforcement of Support Act to determine that the [petitioner] is a parent of a particular child or to determine that a [respondent] is a parent of that child.

(b) In a proceeding to determine parentage, a responding tribunal of this State shall apply the [Uniform Parentage Act; procedural and substantive law of this State,] and the rules of this State on choice of law.

### § 701. Proceeding to Determine Parentage.

(a) A tribunal of this State may serve as an initiating or responding tribunal in a proceeding brought under this [Act] or a law substantially similar to this [Act], the Uniform Reciprocal Enforcement of Support Act, or the Revised Uniform Reciprocal Enforcement of Support Act to determine that the [petitioner] is a parent of a particular child or to determine that a [respondent] is a parent of that child.

(b) In a proceeding to determine parentage, a responding tribunal of this State shall apply the [Uniform Parentage Act; procedural and substantive law of this State,] and the rules of this State on choice of law.

## ARTICLE 8
## INTERSTATE RENDITION

### § 801. Grounds for Rendition.

(a) For purposes of this article, "governor" includes an individual performing the functions of governor or the executive authority of a state covered by this [Act].

(b) The governor of this State may:

(1) demand that the governor of another state surrender an individual found in the other state who is charged criminally in this State with having failed to provide for the support of an obligee;  or

(2) on the demand by the governor of another state, surrender an individual found in this State who is charged criminally in the other state with having failed to provide for the support of an obligee.

(c) A provision for extradition of individuals not inconsistent with this [Act] applies to the demand even if the individual whose surrender is demanded was not in the demanding state when the crime was allegedly committed and has not fled therefrom.

## § 802. Condition of Rendition.

(a) Before making demand that the governor of another state surrender an individual charged criminally in this State with having failed to provide for the support of an obligee, the governor of this State may require a prosecutor of this State to demonstrate that at least [60] days previously the obligee had initiated proceedings for support pursuant to this [Act] or that the proceeding would be of no avail.

(b) If, under this [Act] or a law substantially similar to this [Act], the Uniform Reciprocal Enforcement of Support Act, or the Revised Uniform Reciprocal Enforcement of Support Act, the governor of another state makes a demand that the governor of this State surrender an individual charged criminally in that state with having failed to provide for the support of a child or other individual to whom a duty of support is owed, the governor may require a prosecutor to investigate the demand and report whether a proceeding for support has been initiated or would be effective.  If it appears that a proceeding would be effective but has not been initiated, the governor may delay honoring the demand for a reasonable time to permit the initiation of a proceeding.

(c) If a proceeding for support has been initiated and the individual whose rendition is demanded prevails, the governor may decline to honor the demand. If the [petitioner] prevails and the individual whose rendition is demanded is subject to a support order, the governor may decline to honor the demand if the individual is complying with the support order.

*[ED.—The provisions of Article 9, dealing with uniformity of application and construction, severability, repeals, effective date, and short title, have been omitted.]*

# UNIFORM MARRIAGE AND DIVORCE ACT (1970)
## 9A U.L.A. 156 (1987)

*[The Uniform Marriage and Divorce Act is reprinted with permission from the National Conference of Commissioners on State Laws.]*

### § 101. [Short Title]

This Act may be cited as the "Uniform Marriage and Divorce Act."

### § 102. [Purposes:  Rules of Construction]

This Act shall be liberally construed and applied to promote its underlying purposes, which are to:

(1) provide adequate procedures for the solemnization and registration of marriage;

(2) strengthen and preserve the integrity of marriage and safeguard family relationships;

(3) promote the amicable settlement of disputes that have arisen between parties to a marriage;

(4) mitigate the potential harm to the spouses and their children caused by the process of legal dissolution of marriage;

(5) make reasonable provision for spouse and minor children during and after litigation;  and

(6) make the law of legal dissolution of marriage effective for dealing with the realities of matrimonial experience by making irretrievable breakdown of the marriage relationship the sole basis for its dissolution.

### § 201. [Formalities]

Marriage is a personal relationship between a man and a woman arising out of a civil contract to which the consent of the parties is essential.  A marriage licensed, solemnized, and registered as provided in this Act is valid in this State. A marriage may be contracted, maintained, invalidated, or dissolved only as provided by law.

### § 202. [Marriage License and Marriage Certificate]

(a) The [Secretary of State, Commissioner of Public Health] shall prescribe the form for an application for a marriage license, which shall include the following information:

(1) name, sex, occupation, address, social security number, date and place of birth of each party to the proposed marriage;

(2) if either party was previously married, his name, and the date, place, and court in which the marriage was dissolved or declared invalid or the date and place of death of the former spouse;

(3) name and address of the parents or guardian of each party; and

(4) whether the parties are related to each other and, if so, their relationship.

(5) the name and date of birth of any child of which both parties are parents, born before the making of the application, unless their parental rights and the parent and child relationship with respect to the child have been terminated.

(b) The [Secretary of State, Commissioner of Public Health] shall prescribe the forms for the marriage license, the marriage certificate, and the consent to marriage.

### § 203. [License to Marry]

When a marriage application has been completed and signed by both parties to a prospective marriage and at least one party has appeared before the [marriage license] clerk and paid the marriage license fee of [$_____], the [marriage license] clerk shall issue a license to marry and a marriage certificate form upon being furnished:

(1) satisfactory proof that each party to the marriage will have attained the age of 18 years at the time the marriage license is effective, or will have attained the age of 16 years and has either the consent to the marriage of both parents or his guardian, or judicial approval; [or, if under the age of 16 years, has both the consent of both parents or his guardian and judicial approval;] and

(2) satisfactory proof that the marriage is not prohibited; [and]

[ (3) a certificate of the results of any medical examination required by the laws of this State].

### § 204. [License, Effective Date]

A license to marry becomes effective throughout this state 3 days after the date of issuance, unless the [_____] court orders that the license is effective when issued, and expires 180 days after it becomes effective.

### § 205. [Judicial Approval]

(a) The [_____] court, after a reasonable effort has been made to notify the parents or guardian of each underaged party, may order the [marriage license] clerk to issue a marriage license and a marriage certificate form:

[ (1) ] to a party aged 16 or 17 years who has no parent capable of consenting to his marriage, or whose parent or guardian has not consented to his marriage; [or

(2) to a party under the age of 16 years who has the consent of both parents

to his marriage, if capable of giving consent, or his guardian].

(b) A marriage license and a marriage certificate form may be issued under this section only if the court finds that the underaged party is capable of assuming the responsibilities of marriage and the marriage will serve his best interest. Pregnancy alone does not establish that the best interest of the party will be served.

(c) The [_____] court shall authorize performance of a marriage by proxy upon the showing required by the provisions on solemnization.

## § 206. [Solemnization and Registration]

(a) A marriage may be solemnized by a judge of a court of record, by a public official whose powers include solemnization of marriages, or in accordance with any mode of solemnization recognized by any religious denomination, Indian Nation or Tribe, or Native Group. Either the person solemnizing the marriage, or, if no individual acting alone solemnized the marriage, a party to the marriage, shall complete the marriage certificate form and forward it to the [marriage license] clerk.

(b) If a party to a marriage is unable to be present at the solemnization, he may authorize in writing a third person to act as his proxy. If the person solemnizing the marriage is satisfied that the absent party is unable to be present and has consented to the marriage, he may solemnize the marriage by proxy. If he is not satisfied, the parties may petition the [_____] court for an order permitting the marriage to be solemnized by proxy.

(c) Upon receipt of the marriage certificate, the [marriage license] clerk shall register the marriage.

(d) The solemnization of the marriage is not invalidated by the fact that the person solemnizing the marriage was not legally qualified to solemnize it, if neither party to the marriage believed him to be so qualified.

## § 207. [Prohibited Marriages]

(a) The following marriages are prohibited:

(1) a marriage entered into prior to the dissolution of an earlier marriage of one of the parties;

(2) a marriage between an ancestor and a descendant, or between a brother and a sister, whether the relationship is by the half or the whole blood, or by adoption;

(3) a marriage between an uncle and a niece or between an aunt and a nephew, whether the relationship is by the half or the whole blood, except as to marriages permitted by the established customs of aboriginal cultures.

(b) Parties to a marriage prohibited under this section who cohabit after removal of the impediment are lawfully married as of the date of the removal of the impediment.

(c) Children born of a prohibited marriage are legitimate.

## § 208. [Declaration of Invalidity]

(a) The [_____] court shall enter its decree declaring the invalidity of a marriage entered into under the following circumstances:

(1) a party lacked capacity to consent to the marriage at the time the marriage was solemnized, either because of mental incapacity or infirmity or because of the influence of alcohol, drugs, or other incapacitating substances, or a party was induced to enter into a marriage by force or duress, or by fraud involving the essentials of marriage;

(2) a party lacks the physical capacity to consummate the marriage by sexual intercourse, and at the time the marriage was solemnized the other party did not know of the incapacity;

(3) a party [was under the age of 16 years and did not have the consent of his parents or guardian and judicial approval or] was aged 16 or 17 years and did not have the consent of his parents or guardian or judicial approval;  or

(4) the marriage is prohibited.

(b) A declaration of invalidity under subsection (a)(1) through (3) may be sought by any of the following persons and must be commenced within the times specified, but in no event may a declaration of invalidity be sought after the death of either party to the marriage:

(1) for a reason set forth in subsection (a)(1), by either party or by the legal representative of the party who lacked capacity to consent, no later than 90 days after the petitioner obtained knowledge of the described condition;

(2) for the reason set forth in subsection (a)(2), by either party, no later than one year after the petitioner obtained knowledge of the described condition;

(3) for the reason set forth in subsection (a)(3), by the underaged party, his parent or guardian, prior to the time the underaged party reaches the age at which he could have married without satisfying the omitted requirement.

Alternative A

[ (c) A declaration of invalidity for the reason set forth in subsection (a)(4) may be sought by either party, the legal spouse in case of a bigamous marriage, the [appropriate state official], or a child of either party, at any time prior to the death of one of the parties.]

Alternative B

[ (c) A declaration of invalidity for the reason set forth in subsection (a)(4) may be sought by either party, the legal spouse in case of a bigamous marriage, the [appropriate state official] or a child of either party, at any time, not to exceed

5 years following the death of either party.]

(d) Children born of a marriage declared invalid are legitimate.

(e) Unless the court finds, after a consideration of all relevant circumstances, including the effect of a retroactive decree on third parties, that the interests of justice would be served by making the decree not retroactive, it shall declare the marriage invalid as of the date of the marriage. The provisions of this Act relating to property rights of the spouses, maintenance, support, and custody of children on dissolution of marriage are applicable to non-retroactive decrees of invalidity.

## § 209. [Putative Spouse].

Any person who has cohabited with another to whom he is not legally married in the good faith belief that he was married to that person is a putative spouse until knowledge of the fact that he is not legally married terminates his status and prevents acquisition of further rights. A putative spouse acquires the rights conferred upon a legal spouse, including the right to maintenance following termination of his status, whether or not the marriage is prohibited (Section 207) or declared invalid (Section 208). If there is a legal spouse or other putative spouses, rights acquired by a putative spouse do not supersede the rights of the legal spouse or those acquired by other putative spouses, but the court shall apportion property, maintenance, and support rights among the claimants as appropriate in the circumstances and in the interests of justice.

## § 210. [Application].

All marriages contracted within this State prior to the effective date of this Act, or outside this State, that were valid at the time of the contract or subsequently validated by the laws of the place in which they were contracted or by the domicil of the parties, are valid in this State.

## [§ 211. [Invalidity of Common Law Marriage] [ALTERNATIVE B].

Common law marriages contracted in this State after the effective date of this Act are invalid.]

## § 302. [Dissolution of Marriage;  Legal Separation].

(a) The [_____] court shall enter a decree of dissolution of marriage if:

(1) the court finds that one of the parties, at the time the action was commenced, was domiciled in this State, or was stationed in this State while a member of the armed services, and that the domicil or military presence has been maintained for 90 days next preceding the making of the findings;

(2) the court finds that the marriage is irretrievably broken, if the finding is supported by evidence that (i) the parties have lived separate and apart for a

period of more than 180 days next preceding the commencement of the proceeding, or (ii) there is serious marital discord adversely affecting the attitude of one or both of the parties toward the marriage;

(3) the court finds that the conciliation provisions of Section 305 either do not apply or have been met;

(4) to the extent it has jurisdiction to do so, the court has considered, approved, or provided for child custody, the support of any child entitled to support, the maintenance of either spouse, and the disposition of property; or has provided for a separate, later hearing to complete these matters.

(b) If a party requests a decree of legal separation rather than a decree of dissolution of marriage, the court shall grant the decree in that form unless the other party objects.

## § 303. [Procedure; Commencement; Pleadings; Abolition of Existing Defenses].

(a) All proceedings under this Act are commenced in the manner provided by the [Rules of Civil Practice].

(b) The verified petition in a proceeding for dissolution of marriage or legal separation shall allege that the marriage is irretrievably broken and shall set forth:

(1) the age, occupation, and residence of each party and his length of residence in this State;

(2) the date of the marriage and the place at which it was registered;

(3) that the jurisdictional requirements of Section 302 exist and the marriage is irretrievably broken in that either (i) the parties have lived separate and apart for a period of more than 180 days next preceding the commencement of the proceeding or (ii) there is serious marital discord adversely affecting the attitude of one or both of the parties toward the marriage, and there is no reasonable prospect of reconciliation;

(4) the names, ages, and addresses of all living children of the marriage, and whether the wife is pregnant;

(5) any arrangements as to support, custody, and visitation of the children and maintenance of a spouse;  and

(6) the relief sought.

(c) Either or both parties to the marriage may initiate the proceeding.

(d) If a proceeding is commenced by one of the parties, the other party must be served in the manner provided by the [Rules of Civil Practice] and may within [30] days after the date of service file a verified response.

(e) Previously existing defenses to divorce and legal separation, including but not limited to condonation, connivance, collusion, recrimination, insanity, and lapse of time, are abolished.

(f) The court may join additional parties proper for the exercise of its authority to implement this Act.

## § 304. [Temporary Order or Temporary Injunction].

(a) In a proceeding for dissolution of marriage or for legal separation, or in a proceeding for disposition of property or for maintenance or support following dissolution of the marriage by a court which lacked personal jurisdiction over the absent spouse, either party may move for temporary maintenance or temporary support of a child of the marriage entitled to support. The motion shall be accompanied by an affidavit setting forth the factual basis for the motion and the amounts requested.

(b) As a part of a motion for temporary maintenance or support or by independent motion accompanied by affidavit, either party may request the court to issue a temporary injunction for any of the following relief:

(1) restraining any person from transferring, encumbering, concealing, or otherwise disposing of any property except in the usual course of business or for the necessities of life, and, if so restrained, requiring him to notify the moving party of any proposed extraordinary expenditures made after the order is issued;

(2) enjoining a party from molesting or disturbing the peace of the other party or of any child;

(3) excluding a party from the family home or from the home of the other party upon a showing that physical or emotional harm would otherwise result;

(4) enjoining a party from removing a child from the jurisdiction of the court; and

(5) providing other injunctive relief proper in the circumstances.

(c) The court may issue a temporary restraining order without requiring notice to the other party only if it finds on the basis of the moving affidavit or other evidence that irreparable injury will result to the moving party if no order is issued until the time for responding has elapsed.

(d) A response may be filed within [20] days after service of notice of motion or at the time specified in the temporary restraining order.

(e) On the basis of the showing made and in conformity with Sections 308 and 309, the court may issue a temporary injunction and an order for temporary maintenance or support in amounts and on terms just and proper in the circumstance.

(f) A temporary order or temporary injunction:

(1) does not prejudice the rights of the parties or the child which are to be adjudicated at subsequent hearings in the proceeding;

(2) may be revoked or modified before final decree on a showing by affidavit of the facts necessary to revocation or modification of a final decree under Section 316; and

(3) terminates when the final decree is entered or when the petition for dissolution or legal separation is voluntarily dismissed.

## § 305. [Irretrievable Breakdown].

(a) If both of the parties by petition or otherwise have stated under oath or affirmation that the marriage is irretrievably broken, or one of the parties has so stated and the other has not denied it, the court, after hearing, shall make a finding whether the marriage is irretrievably broken.

(b) If one of the parties has denied under oath or affirmation that the marriage is irretrievably broken, the court shall consider all relevant factors, including the circumstances that gave rise to filing the petition and the prospect of reconciliation, and shall:

(1) make a finding whether the marriage is irretrievably broken;  or

(2) continue the matter for further hearing not fewer than 30 nor more than 60 days later, or as soon thereafter as the matter may be reached on the court's calendar, and may suggest to the parties that they seek counseling. The court, at the request of either party shall, or on its own motion may, order a conciliation conference.  At the adjourned hearing the court shall make a finding whether the marriage is irretrievably broken.

(c) A finding of irretrievable breakdown is a determination that there is no reasonable prospect of reconciliation.

## § 306. [Separation Agreement].

(a) To promote amicable settlement of disputes between parties to a marriage attendant upon their separation or the dissolution of their marriage, the parties may enter into a written separation agreement containing provisions for disposition of any property owned by either of them, maintenance of either of them, and support, custody, and visitation of their children.

(b) In a proceeding for dissolution of marriage or for legal separation, the terms of the separation agreement, except those providing for the support, custody, and visitation of children, are binding upon the court unless it finds, after considering the economic circumstances of the parties and any other relevant evidence produced by the parties, on their own motion or on request of the court, that the separation agreement is unconscionable.

(c) If the court finds the separation agreement unconscionable, it may request the parties to submit a revised separation agreement or may make orders for the disposition of property, maintenance, and support.

(d) If the court finds that the separation agreement is not unconscionable as to disposition of property or maintenance, and not unsatisfactory as to support:

(1) unless the separation agreement provides to the contrary, its terms shall be set forth in the decree of dissolution or legal separation and the parties shall be

ordered to perform them, or

(2) if the separation agreement provides that its terms shall not be set forth in the decree, the decree shall identify the separation agreement and state that the court has found the terms not unconscionable.

(e) Terms of the agreement set forth in the decree are enforceable by all remedies available for enforcement of a judgment, including contempt, and are enforceable as contract terms.

(f) Except for terms concerning the support, custody, or visitation of children, the decree may expressly preclude or limit modification of terms set forth in the decree if the separation agreement so provides. Otherwise, terms of a separation agreement set forth in the decree are automatically modified by modification of the decree.

### § 307. [Disposition of Property] [ALTERNATIVE A].

(a) In a proceeding for dissolution of a marriage, legal separation, or disposition of property following a decree of dissolution of marriage or legal separation by a court which lacked personal jurisdiction over the absent spouse or lacked jurisdiction to dispose of the property, the court, without regard to marital misconduct, shall, and in a proceeding for legal separation may, finally equitably apportion between the parties the property and assets belonging to either or both however and whenever acquired, and whether the title thereto is in the name of the husband or wife or both. In making apportionment the court shall consider the duration of the marriage, and prior marriage of either party, antenuptial agreement of the parties, the age, health, station, occupation, amount and sources of income, vocational skills, employability, estate, liabilities, and needs of each of the parties, custodial provisions, whether the apportionment is in lieu of or in addition to maintenance, and the opportunity of each for future acquisition of capital assets and income. The court shall also consider the contribution or dissipation of each party in the acquisition, preservation, depreciation, or appreciation in value of the respective estates, and the contribution of a spouse as a homemaker or to the family unit.

(b) In a proceeding, the court may protect and promote the best interests of the children by setting aside a portion of the jointly and separately held estates of the parties in a separate fund or trust for the support, maintenance, education, and general welfare of any minor, dependent, or incompetent children of the parties.

### § 307. [Disposition of Property] [ALTERNATIVE B].

In a proceeding for dissolution of the marriage, legal separation, or disposition of property following a decree of dissolution of the marriage or legal separation by a court which lacked personal jurisdiction over the absent spouse or lacked jurisdiction to dispose of the property, the court shall assign each spouse's separate property to that spouse. It also shall divide community property, without regard to marital misconduct, in just proportions after considering all relevant factors including:

(1) contribution of each spouse to acquisition of the marital property, including contribution of a spouse as homemaker;

(2) value of the property set apart to each spouse;

(3) duration of the marriage; and

(4) economic circumstances of each spouse when the division of property is to become effective, including the desirability of awarding the family home or the right to live therein for a reasonable period to the spouse having custody of any children.

## § 308. [Maintenance].

(a) In a proceeding for dissolution of marriage, legal separation, or maintenance following a decree of dissolution of the marriage by a court which lacked personal jurisdiction over the absent spouse, the court may grant a maintenance order for either spouse only if it finds that the spouse seeking maintenance:

(1) lacks sufficient property to provide for his reasonable needs; and

(2) is unable to support himself through appropriate employment or is the custodian of a child whose condition or circumstances make it appropriate that the custodian not be required to seek employment outside the home.

(b) The maintenance order shall be in amounts and for periods of time the court deems just, without regard to marital misconduct, and after considering all relevant factors including:

(1) the financial resources of the party seeking maintenance, including marital property apportioned to him, his ability to meet his needs independently, and the extent to which a provision for support of a child living with the party includes a sum for that party as custodian;

(2) the time necessary to acquire sufficient education or training to enable the party seeking maintenance to find appropriate employment;

(3) the standard of living established during the marriage;

(4) the duration of the marriage;

(5) the age and the physical and emotional condition of the spouse seeking maintenance; and

(6) the ability of the spouse from whom maintenance is sought to meet his needs while meeting those of the spouse seeking maintenance.

## § 309. [Child Support].

In a proceeding for dissolution of marriage, legal separation, maintenance, or child support, the court may order either or both parents owing a duty of support to a child to pay an amount reasonable or necessary for his support, without regard to marital misconduct, after considering all relevant factors including:

(1) the financial resources of the child;

(2) the financial resources of the custodial parent;

(3) the standard of living the child would have enjoyed had the marriage not been dissolved;

(4) the physical and emotional condition of the child and his educational needs; and

(5) the financial resources and needs of the noncustodial parent.

## § 310. [Representation of Child].

The court may appoint an attorney to represent the interests of a minor or dependent child with respect to his support, custody, and visitation. The court shall enter an order for costs, fees, and disbursements in favor of the child's attorney. The order shall be made against either or both parents, except that, if the responsible party is indigent, the costs, fees, and disbursements shall be borne by the [appropriate agency].

## § 311. [Payment of Maintenance or Support to Court].

(a) Upon its own motion or upon motion of either party, the court may order at any time that maintenance or support payments be made to the [clerk of court, court trustee, probation officer] as trustee for remittance to the person entitled to receive the payments.

(b) The [clerk of court, court trustee, probation officer] shall maintain records listing the amount of payments, the date payments are required to be made, and the names and addresses of the parties affected by the order.

(c) The parties affected by the order shall inform the [clerk of court, court trustee, probation officer] of any change of address or of other condition that may affect the administration of the order.

(d) If a party fails to make a required payment, the [clerk of court, court trustee, probation officer] shall send by registered or certified mail notice of the arrearage to the obligor. If payment of the sum due is not made to the [clerk of court, court trustee, probation officer] within 10 days after sending notice, the [clerk of court, court trustee, probation officer] shall certify the amount due to the [prosecuting attorney]. The [prosecuting attorney] shall promptly initiate contempt proceedings against the obligator.

(e) The [prosecuting attorney] shall assist the court on behalf of a person entitled to receive maintenance or support in all proceedings initiated under this section to enforce compliance with the order. The person to whom maintenance or support is awarded may also initiate action to collect arrearages.

(f) If the person obligated to pay support has left or is beyond the jurisdiction of the court, the [prosecuting attorney] may institute any other proceeding available under the laws of this State for enforcement of the duties of support and maintenance.

### § 312. [Assignments].

The court may order the person obligated to pay support or maintenance to make an assignment of a part of his periodic earnings or trust income to the person entitled to receive the payments.  The assignment is binding on the employer, trustee, or other payor of the funds 2 weeks after service upon him of notice that it has been made.  The payor shall withhold from the earnings or trust income payable to the person obligated to support the amount specified in the assignment and shall transmit the payments to the person specified in the order. The payor may deduct from each payment a sum not exceeding [$1.00] as reimbursement for costs.  An employer shall not discharge or otherwise discipline an employee as a result of a wage or salary assignment authorized by this section.

### § 313. [Attorney's Fees].

The court from time to time after considering the financial resources of both parties may order a party to pay a reasonable amount for the cost to the other party of maintaining or defending any proceeding under this Act and for attorney's fees, including sums for legal services rendered and costs incurred prior to the commencement of the proceeding or after entry of judgment.  The court may order that the amount be paid directly to the attorney, who may enforce the order in his name.

### § 314. [Decree].

(a) A decree of dissolution of marriage or of legal separation is final when entered, subject to the right of appeal.  An appeal from the decree of dissolution that does not challenge the finding that the marriage is irretrievably broken does not delay the finality of that provision of the decree which dissolves the marriage beyond the time for appealing from that provision, and either of the parties may remarry pending appeal.

(b) No earlier than 6 months after entry of a decree of legal separation, the court on motion of either party shall convert the decree to a decree of dissolution of marriage.

(c) The Clerk of Court shall give notice of the entry of a decree of dissolution or legal separation:

(1) if the marriage is registered in this State, to the [marriage license] clerk of the [county, judicial district] where the marriage is registered who shall enter

the fact of dissolution or separation in the [Registry of Marriage];  or

(2) if the marriage is registered in another jurisdiction, to the appropriate official of that jurisdiction, with the request that he enter the fact of dissolution in the appropriate record.

(d) Upon request by a wife whose marriage is dissolved or declared invalid, the court may, and if there are no children of the parties shall, order her maiden name or a former name restored.

### § 315. [Independence of Provisions of Decree or Temporary Order].

If a party fails to comply with a provision of a decree or temporary order or injunction, the obligation of the other party to make payments for support or maintenance or to permit visitation is not suspended;  but he may move the court to grant an appropriate order.

### § 316. [Modification and Termination of Provisions for Maintenance, Support and Property Disposition].

(a) Except as otherwise provided in subsection (f) of Section 306, the provisions of any decree respecting maintenance or support may be modified only as to installments accruing subsequent to the motion for modification and only upon a showing of changed circumstances so substantial and continuing as to make the terms unconscionable.  The provisions as to property disposition may not be revoked or modified, unless the court finds the existence of conditions that justify the reopening of a judgment under the laws of this state.

(b) Unless otherwise agreed in writing or expressly provided in the decree, the obligation to pay future maintenance is terminated upon the death of either party or the remarriage of the party receiving maintenance.

(c) Unless otherwise agreed in writing or expressly provided in the decree, provisions for the support of a child are terminated by emancipation of the child but not by the death of a parent obligated to support the child.  When a parent obligated to pay support dies, the amount of support may be modified, revoked, or commuted to a lump sum payment, to the extent just and appropriate in the circumstances.

### § 401. [Jurisdiction;  Commencement of Proceeding].

(a) A court of this State competent to decide child custody matters has jurisdiction to make a child custody determination by initial or modification decree if:

(1) this State (i) is the home state of the child at the time of commencement of the proceeding, or (ii) had been the child's home state within 6 months before commencement of the proceeding and the child is absent from this State because of his removal or retention by a person claiming his custody or

for other reason, and a parent or person acting as parent continues to live in this State;  or

(2) it is in the best interest of the child that a court of this State assume jurisdiction because (i) the child and his parents, or the child and at least one contestant, have a significant connection with this State, and (ii) there is available in this State substantial evidence concerning the child's present or future care, protection, training, and personal relationships;  or

(3) the child is physically present in this State and (i) has been abandoned or (ii) it is necessary in an emergency to protect him because he has been subjected to or threatened with mistreatment or abuse or is neglected or dependent;  or

(4)(i) no other state has jurisdiction under prerequisites substantially in accordance with paragraphs (1), (2) or (3), or another state has declined to exercise jurisdiction on the ground that this State is the more appropriate forum to determine custody of the child, and (ii) it is in his best interest that the court assume jurisdiction.

(b) Except under paragraphs (3) and (4) of subsection (a), physical presence in this State of the child, or of the child and one of the contestants, is not alone sufficient to confer jurisdiction on a court of this State to make a child custody determination.

(c) Physical presence of the child, while desirable, is not a prerequisite for jurisdiction to determine his custody.

(d) A child custody proceeding is commenced in the [_____] court:

(1) by a parent, by filing a petition

(i) for dissolution or legal separation;  or

(ii) for custody of the child in the [county, judicial district] in which he is permanently resident or found;  or

(2) by a person other than a parent, by filing a petition for custody of the child in the [county, judicial district] in which he is permanently resident or found, but only if he is not in the physical custody of one of his parents.

(e) Notice of a child custody proceeding shall be given to the child's parent, guardian, and custodian, who may appear, be heard, and file a responsive pleading.  The court, upon a showing of good cause, may permit intervention of other interested parties.

## § 402. [Best Interest of Child].

The court shall determine custody in accordance with the best interest of the child.  The court shall consider all relevant factors including:

(1) the wishes of the child's parent or parents as to his custody;

(2) the wishes of the child as to his custodian;

(3) the interaction and interrelationship of the child with his parent or

parents, his siblings, and any other person who may significantly affect the child's best interest;

(4) the child's adjustment to his home, school, and community; and

(5) the mental and physical health of all individuals involved.

The court shall not consider conduct of a proposed custodian that does not affect his relationship to the child.

## § 403. [Temporary Orders].

(a) A party to a custody proceeding may move for a temporary custody order. The motion must be supported by an affidavit as provided in Section 410. The court may award temporary custody under the standards of Section 402 after a hearing, or, if there is no objection, solely on the basis of the affidavits.

(b) If a proceeding for dissolution of marriage or legal separation is dismissed, any temporary custody order is vacated unless a parent or the child's custodian moves that the proceeding continue as a custody proceeding and the court finds, after a hearing, that the circumstances of the parents and the best interest of the child requires that a custody decree be issued.

(c) If a custody proceeding commenced in the absence of a petition for dissolution of marriage or legal separation under subsection (1)(ii) or (2) of Section 401 is dismissed, any temporary custody order is vacated.

## § 404. [Interviews].

(a) The court may interview the child in chambers to ascertain the child's wishes as to his custodian and as to visitation. The court may permit counsel to be present at the interview. The court shall cause a record of the interview to be made and to be part of the record in the case.

(b) The court may seek the advice of professional personnel, whether or not employed by the court on a regular basis. The advice given shall be in writing and made available by the court to counsel upon request. Counsel may examine as a witness any professional personnel consulted by the court.

## § 405. [Investigations and Reports].

(a) In contested custody proceedings, and in other custody proceedings if a parent or the child's custodian so requests, the court may order an investigation and report concerning custodial arrangements for the child. The investigation and report may be made by [the court social service agency, the staff of the juvenile court, the local probation or welfare department, or a private agency employed by the court for the purpose].

(b) In preparing his report concerning a child, the investigator may consult any person who may have information about the child and his potential custodial arrangements. Upon order of the court, the investigator may refer the child to professional personnel for diagnosis. The investigator may consult with and obtain information from medical, psychiatric, or other expert persons who have served the child in the past without obtaining the consent of the parent or the child's custodian; but the child's consent must be obtained if he has reached the age of 16, unless the court finds that he lacks mental capacity to consent. If the requirements of subsection (c) are fulfilled, the investigator's report may be received in evidence at the hearing.

(c) The court shall mail the investigator's report to counsel and to any party not represented by counsel at least 10 days prior to the hearing. The investigator shall make available to counsel and to any party not represented by counsel the investigator's file of underlying data, and reports, complete texts of diagnostic reports made to the investigator pursuant to the provisions of subsection (b), and the names and addresses of all persons whom the investigator has consulted. Any party to the proceeding may call the investigator and any person whom he has consulted for cross-examination. A party may not waive his right of cross-examination prior to the hearing.

## § 406. [Hearings].

(a) Custody proceedings shall receive priority in being set for hearing.

(b) The court may tax as costs the payment of necessary travel and other expenses incurred by any person whose presence at the hearing the court deems necessary to determine the best interest of the child.

(c) The court without a jury shall determine questions of law and fact. If it finds that a public hearing may be detrimental to the child's best interest, the court may exclude the public from a custody hearing, but may admit any person who has a direct and legitimate interest in the particular case or a legitimate educational or research interest in the work of the court.

(d) If the court finds it necessary to protect the child's welfare that the record of any interview, report, investigation, or testimony in a custody proceeding be kept secret, the court may make an appropriate order sealing the record.

## § 407. [Visitation].

(a) A parent not granted custody of the child is entitled to reasonable visitation rights unless the court finds, after a hearing, that visitation would endanger seriously the child's physical, mental, moral, or emotional health.

(b) The court may modify an order granting or denying visitation rights whenever modification would serve the best interest of the child; but the court shall not restrict a parent's visitation rights unless it finds that the visitation would endanger seriously the child's physical, mental, moral, or emotional health.

## § 408. [Judicial Supervision].

(a) Except as otherwise agreed by the parties in writing at the time of the custody decree, the custodian may determine the child's upbringing, including his education, health care, and religious training, unless the court after hearing, finds, upon motion by the noncustodial parent, that in the absence of a specific limitation of the custodian's authority, the child's physical health would be endangered or his emotional development significantly impaired.

(b) If both parents or all contestants agree to the order, or if the court finds that in the absence of the order the child's physical health would be endangered or his emotional development significantly impaired, the court may order the [local probation or welfare department, court social service agency] to exercise continuing supervision over the case to assure that the custodial or visitation terms of the decree are carried out.

## § 409. [Modification].

(a) No motion to modify a custody decree may be made earlier than 2 years after its date, unless the court permits it to be made on the basis of affidavits that there is reason to believe the child's present environment may endanger seriously his physical, mental, moral, or emotional health.

(b) If a court of this State has jurisdiction pursuant to the Uniform Child Custody Jurisdiction Act, the court shall not modify a prior custody decree unless it finds, upon the basis of facts that have arisen since the prior decree or that were unknown to the court at the time of entry of the prior decree, that a change has occurred in the circumstances of the child or his custodian, and that the modification is necessary to serve the best interest of the child. In applying these standards the court shall retain the custodian appointed pursuant to the prior decree unless:

(1) the custodian agrees to the modification;

(2) the child has been integrated into the family of the petitioner with consent of the custodian; or

(3) the child's present environment endangers seriously his physical, mental, moral, or emotional health, and the harm likely to be caused by a change of environment is outweighed by its advantages to him.

(c) Attorney fees and costs shall be assessed against a party seeking modification if the court finds that the modification action is vexatious and constitutes harassment.

## § 410. [Affidavit Practice].

A party seeking a temporary custody order or modification of a custody decree shall submit together with his moving papers an affidavit setting forth facts supporting the requested order or modification and shall give notice, together with a copy of his affidavit, to other parties to the proceeding, who may file opposing affidavits. The court shall deny the motion unless it finds that adequate cause for hearing the motion is established by the affidavits, in which case it shall set a date for hearing on an order to show cause why the requested order or modification should not be granted.

*[ED.—Sections 501-503 dealing with time of taking effect, application to pending actions, and severability, and § 105, dealing with general repealer, have been omitted.]*

### § 504. [Specific Repealer].

The following acts and all other acts and parts of acts inconsistent herewith are hereby repealed: [Here should follow the acts to be specifically repealed, including any acts regulating:

(1) marriage, including grounds for annulment and provisions for void marriages;

(2) existing grounds for divorce and legal separation;

(3) existing defenses to divorce and legal separation, including but not limited to condonation, connivance, collusion, recrimination, insanity, and lapse of time; and

(4) alimony, child support, custody, and division of spouses' property in the event of a divorce and judicial proceedings designed to modify the financial or custody provisions of divorce decrees].

### § 506. [Laws Not Repealed].

This Act does not repeal: [Here should follow the acts not to be repealed, including any acts regulating or prescribing:

(1) the contents of and forms for marriage licenses and methods of registering marriages and providing for license or registration fees;

(2) the validity of premarital agreements between spouses concerning their marital property rights;

(3) marital property rights during a marriage or when the marriage terminates by the death of one of the spouses;

(4) the scope and extent of the duty of a parent to support a child of the marriage;

(5) custody of and support duty owed to an illegitimate child;

(6) the Uniform Child Custody Jurisdiction Act; and

(7) any applicable laws relating to wage assignments, garnishments, and exemptions other than those providing for family support and maintenance].

# UNIFORM PREMARITAL AGREEMENT ACT (1983)
# 9B U.L.A. 369 (1987)

*[Reproduced with permission from the National Conference of Commissioners on Uniform State Laws]*

## § 1. Definitions
As used in this Act:

(1) "Premarital agreement" means an agreement between prospective spouses made in contemplation of marriage and to be effective upon marriage.

(2) "Property" means an interest, present or future, legal or equitable, vested or contingent, in real or personal property, including income and earnings.

## § 2. Formalities
A premarital agreement must be in writing and signed by both parties. It is enforceable without consideration.

## § 3. Content
(a) Parties to a premarital agreement may contract with respect to:

(1) the rights and obligations of each of the parties in any of the property of either or both of them whenever and wherever acquired or located;

(2) the right to buy, sell, use, transfer, exchange, abandon, lease, consume, expend, assign, create a security interest in, mortgage, encumber, dispose of, or otherwise manage and control property;

(3) the disposition of property upon separation, marital dissolution, death, or the occurrence or nonoccurrence of any other event;

(4) the modification or elimination of spousal support;

(5) the making of a will, trust, or other arrangement to carry out the provisions of the agreement;

(6) the ownership rights in and disposition of the death benefit from a life insurance policy;

(7) the choice of law governing the construction of the agreement; and

(8) any other matter, including their personal rights and obligations, not in violation of public policy or a statute imposing a criminal penalty.

(b) The right of a child to support may not be adversely affected by a premarital agreement.

## § 4. Effect of Marriage
A premarital agreement becomes effective upon marriage.

## § 5. Amendment, Revocation

After marriage, a premarital agreement may be amended or revoked only by a written agreement signed by the parties. The amended agreement or the revocation is enforceable without consideration.

## § 6. Enforcement

(a) A premarital agreement is not enforceable if the party against whom enforcement is sought proves that:

(1) that party did not execute the agreement voluntarily; or　(2) the agreement was unconscionable when it was executed and, before　execution of the agreement, that party:

(i) was not provided a fair and reasonable disclosure of the property or financial obligations of the other party;

(ii) did not voluntarily and expressly waive, in writing, any right to disclosure of the property or financial obligations of the other party beyond the disclosure provided; and

(iii) did not have, or reasonably could not have had, an adequate knowledge　of the property or financial obligations of the other party.

(b) If a provision of a premarital agreement modifies or eliminates spousal support and that modification or elimination causes one party to the agreement to be eligible for support under a program of public assistance at the time of separation or marital dissolution, a court, notwithstanding the terms of the agreement, may require the other party to provide support to the extent　necessary to avoid that eligibility.

(c) An issue of unconscionability of a premarital agreement shall be decided　by the court as a matter of law.

## § 7. Enforcement:  Void Marriage

If a marriage is determined to be void, an agreement that would otherwise have  been a premarital agreement is enforceable only to the extent necessary to avoid an inequitable result.

## § 8. Limitation of Actions.

Any statute of limitations applicable to an action asserting a claim for relief under a premarital agreement is tolled during the marriage of the  parties to the agreement. However, equitable defenses limiting the time for  enforcement, including laches and estoppel, are available to either party.

*[ED.—Sections 9 through 13, dealing with application and construction, the short title of the Act, severability, time of effect and repeals, have been omitted.]*

# UNIFORM PUTATIVE AND UNKNOWN FATHERS ACT (1988)

*[Reproduced with permission from the National Conference of Commissioners on Uniform State Laws]*

## § 1. Definitions

In this [Act]:

(1) "Man" means a male individual of any age;

(2) "Putative father" means a man who claims to be, or is named as, the biological father or a possible biological father of a particular child, and whose paternity of that child has not been judicially determined, excluding:

(i) a man whose parental rights with respect to that child have been previously judicially terminated or declared not to exist;

(ii) a donor of semen used in artificial insemination, whose identity is not known by the mother of the resulting child or whose semen was donated under circumstances indicating that the donor did not anticipate having an interest in the resulting child;

(iii) a man who is or was married to the mother of a particular child, and the child is born during the marriage [or within 300 days after the marriage was terminated by death, annulment, declaration of invalidity, divorce, or marital dissolution, or after a decree of separation was entered by a court];

(iv) a man who, before the birth of a particular child, attempted to marry the mother of the child in apparent compliance with law, although the attempted marriage is, or could be declared, invalid, and

(A) if the attempted marriage could be declared invalid only by a court, the child is born during the attempted marriage [, or within 300 days after its termination by death, annulment, declaration of invalidity, divorce, or marital dissolution]; or

(B) if the attempted marriage is invalid without a court order, the child is born during, or within 300 days after the termination of, cohabitation; and

(v) a man who, after the birth of a particular child, married or attempted to marry the mother of the child in apparent compliance with law, although the attempted marriage is, or could be declared, invalid, and

(A) has acknowledged his paternity of the child in a writing filed with the [appropriate court or Vital Statistics Bureau],

(B) with his consent, he is named as the child's biological father on the child's birth certificate, or

(C) is obligated to support the child under a written promise or by court order;

(3) "Unknown father" means a particular child's biological father, whose identity is unascertained. However, the term does not include a donor of semen used in artificial insemination or in vitro fertilization whose identity is not known to the mother of the resulting child or whose semen was donated under circumstances indicating that the donor did not anticipate having an interest in the resulting child.

## [§ 2. Right to Determination of Paternity

(a) A putative father may bring an action to determine whether he is the biological father of a particular child [, in accordance with [applicable state law],] at any time, unless his paternity or his possible parental rights have already been determined or are in issue in a pending action.

(b) An agreement between a putative father and the mother or between him and the child does not bar an action under this section [, unless the agreement has been judicially approved [under applicable state law].]

## § 3. Notice of Judicial Proceedings for Adoption or Termination of Parental Rights

(a) In an adoption or other judicial proceeding that might result in termination of any man's parental rights with respect to a child, the person seeking termination shall give notice to every putative father of that child known to that person.

(b) The notice must be given at a time and place and in a manner (i) appropriate under the [rules of civil procedure for the service of process in a civil action in this State] or (ii) at a time and place and in a manner as the court directs to provide actual notice.

(c) A putative father may participate as a party in a proceeding described in subsection (a).

(d) If, at any time in the proceeding, it appears to the court that there is a putative father of the child who has not been given notice, the court shall require notice to be given to him in accordance with subsection (b).

(e) If, at any time in the proceeding, it appears to the court that an unknown father might not have been given notice, the court shall determine whether he can be identified. The determination must be based on evidence that includes inquiry of appropriate persons in an effort to identify the unknown father for the purpose of providing notice. The inquiry must include:

(1) whether the mother was married at the time of conception of the child or at a later time;

(2) whether the mother was cohabiting with a man at the probable time of conception of the child;

(3) whether the mother has received support payments or promises of support, other than from a governmental agency, with respect to the child or because of her pregnancy;

(4) whether the mother has named any man as the biological father in connection with applying for or receiving public assistance; and

(5) whether any man has formally or informally acknowledged or claimed paternity of the child in any jurisdiction in which the mother resided at the time of or since conception of the child or in which the child has resided or resides at the time of the inquiry.

(f) If the inquiry required by subsection (e) identifies any man as the unknown father, notice of the proceeding must be given to each in accordance with subsection (b). If the inquiry so identifies a man, but his whereabouts are unknown, the court shall proceed in accordance with subsections (b) and (g).

(g) If, after the inquiry required by subsection (e), it appears that there might be an unknown father of the child, the court shall consider whether publication or public posting of notice of the proceeding is likely to lead to actual notice to him. The court may order publication or public posting of notice only if, on the basis of all information available, the court determines that the publication or posting is likely to lead to actual notice to him.

## § 4. Notice of Judicial Proceedings Regarding Custody or Visitation

(a) The petitioner in a judicial proceeding to change or establish legal or physical custody of or visitation rights with respect to a child shall give notice to every putative father of that child known to the petitioner, except a proceeding for annulment, declaration of invalidity, divorce, marital dissolution, legal separation, modification of child custody, or determination of paternity.

(b) The notice must be given (i) at a time and place and in a manner appropriate under the [rules of civil procedure for the service of process in a civil action in this State] or (ii) as the court directs and determines will likely provide actual notice.

(c) If, at any time in the proceeding, it appears to the court that there is a putative father of the child who has not been given notice of the proceeding, the court shall require notice of the proceeding to be given to him in accordance with subsection (b).

(d) If, at any time in the proceeding, it appears to the court that an unknown father might not have been given notice of the proceeding, the court may attempt to identify him pursuant to Section 3(e) and require notice of the proceeding to be given to him pursuant to Section 3(f) and (g).

(e) A putative father may participate as a party in a proceeding described in subsection (a).

## § 5. Factors in Determining Parental Rights of Father

In determining whether to preserve or terminate the parental rights of a putative father in a proceeding governed by Section 3 or 4, the court shall consider all of the following factors that are pertinent:

(1) the age of the child;

(2) the nature and quality of any relationship between the man and the child;

(3) the reasons for any lack of a relationship between the man and the child;

(4) whether a parent and child relationship has been established between the child and another man;

(5) whether the child has been abused or neglected;

(6) whether the man has a history of substance abuse or of abuse of the mother or the child;

(7) any proposed plan for the child;

(8) whether the man seeks custody and is able to provide the child with emotional or financial support and a home, whether or not he has had opportunity to establish a parental relationship with the child;

(9) whether the man visits the child, has shown any interest in visitation, or, desiring visitation, has been effectively denied opportunity to visit the child;

(10) whether the man is providing financial support for the child according to his means;

(11) whether the man provided emotional or financial support for the mother during her prenatal, natal, and postnatal care;

(12) the circumstances of the child's conception, including whether the child was conceived as a result of incest or forcible rape;

(13) whether the man has formally or informally acknowledged or declared his possible paternity of the child; and

(14) other factors the court considers relevant to the standards stated in Section 6(d) and (g).

## § 6. Court Determinations and Orders

(a) If a man appears in a proceeding described in Section 3, other than as a petitioner or prospective adoptive parent, the court may:

(1) [in accordance with [applicable state law],] determine whether the man is the biological father of the child and, if the court determines that he is, enter an order in accordance with subsection (d); or

(2) without determining paternity, and consistent with the standards in subsection (d), enter an order, after considering the factors in Section 5, terminating any parental rights he may have, or declaring that he has no parental rights, with respect to the child.

(b) If the court makes an order under subsection (a), the court may also make an order (i) terminating the parental rights of any other man given notice who does not appear, or (ii) declaring that no man has any parental rights with respect to the child.

(c) If a man who appears in a proceeding described in Section 3 is determined by the court to be the father, the court, after considering evidence of the factors in Section 5, shall determine (i) whether a familial bond between the father and the child has been established; or (ii) whether the failure to establish a familial bond is justified, and the father has the desire and potential to establish the bond.

(d) If the court makes an affirmative determination under subsection (c), the court may terminate the parental rights of the father[, in accordance with [applicable state law],] only if failure to do so would be detrimental to the child. If the court does not make an affirmative determination, it may terminate the parental rights of the father if doing so is in the best interest of the child.

(e) If no man appears in a proceeding described in Section 3, the court may enter an order:

(1) terminating with respect to the child the parental rights of any man given notice; or

(2) declaring that no putative father or unknown father has any parental rights with respect to the child.

(f) If the court does not require notice under Section 3, it shall enter an order declaring that no putative father or unknown father has any parental rights with respect to the child.

(g) If a man appears in a proceeding described in Section 4 and requests custody or visitation based on a claim of paternity, the court shall either determine[, in accordance with [applicable state law],] whether he is the biological father of the child or, after considering the factors in Section 5, deny him the custody of or visitation with the child. If the court determines that he is the biological father, the court shall determine, after considering evidence of the factors listed in Section 5, whether or not to grant him custody or visitation and shall make such other orders as are appropriate. All orders issued under this subsection must be in the child's best interest.

(h) A court order under subsection (a)(2), (b), (d), or (e) terminating the parental rights of a man, or declaring that no man has parental rights, with respect to the child, is not a determination that the man is or is not the biological father of the child.

(i) [Six months] after the date of issuance of an order under this section terminating parental rights or declaring that no man has parental rights, no person may directly or collaterally challenge the order upon any ground, including fraud, misrepresentation, failure to give a required notice, or lack of jurisdiction over the parties or of the subject matter. The running of this period of limitation may not be extended for any reason.

[ED.—*Sections 7 through 10, dealing with short title, severability, effective date and repeals, have been omitted.*]

# UNIFORM STATUS OF CHILDREN OF ASSISTED CONCEPTION ACT (1988)

## 9B U.L.A. 152 (Supp.1994)

*[Reproduced with permission from the National Conference of Commissioners on Uniform State Laws.]*

### § 1. Definitions.

In this [Act]:

(1) "Assisted conception" means a pregnancy resulting from (i) fertilizing an egg of a woman with sperm of a man by means other than sexual intercourse or (ii) implanting an embryo, but the term does not include the pregnancy of a wife resulting from fertilizing her egg with sperm of her husband.

(2) "Donor" means an individual [other than a surrogate] who produces egg or sperm used for assisted conception, whether or not a payment is made for the egg or sperm used, but does not include a woman who gives birth to a resulting child.

[(3) "Intended parents," means a man and woman, married to each other, who enter into an agreement under this [Act] providing that they will be the parents of a child born to a surrogate through assisted conception using egg or sperm of one or both of the intended parents.]

(4) "Surrogate" means an adult woman who enters into an agreement to bear a child conceived through assisted conception for intended parents.

### § 2. Maternity.

[Except as provided in Sections 5 through 9,] a woman who gives birth to a child is the child's mother.

### § 3. Assisted Conception by Married Woman.

[Except as provided in Sections 5 through 9,] the husband of a woman who bears a child through assisted conception is the father of the child, notwithstanding a declaration of invalidity or annulment of the marriage obtained after the assisted conception, unless within two years after learning of the child's birth he commences an action in which the mother and child are parties and in which it is determined that he did not consent to the assisted conception.

### § 4. Parental Status of Donors and Deceased Persons.

[Except as otherwise provided in Sections 5 through 9:]

(a) A donor is not the parent of a child conceived through assisted conception.

(b) An individual who dies before implantation of an embryo, or before a child is conceived other than through sexual intercourse, using the individual's egg or sperm, is not a parent of the resulting child.

## ALTERNATIVE A

### Comment

A state which chooses Alternative A should also consider section 1(3) and the bracketed language in sections 1(2), 2, 3 and 4.

## [§ 5. Surrogacy Agreement.

(a) A surrogate, her husband, if she is married, and intended parents may enter into a written agreement whereby the surrogate relinquishes all her rights and duties as a parent of a child conceived through assisted conception, and the intended parents may become the parents of the child pursuant to Section 8.

(b) If the agreement is not approved by the court under Section 6 before conception, the agreement is void and the surrogate is the mother of a resulting child and the surrogate's husband, if a party to the agreement, is the father of the child. If the surrogate's husband is not a party to the agreement or the surrogate is unmarried, paternity of the child is governed by [the Uniform Parentage Act].

## § 6. Petition and Hearing for Approval of Surrogacy.

(a) The intended parents and the surrogate may file a petition in the [appropriate court] to approve a surrogacy agreement if one of them is a resident of this State. The surrogate's husband, if she is married, must join in the petition. A copy of the agreement must be attached to the petition. The court shall name a [guardian ad litem] to represent the interests of any child to be conceived by the surrogate through assisted conception and [shall] [may] appoint counsel to represent the surrogate.

(b) The court shall hold a hearing on the petition and shall enter an order approving the surrogacy agreement, authorizing assisted conception for a period of 12 months after the date of the order, declaring the intended parents to be the parents of a child to be conceived through assisted conception pursuant to the agreement and discharging the guardian ad litem and attorney for the surrogate, upon finding that:

(1) the court has jurisdiction and all parties have submitted to its jurisdiction under subsection (e) and have agreed that the law of this State shall govern all matters arising under this [Act] and the agreement;

(2) the intended mother is unable to bear a child or is unable to do so without unreasonable risk to an unborn child or to the physical or mental health

of the intended mother or child, and the finding is supported by medical evidence;

(3) the [relevant child welfare agency] has made a home study of the intended parents and the surrogate and a copy of the report of the home study has been filed with the court;

(4) the intended parents, the surrogate, and the surrogate's husband, if any, meet the standards of fitness applicable to adoptive parents in this State;

(5) all parties have voluntarily entered into the agreement and understand its terms and the nature, and meaning, and the effect of the proceeding;

(6) the surrogate has had at least one pregnancy and delivery and bearing another child will not pose an unreasonable risk to the unborn child or to the physical or mental health of the surrogate or the child, and this finding is supported by medical evidence;

(7) all parties have received counseling concerning the effect of the surrogacy by [a qualified health-care professional or social worker] and a report containing conclusions about the capacity of the parties to enter into and fulfill the agreement has been filed with the court;

(8) a report of the results of any medical or psychological examination or genetic screening agreed to by the parties or required by law has been filed with the court and made available to the parties;

(9) adequate provision has been made for all reasonable health care costs associated with the surrogacy until the child's birth including responsibility for such costs if the agreement is terminated under Section 7; and

(10) the agreement will not be substantially detrimental to the interest of any of the affected individuals.

(c) Unless otherwise provided in the surrogacy agreement, all court costs, attorney's fees, and other costs and expenses associated with the hearing shall be assessed against the intended parents.

(d) Notwithstanding any other law concerning judicial proceedings or vital statistics, the court shall conduct all hearings and proceedings under this section in camera. The court shall keep all records confidential and subject to inspection under the same standards applicable to adoptions. At the request of any party, the court shall take steps necessary to insure that the identities of the parties are not disclosed.

(e) The court conducting the hearing has exclusive and continuing jurisdiction of all matters arising out of the surrogacy until a child born after entry of an order under this section is 180 days old.

## § 7. Termination of Surrogacy Agreement.

(a) After entry of an order under Section 6, but before the surrogate becomes pregnant through assisted conception, the court for cause, or the surrogate, her husband, or the intended parents may terminate the agreement by giving written notice of termination to all other parties and filing notice of the termination with the court. Thereupon, the court shall vacate the order entered under Section 6.

(b) A surrogate who has provided an egg for the assisted conception pursuant to an agreement approved under Section 6 may terminate the agreement by filing written notice with the court within 180 days after the last insemination pursuant to the agreement. Upon finding, after notice to the parties to the agreement and hearing, that the surrogate has voluntarily terminated the surrogacy agreement and understands the nature, meaning, and effect of the termination the court shall vacate the order entered under Section 6.

(c) The surrogate is not liable to the intended parents for terminating the agreement pursuant to this section.

## § 8. Parentage Under Approved Surrogacy.

(a) The following rules of parentage apply to surrogacy agreements approved under Section 6:

(1) Upon birth of a child to the surrogate, the intended parents are the parents of the child and the surrogate and her husband, if she is married, are not parents of the child unless the court vacates the order pursuant to Section 7(b).

(2) If, after notice of termination by the surrogate, the court vacates the order under Section 7(b) the surrogate is the mother of the resulting child, and her husband, if a party to the agreement, is the father. If the surrogate's husband is not a party to the agreement or the surrogate is unmarried, paternity of the child is governed by [the Uniform Parentage Act].

(b) Upon birth of the child, the intended parents shall file a written notice with the court that a child has been born to the surrogate within 300 days after assisted conception. Thereupon, the court shall enter an order directing the [Department of Vital Statistics] to issue a new birth certificate naming the intended parents as parents and to seal the original birth certificate in the records of the [Department of Vital Statistics].

## § 9. Surrogacy:  Miscellaneous Provisions.

(a) A surrogacy agreement that is the basis of an order under Section 6 may provide for the payment of consideration.

(b) A surrogacy agreement may not limit the right of the surrogate to make decisions regarding her health care or that of the embryo or fetus.

(c) After the entry of an order under Section 6, the marriage of the surrogate does not affect the validity of the order, and her husband's consent to the surrogacy agreement is not required, nor is he the father of any resulting child.

(d) A child born to a surrogate within 300 days after assisted conception pursuant to an order under Section 6 is presumed to result from the assisted conception. The presumption is conclusive as to all persons who have notice of the birth and who do not commence within 180 days after notice, an action to assert the contrary in which the child and the parties to the agreement are named as parties. The action must be filed in the court that issued the order under Section 6.

(e) A health care provider is not liable for recognizing the surrogate as the mother before receipt of a copy of the order entered under Section 6 or for recognizing the intended parents as parents after receipt of an order entered under Section 6.]

[END OF ALTERNATIVE A]

ALTERNATIVE B

**Comment**

A state which chooses Alternative B shall also consider sections 10, 11, 12, 13, 14, 15 and 16, renumbered 6, 7, 8, 9, 10, 11 and 12, respectively.

**[§ 5. Surrogate Agreements.**

An agreement in which a woman agrees to become a surrogate or to relinquish her rights and duties as parent of a child conceived through assisted conception is void. However, she is the mother of a resulting child and the surrogate's husband, if a party to the agreement, is the father of the child. If her husband is not a party to the agreement or the surrogate is unmarried, paternity of the child is governed by [the Uniform Parentage Act].]

[END OF ALTERNATIVE B]

**§ 10. Parent and Child Relationship;  Status of Child.**

(a) A child whose status as a child is declared or negated by this [Act] is the child only of his or her parents as determined under this [Act].

(b) Unless superseded by later events forming or terminating a parent and child relationship, the status of parent and child declared or negated by this [Act] as to a given individual and a child born alive controls for purposes of:

(1) intestate succession;

(2) probate law exemptions, allowances, or other protections for children in a parent's estate;  and

(3) determining eligibility of the child or its descendants to share in a donative transfer from any person as a member of a class determined by reference to the relationship.

*[ED.—Sections 11 through 15, dealing with uniformity of application and construction, severability, short title, effective date and repeals, have not been included.]*

## § 16.  Application to Existing Relationships.

This [Act] applies to surrogacy agreements entered into after its effective date.

*[ED.—Section 14, dealing with effective date, also provides that the provisions of the Act are to be applied prospectively.]*

# PART II.  FEDERAL LAWS

## BANKRUPTCY—EXEMPTIONS AND DISCHARGE
## UNITED STATES CODE ANNOTATED, TITLE 11
### (Selected Family Law Provisions)

### § 362.  Automatic stay

(a) Except as provided in subsection (b) of this section, a petition filed under section 301, 302, or 303 of this title, or an application filed under section 5(a)(3) of the Securities Investor Protection Act of 1970, operates as a stay, applicable to all entities, of--

(1) the commencement or continuation, including the issuance or employment of process, of a judicial, administrative, or other action or proceeding against the debtor that was or could have been commenced before the commencement of the case under this title, or to recover a claim against the debtor that arose before the commencement of the case under this title;

. . .

(3) any act to obtain possession of property of the estate or of property from the estate or to exercise control over property of the estate;

(4) any act to create, perfect, or enforce any lien against property of the estate;

. . .

(6) any act to collect, assess, or recover a claim against the debtor that arose before the commencement of the case under this title;

. . .

(b) The filing of a petition under section 301, 302, or 303 of this title, or of an application under section 5(a)(3) of the Securities Investor Protection Act of 1970, does not operate as a stay . . .

(2) under subsection (a) of this section--

(A) of the commencement or continuation of an action or proceeding for--

(i) the establishment of paternity;  or

(ii) the establishment or modification of an order for alimony, maintenance, or support;  or

(B) of the collection of alimony, maintenance, or support from property that is not property of the estate; . . .

### § 507.  Priorities

(a) The following expenses and claims have priority in the following order:

(1) First, administrative expenses allowed under section 503(b) of this title, and any fees and charges assessed against the estate under chapter 123 of title 28.

(2) Second, unsecured claims allowed under section 502(f) of this title.

(3) Third, allowed unsecured claims, but only to the extent of $4,000 for each individual or corporation, as the case may be, earned within 90 days before the date of the filing of the petition or the date of the cessation of the debtor's business, whichever occurs first, for--

(A) wages, salaries, or commissions, including vacation, severance, and sick leave pay earned by an individual;  or

(B) sales commissions earned by an individual or by a corporation with only 1 employee, acting as an independent contractor in the sale of goods or services for the debtor in the ordinary course of the debtor's business if, and only if, during the 12 months preceding that date, at least 75 percent of the amount that the individual or corporation earned by acting as an independent contractor in the sale of goods or services was earned from the debtor;

(4) Fourth, allowed unsecured claims for contributions to an employee benefit plan--

(A) arising from services rendered within 180 days before the date of the filing of the petition or the date of the cessation of the debtor's business, whichever occurs first;  but only

(B) for each such plan, to the extent of--

(i) the number of employees covered by each such plan multiplied by $4,000;  less

(ii) the aggregate amount paid to such employees under paragraph (3) of this subsection, plus the aggregate amount paid by the estate on behalf of such employees to any other employee benefit plan.

(5) Fifth, allowed unsecured claims of persons--

(A) engaged in the production or raising of grain, as defined in section 557(b) of this title, against a debtor who owns or operates a grain storage facility, as defined in section 557(b) of this title, for grain or the proceeds of grain, or

(B) engaged as a United States fisherman against a debtor who has acquired fish or fish produce from a fisherman through a sale or conversion, and who is engaged in operating a fish produce storage or processing facility--

but only to the extent of $4,000 for each such individual.

(6) Sixth, allowed unsecured claims of individuals, to the extent of $1,800 for each such individual, arising from the deposit, before the commencement of the case, of money in connection with the purchase, lease, or rental of property, or the purchase of services, for the personal, family, or household use of such individuals, that were not delivered or provided.

(7) Seventh, allowed claims for debts to a spouse, former spouse, or child of the debtor, for alimony to, maintenance for, or support of such spouse or child, in connection with a separation agreement, divorce decree or other order of a court of record, determination made in accordance with State or territorial law by a

governmental unit, or property settlement agreement, but not to the extent that such debt--

(A) is assigned to another entity, voluntarily, by operation of law, or otherwise; or

(B) includes a liability designated as alimony, maintenance, or support, unless such liability is actually in the nature of alimony, maintenance or support.

. . .

## § 522. Exemptions

(a) In this section--

(1) "dependent" includes spouse, whether or not actually dependent; and

(2) "value" means fair market value as of the date of the filing of the petition or, with respect to property that becomes property of the estate after such date, as of the date such property becomes property of the estate.

(b) Notwithstanding section 541 of this title, an individual debtor may exempt from property of the estate the property listed in either paragraph (1) or, in the alternative, paragraph (2) of this subsection. In joint cases filed under section 302 of this title and individual cases filed under section 301 or 303 of this title by or against debtors who are husband and wife, and whose estates are ordered to be jointly administered under Rule 1015(b) of the Federal Rules of Bankruptcy Procedure, one debtor may not elect to exempt property listed in paragraph (1) and the other debtor elect to exempt property listed in paragraph (2) of this subsection. If the parties cannot agree on the alternative to be elected, they shall be deemed to elect paragraph (1), where such election is permitted under the law of the jurisdiction where the case is filed. Such property is--

(1) property that is specified under subsection (d) of this section, unless the State law that is applicable to the debtor under paragraph (2)(A) of this subsection specifically does not so authorize; or, in the alternative,

(2)(A) any property that is exempt under Federal law, other than subsection (d) of this section, or State or local law that is applicable on the date of the filing of the petition at the place in which the debtor's domicile has been located for the 180 days immediately preceding the date of the filing of the petition, or for a longer portion of such 180-day period than in any other place; and

(B) any interest in property in which the debtor had, immediately before the commencement of the case, an interest as a tenant by the entirety or joint tenant to the extent that such interest as a tenant by the entirety or joint tenant is exempt from process under applicable nonbankruptcy law.

(c) Unless the case is dismissed, property exempted under this section is not liable during or after the case for any debt of the debtor that arose, or that is determined under section 502 of this title as if such debt had arisen, before the commencement of the case, except--

      (1) a debt of a kind specified in section 523(a)(1) or 523(a)(5) of this title;

      (2) a debt secured by a lien that is--

(A)(i) not avoided under subsection (f) or (g) of this section or under section 544, 545, 547, 548, 549, or 724(a) of this title;  and

      (ii) not void under section 506(d) of this title;  or

      (B) a tax lien, notice of which is properly filed;  or

      (3) a debt of a kind specified in section 523(a)(4) or 523(a)(6) of this title owed by an institution-affiliated party of an insured depository institution to a Federal depository institutions regulatory agency acting in its capacity as conservator, receiver, or liquidating agent for such institution.

      (d) The following property may be exempted under subsection (b)(1) of this section:

      (1) The debtor's aggregate interest, not to exceed $15,000 in value, in real property or personal property that the debtor or a dependent of the debtor uses as a residence, in a cooperative that owns property that the debtor or a dependent of the debtor uses as a residence, or in a burial plot for the debtor or a dependent of the debtor.

      (2) The debtor's interest, not to exceed $2,400 in value, in one motor vehicle.

      (3) The debtor's interest, not to exceed $400 in value in any particular item or $8,000 in aggregate value, in household furnishings, household goods, wearing apparel, appliances, books, animals, crops, or musical instruments, that are held primarily for the personal, family, or household use of the debtor or a dependent of the debtor.

      (4) The debtor's aggregate interest, not to exceed $1,000 in value, in jewelry held primarily for the personal, family, or household use of the debtor or a dependent of the debtor.

      (5) The debtor's aggregate interest in any property, not to exceed in value $800 plus up to $7,500 of any unused amount of the exemption provided under paragraph (1) of this subsection.

      (6) The debtor's aggregate interest, not to exceed $1,500 in value, in any implements, professional books, or tools, of the trade of the debtor or the trade of a dependent of the debtor.

      (7) Any unmatured life insurance contract owned by the debtor, other than a credit life insurance contract.

      (8) The debtor's aggregate interest, not to exceed in value $8,000 less any amount of property of the estate transferred in the manner specified in section 542(d) of this title, in any accrued dividend or interest under, or loan value of, any unmatured life insurance contract owned by the debtor under which the insured is the debtor or an individual of whom the debtor is a dependent.

(9) Professionally prescribed health aids for the debtor or a dependent of the debtor.

(10) The debtor's right to receive--

(A) a social security benefit, unemployment compensation, or a local public assistance benefit;

(B) a veterans' benefit;

(C) a disability, illness, or unemployment benefit;

(D) alimony, support, or separate maintenance, to the extent reasonably necessary for the support of the debtor and any dependent of the debtor;

(E) a payment under a stock bonus, pension, profitsharing, annuity, or similar plan or contract on account of illness, disability, death, age, or length of service, to the extent reasonably necessary for the support of the debtor and any dependent of the debtor, unless--

(i) such plan or contract was established by or under the auspices of an insider that employed the debtor at the time the debtor's rights under such plan or contract arose;

(ii) such payment is on account of age or length of service; and

(iii) such plan or contract does not qualify under section 401(a), 403(a), 403(b), or 408 of the Internal Revenue Code of 1986.

(11) The debtor's right to receive, or property that is traceable to--

(A) an award under a crime victim's reparation law;

(B) a payment on account of the wrongful death of an individual of whom the debtor was a dependent, to the extent reasonably necessary for the support of the debtor and any dependent of the debtor;

(C) a payment under a life insurance contract that insured the life of an individual of whom the debtor was a dependent on the date of such individual's death, to the extent reasonably necessary for the support of the debtor and any dependent of the debtor;

(D) a payment, not to exceed $15,000, on account of personal bodily injury, not including pain and suffering or compensation for actual pecuniary loss, of the debtor or an individual of whom the debtor is a dependent; or

(E) a payment in compensation of loss of future earnings of the debtor or an individual of whom the debtor is or was a dependent, to the extent reasonably necessary for the support of the debtor and any dependent of the debtor.

(e) A waiver of an exemption executed in favor of a creditor that holds an unsecured claim against the debtor is unenforceable in a case under this title with respect to such claim against property that the debtor may exempt under subsection (b) of this section. A waiver by the debtor of a power under subsection (f) or (h) of this section to avoid a transfer, under subsection (g) or (i) of this section to exempt property, or under subsection (i) of this section to recover property or to preserve a transfer, is unenforceable in a case under this title.

(f)(1) Notwithstanding any waiver of exemptions but subject to paragraph (3), the debtor may avoid the fixing of a lien on an interest of the debtor in property to the extent that such lien impairs an exemption to which the debtor would have been entitled under subsection (b) of this section, if such lien is--

(A) a judicial lien, other than a judicial lien that secures a debt--

(i) to a spouse, former spouse, or child of the debtor, for alimony to, maintenance for, or support of such spouse or child, in connection with a separation agreement, divorce decree or other order of a court of record, determination made in accordance with State or territorial law by a governmental unit, or property settlement agreement; and

(ii) to the extent that such debt--

(I) is not assigned to another entity, voluntarily, by operation of law, or otherwise; and

(II) includes a liability designated as alimony, maintenance, or support, unless such liability is actually in the nature of alimony, maintenance or support.[1]; or

(B) a nonpossessory, nonpurchase-money security interest in any--

(i) household furnishings, household goods, wearing apparel, appliances, books, animals, crops, musical instruments, or jewelry that are held primarily for the personal, family, or household use of the debtor or a dependent of the debtor;

(ii) implements, professional books, or tools, of the trade of the debtor or the trade of a dependent of the debtor; or

(iii) professionally prescribed health aids for the debtor or a dependent of the debtor.

(2)(A) For the purposes of this subsection, a lien shall be considered to impair an exemption to the extent that the sum of--

(i) the lien;

(ii) all other liens on the property; and

(iii) the amount of the exemption that the debtor could claim if there were no liens on the property;

exceeds the value that the debtor's interest in the property would have in the absence of any liens.

(B) In the case of a property subject to more than 1 lien, a lien that has been avoided shall not be considered in making the calculation under subparagraph (A) with respect to other liens.

(C) This paragraph shall not apply with respect to a judgment arising out of a mortgage foreclosure.

(3) In a case in which State law that is applicable to the debtor--

---

[1] So in original. Period probably should not appear.

(A) permits a person to voluntarily waive a right to claim exemptions under subsection (d) or prohibits a debtor from claiming exemptions under subsection (d); and

(B) either permits the debtor to claim exemptions under State law without limitation in amount, except to the extent that the debtor has permitted the fixing of a consensual lien on any property or prohibits avoidance of a consensual lien on property otherwise eligible to be claimed as exempt property; the debtor may not avoid the fixing of a lien on an interest of the debtor or a dependent of the debtor in property if the lien is a nonpossessory, nonpurchase-money security interest in implements, professional books, or tools of the trade of the debtor or a dependent of the debtor or farm animals or crops of the debtor or a dependent of the debtor to the extent the value of such implements, professional books, tools of the trade, animals, and crops exceeds $5,000.

(g) Notwithstanding sections 550 and 551 of this title, the debtor may exempt under subsection (b) of this section property that the trustee recovers under section 510(c)(2), 542, 543, 550, 551, or 553 of this title, to the extent that the debtor could have exempted such property under subsection (b) of this section if such property had not been transferred, if--

(1)(A) such transfer was not a voluntary transfer of such property by the debtor; and

(B) the debtor did not conceal such property; or

(2) the debtor could have avoided such transfer under subsection (f)(2) of this section.

(h) The debtor may avoid a transfer of property of the debtor or recover a setoff to the extent that the debtor could have exempted such property under subsection (g)(1) of this section if the trustee had avoided such transfer, if--

(1) such transfer is avoidable by the trustee under section 544, 545, 547, 548, 549, or 724(a) of this title or recoverable by the trustee under section 553 of this title; and

(2) the trustee does not attempt to avoid such transfer.

(i)(1) If the debtor avoids a transfer or recovers a setoff under subsection (f) or (h) of this section, the debtor may recover in the manner prescribed by, and subject to the limitations of, section 550 of this title, the same as if the trustee had avoided such transfer, and may exempt any property so recovered under subsection (b) of this section.

(2) Notwithstanding section 551 of this title, a transfer avoided under section 544, 545, 547, 548, 549, or 724(a) of this title, under subsection (f) or (h) of this section, or property recovered under section 553 of this title, may be preserved for the benefit of the debtor to the extent that the debtor may exempt such property under subsection (g) of this section or paragraph (1) of this subsection.

(j) Notwithstanding subsections (g) and (i) of this section, the debtor may exempt a particular kind of property under subsections (g) and (i) of this section only to the extent that the debtor has exempted less property in value of such kind than that to which the debtor is entitled under subsection (b) of this section.

(k) Property that the debtor exempts under this section is not liable for payment of any administrative expense except--

(1) the aliquot share of the costs and expenses of avoiding a transfer of property that the debtor exempts under subsection (g) of this section, or of recovery of such property, that is attributable to the value of the portion of such property exempted in relation to the value of the property recovered; and

(2) any costs and expenses of avoiding a transfer under subsection (f) or (h) of this section, or of recovery of property under subsection (i)(1) of this section, that the debtor has not paid.

(l) The debtor shall file a list of property that the debtor claims as exempt under subsection (b) of this section. If the debtor does not file such a list, a dependent of the debtor may file such a list, or may claim property as exempt from property of the estate on behalf of the debtor. Unless a party in interest objects, the property claimed as exempt on such list is exempt.

(m) Subject to the limitation in subsection (b), this section shall apply separately with respect to each debtor in a joint case.

## § 523. Exceptions to discharge

(a) A discharge under section 727, 1141, 1228(a), 1228(b), or 1328(b) of this title does not discharge an individual debtor from any debt

. . .

(5) to a spouse, former spouse, or child of the debtor, for alimony to, maintenance for, or support of such spouse or child, in connection with a separation agreement, divorce decree or other order of a court of record, determination made in accordance with State or territorial law by a governmental unit, or property settlement agreement, but not to the extent that--

(A) such debt is assigned to another entity, voluntarily, by operation of law, or otherwise (other than debts assigned pursuant to section 402(a)(26) of the Social Security Act, or any such debt which has been assigned to the Federal Government or to a State or any political subdivision of such State); or

(B) such debt includes a liability designated as alimony, maintenance, or support, unless such liability is actually in the nature of alimony, maintenance, or support; . . .

(8) for an educational benefit overpayment or loan made, insured or guaranteed by a governmental unit, or made under any program funded in whole or in part by a governmental unit or nonprofit institution, or for an obligation to repay funds received as an educational benefit, scholarship or stipend, unless--

(A) such loan, benefit, scholarship, or stipend overpayment first became due more than 7 years (exclusive of any applicable suspension of the repayment period) before the date of the filing of the petition;  or

(B) excepting such debt from discharge under this paragraph will impose an undue hardship on the debtor and the debtor's dependents; . . .

. . .

(11) provided in any final judgment, unreviewable order, or consent order or decree entered in any court of the United States or of any State, issued by a Federal depository institutions regulatory agency, or contained in any settlement agreement entered into by the debtor, arising from any act of fraud or defalcation while acting in a fiduciary capacity committed with respect to any depository institution or insured credit union;

. . .

(15) not of the kind described in paragraph (5) that is incurred by the debtor in the course of a divorce or separation or in connection with a separation agreement, divorce decree or other order of a court of record, a determination made in accordance with State or territorial law by a governmental unit unless--

(A) the debtor does not have the ability to pay such debt from income or property of the debtor not reasonably necessary to be expended for the maintenance or support of the debtor or a dependent of the debtor and, if the debtor is engaged in a business, for the payment of expenditures necessary for the continuation, preservation, and operation of such business;  or

(B) discharging such debt would result in a benefit to the debtor that outweighs the detrimental consequences to a spouse, former spouse, or child of the debtor; . . .

## § 547. Preferences

(a) In this section--

(1) "inventory" means personal property leased or furnished, held for sale or lease, or to be furnished under a contract for service, raw materials, work in process, or materials used or consumed in a business, including farm products such as crops or livestock, held for sale or lease;

(2) "new value" means money or money's worth in goods, services, or new credit, or release by a transferee of property previously transferred to such transferee in a transaction that is neither void nor voidable by the debtor or the trustee under any applicable law, including proceeds of such property, but does not include an obligation substituted for an existing obligation;

(3) "receivable" means right to payment, whether or not such right has been earned by performance;  and

(4) a debt for a tax is incurred on the day when such tax is last payable without penalty, including any extension.

(b) Except as provided in subsection (c) of this section, the trustee may avoid any transfer of an interest of the debtor in property--

(1) to or for the benefit of a creditor;

(2) for or on account of an antecedent debt owed by the debtor before such transfer was made;

(3) made while the debtor was insolvent;

(4) made--

(A) on or within 90 days before the date of the filing of the petition;  or

(B) between ninety days and one year before the date of the filing of the petition, if such creditor at the time of such transfer was an insider;  and

(5) that enables such creditor to receive more than such creditor would receive if--

(A) the case were a case under chapter 7 of this title;

(B) the transfer had not been made;  and

(C) such creditor received payment of such debt to the extent provided by the provisions of this title.

(c) The trustee may not avoid under this section a transfer--

. . .

(7) to the extent such transfer was a bona fide payment of a debt to a spouse, former spouse, or child of the debtor, for alimony to, maintenance for, or support of such spouse or child, in connection with a separation agreement, divorce decree or other order of a court of record, determination made in accordance with State or territorial law by a governmental unit, or property settlement agreement, but not to the extent that such debt--

(A) is assigned to another entity, voluntarily, by operation of law, or otherwise;  or

(B) includes a liability designated as alimony, maintenance, or support, unless such liability is actually in the nature of alimony, maintenance or support;

. . .

# CHILD SUPPORT RECOVERY ACT OF 1992

## 18 U.S.C.A. § 228

### § 228. Failure to pay legal child support obligations

(a) Offense.--Whoever willfully fails to pay a past due support obligation with respect to a child who resides in another State shall be punished as provided in subsection (b).

(b) Punishment.--The punishment for an offense under this section is--

(1) in the case of a first offense under this section, a fine under this title, imprisonment for not more than 6 months, or both;  and

(2) in any other case, a fine under this title, imprisonment for not more than 2 years, or both.

(c) Restitution.--Upon a conviction under this section, the court shall order restitution under section 3663 in an amount equal to the past due support obligation as it exists at the time of sentencing.

(d) Definitions.--As used in this section--

(1) the term "past due support obligation" means any amount--

(A) determined under a court order or an order of an administrative process pursuant to the law of a State to be due from a person for the support and maintenance of a child or of a child and the parent with whom the child is living;  and

(B) that has remained unpaid for a period longer than one year, or is greater than $5,000;  and

(2) the term "State" includes the District of Columbia, and any other possession or territory of the United States.

# THE INDIAN CHILD WELFARE ACT
## SUBCHAPTER I—CHILD CUSTODY PROCEEDINGS
## 25 U.S.C.A. § 1911 et seq.

### § 1911. Indian tribe jurisdiction over Indian child custody proceedings

(a) Exclusive jurisdiction

An Indian tribe shall have jurisdiction exclusive as to any State over any child custody proceeding involving an Indian child who resides or is domiciled within the reservation of such tribe, except where such jurisdiction is otherwise vested in the State by existing Federal law. Where an Indian child is a ward of a tribal court, the Indian tribe shall retain exclusive jurisdiction, notwithstanding the residence or domicile of the child.

(b) Transfer of proceedings; declination by tribal court

In any State court proceeding for the foster care placement of, or termination of parental rights to, an Indian child not domiciled or residing within the reservation of the Indian child's tribe, the court, in the absence of good cause to the contrary, shall transfer such proceeding to the jurisdiction of the tribe, absent objection by either parent, upon the petition of either parent or the Indian custodian or the Indian child's tribe: Provided, That such transfer shall be subject to declination by the tribal court of such tribe.

(c) State court proceedings; intervention

In any State court proceeding for the foster care placement of, or termination of parental rights to, an Indian child, the Indian custodian of the child and the Indian child's tribe shall have a right to intervene at any point in the proceeding.

(d) Full faith and credit to public acts, records, and judicial proceedings of Indian tribes

The United States, every State, every territory or possession of the United States, and every Indian tribe shall give full faith and credit to the public acts, records, and judicial proceedings of any Indian tribe applicable to Indian child custody proceedings to the same extent that such entities give full faith and credit to the public acts, records, and judicial proceedings of any other entity.

### § 1912. Pending court proceedings

(a) Notice; time for commencement of proceedings; additional time for preparation

In any involuntary proceeding in a State court, where the court knows or has reason to know that an Indian child is involved, the party seeking the foster care placement of, or termination of parental rights to, an Indian child shall notify the parent or Indian custodian and the Indian child's tribe, by registered mail with return receipt requested, of the pending proceedings and of their right of intervention. If the identity or location of the parent or Indian custodian and the tribe cannot be determined, such notice shall be given to the Secretary in like manner, who shall have fifteen days after receipt to provide the requisite notice to the parent or Indian custodian and the tribe. No foster care placement or termination of parental rights proceeding shall be held until at least ten days after receipt of notice by the parent or Indian custodian and the tribe or the Secretary: Provided, That the parent or Indian custodian or the tribe shall, upon request, be granted up to twenty additional days to prepare for such proceeding.

(b) Appointment of counsel

In any case in which the court determines indigency, the parent or Indian custodian shall have the right to court-appointed counsel in any removal, placement, or termination proceeding. The court may, in its discretion, appoint counsel for the child upon a finding that such appointment is in the best interest of the child. Where State law makes no provision for appointment of counsel in such proceedings, the court shall promptly notify the Secretary upon appointment of counsel, and the Secretary, upon certification of the presiding judge, shall pay reasonable fees and expenses out of funds which may be appropriated pursuant to section 13 of this title.

(c) Examination of reports or other documents

Each party to a foster care placement or termination of parental rights proceeding under State law involving an Indian child shall have the right to examine all reports or other documents filed with the court upon which any decision with respect to such action may be based.

(d) Remedial services and rehabilitative programs; preventive measures

Any party seeking to effect a foster care placement of, or termination of parental rights to, an Indian child under State law shall satisfy the court that active efforts have been made to provide remedial services and rehabilitative programs designed to prevent the breakup of the Indian family and that these efforts have proved unsuccessful.

(e) Foster care placement orders; evidence; determination of damage to child

No foster care placement may be ordered in such proceeding in the absence of a determination, supported by clear and convincing evidence, including testimony of qualified expert witnesses, that the continued custody of the child by the parent or Indian custodian is likely to result in serious emotional or physical damage to the child.

(f) Parental rights termination orders; evidence; determination of damage to child

No termination of parental rights may be ordered in such proceeding in the absence of a determination, supported by evidence beyond a reasonable doubt, including testimony of qualified expert witnesses, that the continued custody of the child by the parent or Indian custodian is likely to result in serious emotional or physical damage to the child.

## § 1913. Parental rights, voluntary termination

(a) Consent; record; certification matters; invalid consents

Where any parent or Indian custodian voluntarily consents to a foster care placement or to termination of parental rights, such consent shall not be valid unless executed in writing and recorded before a judge of a court of competent jurisdiction and accompanied by the presiding judge's certificate that the terms and consequences of the consent were fully explained in detail and were fully understood by the parent or Indian custodian. The court shall also certify that either the parent or Indian custodian fully understood the explanation in English or that it was interpreted into a language that the parent or Indian custodian understood. Any consent given prior to, or within ten days after, birth of the Indian child shall not be valid.

(b) Foster care placement; withdrawal of consent

Any parent or Indian custodian may withdraw consent to a foster care placement under State law at any time and, upon such withdrawal, the child shall be returned to the parent or Indian custodian.

(c) Voluntary termination of parental rights or adoptive placement; withdrawal of consent; return of custody

In any voluntary proceeding for termination of parental rights to, or adoptive placement of, an Indian child, the consent of the parent may be withdrawn for any reason at any time prior to the entry of a final decree of termination or adoption, as the case may be, and the child shall be returned to the parent.

(d) Collateral attack;  vacation of decree and return of custody;  limitations

After the entry of a final decree of adoption of an Indian child in any State court, the parent may withdraw consent thereto upon the grounds that consent was obtained through fraud or duress and may petition the court to vacate such decree.  Upon a finding that such consent was obtained through fraud or duress, the court shall vacate such decree and return the child to the parent.  No adoption which has been effective for at least two years may be invalidated under the provisions of this subsection unless otherwise permitted under State law.

## § 1914. Petition to court of competent jurisdiction to invalidate action upon showing of certain violations

Any Indian child who is the subject of any action for foster care placement or termination of parental rights under State law, any parent or Indian custodian from whose custody such child was removed, and the Indian child's tribe may petition any court of competent jurisdiction to invalidate such action upon a showing that such action violated any provision of sections 1911, 1912, and 1913 of this title.

## § 1915. Placement of Indian children

(a) Adoptive placements;  preferences

In any adoptive placement of an Indian child under State law, a preference shall be given, in the absence of good cause to the contrary, to a placement with (1) a member of the child's extended family;  (2) other members of the Indian child's tribe;  or (3) other Indian families.

(b) Foster care or preadoptive placements;  criteria;  preferences

Any child accepted for foster care or preadoptive placement shall be placed in the least restrictive setting which most approximates a family and in which his special needs, if any, may be met.  The child shall also be placed within reasonable proximity to his or her home, taking into account any special needs of the child.  In any foster care or preadoptive placement, a preference shall be given, in the absence of good cause to the contrary, to a placement with--

(i) a member of the Indian child's extended family;

(ii) a foster home licensed, approved, or specified by the Indian child's tribe;

(iii) an Indian foster home licensed or approved by an authorized non-Indian licensing authority;  or

(iv) an institution for children approved by an Indian tribe or operated by an Indian organization which has a program suitable to meet the Indian child's needs.

(c) Tribal resolution for different order of preference;  personal preference considered;  anonymity in application of preferences

In the case of a placement under subsection (a) or (b) of this section, if the Indian child's tribe shall establish a different order of preference by resolution, the agency or court effecting the placement shall follow such order so long as the placement is the least restrictive setting appropriate to the particular needs of the child, as provided in subsection (b) of this section. Where appropriate, the preference of the Indian child or parent shall be considered:  Provided, That where a consenting parent evidences a desire for anonymity, the court or agency shall give weight to such desire in applying the preferences.

(d) Social and cultural standards applicable

The standards to be applied in meeting the preference requirements of this section shall be the prevailing social and cultural standards of the Indian community in which the parent or extended family resides or with which the parent or extended family members maintain social and cultural ties.

(e) Record of placement;  availability

A record of each such placement, under State law, of an Indian child shall be maintained by the State in which the placement was made, evidencing the efforts to comply with the order of preference specified in this section.  Such record shall be made available at any time upon the request of the Secretary or the Indian child's tribe.

## § 1916. Return of custody

(a) Petition;  best interests of child

Notwithstanding State law to the contrary, whenever a final decree of adoption of an Indian child has been vacated or set aside or the adoptive parents voluntarily consent to the termination of their parental rights to the child, a biological parent or prior Indian custodian may petition for return of custody and the court shall grant such petition unless there is a showing, in a proceeding subject to the provisions of section 1912 of this title, that such return of custody is not in the best interests of the child.

(b) Removal from foster care home;  placement procedure

Whenever an Indian child is removed from a foster care home or institution for the purpose of further foster care, preadoptive, or adoptive placement, such placement shall be in accordance with the provisions of this chapter, except in the case where an Indian child is being returned to the parent or Indian custodian from whose custody the child was originally removed.

## § 1917. Tribal affiliation information and other information for protection of rights from tribal relationship; application of subject of adoptive placement; disclosure by court

Upon application by an Indian individual who has reached the age of eighteen and who was the subject of an adoptive placement, the court which entered the final decree shall inform such individual of the tribal affiliation, if any, of the individual's biological parents and provide such other information as may be necessary to protect any rights flowing from the individual's tribal relationship.

## § 1918. Reassumption of jurisdiction over child custody proceedings

(a) Petition; suitable plan; approval by Secretary

Any Indian tribe which became subject to State jurisdiction pursuant to the provisions of the Act of August 15, 1953 (67 Stat. 588), as amended by Title IV of the Act of April 11, 1968 (82 Stat. 73, 78), or pursuant to any other Federal law, may reassume jurisdiction over child custody proceedings. Before any Indian tribe may reassume jurisdiction over Indian child custody proceedings, such tribe shall present to the Secretary for approval a petition to reassume such jurisdiction which includes a suitable plan to exercise such jurisdiction.

(b) Criteria applicable to consideration by Secretary; partial retrocession

(1) In considering the petition and feasibility of the plan of a tribe under subsection (a) of this section, the Secretary may consider, among other things:

(i) whether or not the tribe maintains a membership roll or alternative provision for clearly identifying the persons who will be affected by the reassumption of jurisdiction by the tribe;

(ii) the size of the reservation or former reservation area which will be affected by retrocession and reassumption of jurisdiction by the tribe;

(iii) the population base of the tribe, or distribution of the population in homogeneous communities or geographic areas; and

(iv) the feasibility of the plan in cases of multitribal occupation of a single reservation or geographic area.

(2) In those cases where the Secretary determines that the jurisdictional provisions of section 1911(a) of this title are not feasible, he is authorized to accept partial retrocession which will enable tribes to exercise referral jurisdiction as provided in section 1911(b) of this title, or, where appropriate, will allow them to exercise exclusive jurisdiction as provided in section 1911(a) of this title over limited community or geographic areas without regard for the reservation status of the area affected.

(c) Approval of petition;  publication in Federal Register;  notice;  reassumption period;  correction of causes for disapproval

If the Secretary approves any petition under subsection (a) of this section, the Secretary shall publish notice of such approval in the Federal Register and shall notify the affected State or States of such approval.  The Indian tribe concerned shall reassume jurisdiction sixty days after publication in the Federal Register of notice of approval.  If the Secretary disapproves any petition under subsection (a) of this section, the Secretary shall provide such technical assistance as may be necessary to enable the tribe to correct any deficiency which the Secretary identified as a cause for disapproval.

(d) Pending actions or proceedings unaffected

Assumption of jurisdiction under this section shall not affect any action or proceeding over which a court has already assumed jurisdiction, except as may be provided pursuant to any agreement under section 1919 of this title.

## § 1919. Agreements between States and Indian tribes

(a) Subject coverage

States and Indian tribes are authorized to enter into agreements with each other respecting care and custody of Indian children and jurisdiction over child custody proceedings, including agreements which may provide for orderly transfer of jurisdiction on a case-by-case basis and agreements which provide for concurrent jurisdiction between States and Indian tribes.

(b) Revocation;  notice;  actions or proceedings unaffected

Such agreements may be revoked by either party upon one hundred and eighty days' written notice to the other party.  Such revocation shall not affect any action or proceeding over which a court has already assumed jurisdiction, unless the agreement provides otherwise.

## § 1920. Improper removal of child from custody;    declination of jurisdiction;  forthwith return of child:  danger exception

Where any petitioner in an Indian child custody proceeding before a State court has improperly removed the child from custody of the parent or Indian custodian or has improperly retained custody after a visit or other temporary relinquishment of custody, the court shall decline jurisdiction over such petition and shall forthwith return the child to his parent or Indian custodian unless returning the child to his parent or custodian would subject the child to a substantial and immediate danger or threat of such danger.

## § 1922. Emergency removal or placement of child;  termination appropriate action

Nothing in this subchapter shall be construed to prevent the emergency removal of an Indian child who is a resident of or is domiciled on a reservation, but temporarily located off the reservation, from his parent or Indian custodian or the emergency placement of such child in a foster home or institution, under applicable State law, in order to prevent imminent physical damage or harm to the child.  The State authority, official, or agency involved shall insure that the emergency removal or placement terminates immediately when such removal or placement is no longer necessary to prevent imminent physical damage or harm to the child and shall expeditiously initiate a child custody proceeding subject to the provisions of this subchapter, transfer the child to the jurisdiction of the appropriate Indian tribe, or restore the child to the parent or Indian custodian, as may be appropriate.

## § 1923. Effective date

None of the provisions of this subchapter, except sections 1911(a), 1918, and 1919 of this title, shall affect a proceeding under State law for foster care placement, termination of parental rights, preadoptive placement, or adoptive placement which was initiated or completed prior to one hundred and eighty days after November 8, 1978, but shall apply to any subsequent proceeding in the same matter or subsequent proceedings affecting the custody or placement of the same child.

# TITLE 18, UNITED STATES CODE ANNOTATED
# INTERNATIONAL PARENTAL KIDNAPING

*[ED.—See, also, The Hague Convention on the Civil Aspects of International Parental Child Abduction, in PART III.)*

### § 1204. International parental kidnapping

(a) Whoever removes a child from the United States or retains a child (who has been in the United States) outside the United States with intent to obstruct the lawful exercise of parental rights shall be fined under this title or imprisoned not more than 3 years, or both.

(b) As used in this section--

(1) the term "child" means a person who has not attained the age of 16 years; and

(2) the term "parental rights", with respect to a child, means the right to physical custody of the child--

(A) whether joint or sole (and includes visiting rights); and

(B) whether arising by operation of law, court order, or legally binding agreement of the parties.

(c) It shall be an affirmative defense under this section that--

(1) the defendant acted within the provisions of a valid court order granting the defendant legal custody or visitation rights and that order was obtained pursuant to the Uniform Child Custody Jurisdiction Act and was in effect at the time of the offense;

(2) the defendant was fleeing an incidence or pattern of domestic violence;

(3) the defendant had physical custody of the child pursuant to a court order granting legal custody or visitation rights and failed to return the child as a result of circumstances beyond the defendant's control, and the defendant notified or made reasonable attempts to notify the other parent or lawful custodian of the child of such circumstances within 24 hours after the visitation period had expired and returned the child as soon as possible.

(d) This section does not detract from The Hague Convention on the Civil Aspects of International Parental Child Abduction, done at The Hague on October 25, 1980.

## PARENTAL KIDNAPING PREVENTION ACT OF 1980
## PUBLIC LAW 96–611, 96TH CONGRESS, 2D SESSION

Sec. 7. (a) The Congress finds that—

(1) there is a large and growing number of cases annually involving disputes between persons claiming rights of custody and visitation of children under the laws, and in the courts, of different States, the District of Columbia, the Commonwealth of Puerto Rico, and the territories and possessions of the United States;

(2) the laws and practices by which the courts of those jurisdictions determine their jurisdiction to decide such disputes, and the effect to be given the decisions of such disputes by the courts of other jurisdictions, are often inconsistent and conflicting;

(3) those characteristics of the law and practice in such cases, along with the limits imposed by a Federal system on the authority of each such jurisdiction to conduct investigations and take other actions outside its own boundaries, contribute to a tendency of parties involved in such disputes to frequently resort to the seizure, restraint, concealment, and interstate transportation of children, the disregard of court orders, excessive relitigation of cases, obtaining of conflicting orders by the courts of various jurisdictions, and interstate travel and communication that is so expensive and time consuming as to disrupt their occupations and commercial activities; and

(4) among the results of those conditions and activities are the failure of the courts of such jurisdictions to give full faith and credit to the judicial proceedings of the other jurisdictions, the deprivation of rights of liberty and property without due process of law, burdens on commerce among such jurisdictions and with foreign nations, and harm to the welfare of children and their parents and other custodians.

(b) For those reasons it is necessary to establish a national system for locating parents and children who travel from one such jurisdiction to another and are concealed in connection with such disputes, and to establish national standards under which the courts of such jurisdictions will determine their jurisdiction to decide such disputes and the effect to be given by each such jurisdiction to such decisions by the courts of other such jurisdictions.

(c) The general purposes of sections 6 to 10 of this Act are to—

(1) promote cooperation between State courts to the end that a determination of custody and visitation is rendered in the State which can best decide the case in the interest of the child;

(2) promote and expand the exchange of information and other forms of mutual assistance between States which are concerned with the same child;

(3) facilitate the enforcement of custody and visitation decrees of sister States;

(4) discourage continuing interstate controversies over child custody in the interest of greater stability of home environment and of secure family relationships for the child;

(5) avoid jurisdictional competition and conflict between State courts in matters of child custody and visitation which have in the past resulted in the shifting of children from State to State with harmful effects on their well-being;  and

(6) deter interstate abductions and other unilateral removals of children undertaken to obtain custody and visitation awards.

Sec. 8. (a) Chapter 115 of title 28, United States Code, is amended by adding immediately after section 1738 the following new section:

**"§ 1738A. Full faith and credit given to child custody determinations**

"(a) The appropriate authorities of every State shall enforce according to its terms, and shall not modify except as provided in subsection (f) of this section, any child custody determination made consistently with the provisions of this section by a court of another State.

"(b) As used in this section, the term—

"(1) "child' means a person under the age of eighteen;

"(2) "contestant' means a person, including a parent, who claims a right to custody or visitation of a child;

"(3) "custody determination' means a judgment, decree, or other order of a court providing for the custody or visitation of a child, and includes permanent and temporary orders, and initial orders and modifications;

"(4) "home State' means the State in which, immediately preceding the time involved, the child lived with his parents, a parent, or a person acting as parent, for at least six consecutive months, and in the case of a child less than six months old, the State in which the child lived from birth with any of such persons. Periods of temporary absence of any of such persons are counted as part of the six-month or other period;

"(5) "modifications' and "modify' refer to a custody determination which modifies, replaces, supersedes, or otherwise is made subsequent to, a prior custody determination concerning the same child, whether made by the same court or not;

"(6) "person acting as a parent' means a person, other than a parent, who has physical custody of a child and who has either been awarded custody by a court or claims a right to custody;

"(7) "physical custody' means actual possession and control of a child; and

"(8) "State' means a State of the United States, the District of Columbia, the Commonwealth of Puerto Rico, or a territory or possession of the United States.

"(c) A child custody determination made by a court of a State is consistent with the provisions of this section only if—

"(1) such court has jurisdiction under the law of such State; and

"(2) one of the following conditions is met:

"(A) such State (i) is the home State of the child on the date of the commencement of the proceeding, or (ii) had been the child's home State within six months before the date of the commencement of the proceeding and the child is absent from such State because of his removal or retention by a contestant or for other reasons, and a contestant continues to live in such State;

"(B)(i) it appears that no other State would have jurisdiction under subparagraph (A), and (ii) it is in the best interest of the child that a court of such State assume jurisdiction because (I) the child and his parents, or the child and at least one contestant, have a significant connection with such State other than mere physical presence in such State, and (II) there is available in such State substantial evidence concerning the child's present or future care, protection, training, and personal relationships;

"(C) the child is physically present in such State and (i) the child has been abandoned, or (ii) it is necessary in an emergency to protect the child because he has been subjected to or threatened with mistreatment or abuse;

"(D)(i) it appears that no other State would have jurisdiction under subparagraph (A), (B), (C), or (E), or another State has declined to exercise jurisdiction on the ground that the State whose jurisdiction is in issue is the more appropriate forum to determine the custody of the child, and (ii) it is in the best interest of the child that such court assume jurisdiction;  or

"(E) the court has continuing jurisdiction pursuant to subsection (d) of this section.

"(d) The jurisdiction of a court of a State which has made a child custody determination consistently with the provisions of this section continues as long as the requirement of subsection (c)(1) of this section continues to be met and such State remains the residence of the child or of any contestant.

"(e) Before a child custody determination is made, reasonable notice and opportunity to be heard shall be given to the contestants, any parent whose parental rights have not been previously terminated and any person who has physical custody of a child.

"(f) A court of a State may modify a determination of the custody of the same child made by a court of another State, if—

"(1) it has jurisdiction to make such a child custody determination; and

"(2) the court of the other State no longer has jurisdiction, or it has declined to exercise such jurisdiction to modify such determination.

"(g) A court of a State shall not exercise jurisdiction in any proceeding for a custody determination commenced during the pendency of a proceeding in a court of another State where such court of that other State is exercising jurisdiction consistently with the provisions of this section to make a custody determination."

(b) The table of sections at the beginning of chapter 115 of title 28, United States Code, is amended by inserting after the item relating to section 1738 the following new item:

"1738A. Full faith and credit given to child custody determinations".

(c) In furtherance of the purposes of section 1738A of title 28, United States Code, as added by subsection (a) of this section, State courts are encouraged to—

(1) afford priority to proceedings for custody determinations; and

(2) award to the person entitled to custody or visitation pursuant to a custody determination which is consistent with the provisions of such section 1738A, necessary travel expenses, attorneys' fees, costs of private investigations, witness fees or expenses, and other expenses incurred in connection with such custody determination in any case in which—

(A) a contestant has, without the consent of the person entitled to custody or visitation pursuant to a custody determination which is consistent with the provisions of such section 1738A, (i) wrongfully removed the child from the physical custody of such person, or (ii) wrongfully retained the child after a visit or other temporary relinquishment of physical custody; or

(B) the court determines it is appropriate.

Sec. 9. . . .

(b) Part D of title IV of the Social Security Act is amended by adding at the end thereof the following new section:

## "USE OF FEDERAL PARENT LOCATOR SERVICE IN CONNECTION WITH THE ENFORCEMENT OR DETERMINATION OF CHILD CUSTODY AND IN CASES OF PARENTAL KIDNAPING OF A CHILD

"Sec. 463. (a) The Secretary shall enter into an agreement with any State which is able and willing to do so, under which the services of the Parent Locator Service established under section 453 shall be made available to such State for the purpose of determining the whereabouts of any absent parent or child when such information is to be used to locate such parent or child for the purpose of—

"(1) enforcing any State or Federal law with respect to the unlawful taking or restraint of a child;  or

"(2) making or enforcing a child custody determination.

"(b) An agreement entered into under this section shall provide that the State agency described in section 454 will, under procedures prescribed by the Secretary in regulations, receive and transmit to the Secretary requests from authorized persons for information as to (or useful in determining) the whereabouts of any absent parent or child when such information is to be used to locate such parent or child for the purpose of—

"(1) enforcing any State or Federal law with respect to the unlawful taking or restraint of a child;  or

"(2) making or enforcing a child custody determination.

"(c) Information authorized to be provided by the Secretary under this section shall be subject to the same conditions with respect to disclosure as information authorized to be provided under section 453, and a request for information by the Secretary under this section shall be considered to be a request for information under section 453 which is authorized to be provided under such section. Only information as to the most recent address and place of employment of any absent parent or child shall be provided under this section.

"(d) For purposes of this section—

"(1) the term "custody determination' means a judgment, decree, or other order of a court providing for the custody or visitation of a child, and includes permanent and temporary orders, and initial orders and modification;

"(2) the term "authorized person' means—

"(A) any agent or attorney of any State having an agreement under this section, who has the duty or authority under the law of such State to enforce a child custody determination;

"(B) any court having jurisdiction to make or enforce such a child custody determination, or any agent of such court;  and

"(C) any agent or attorney of the United States, or of a State having an agreement under this section, who has the duty or authority to investigate, enforce, or bring a prosecution with respect to the unlawful taking or restraint of a child.".

(c) Section 455(a) of such Act is amended by adding after paragraph (3) the following:  "except that no amount shall be paid to any State on account of amounts expended to carry out an agreement which it has entered into pursuant to section 463.".

(d) No agreement entered into under section 463 of the Social Security Act shall become effective before the date on which section 1738A of title 28, United States Code (as added by this title) becomes effective.

Sec. 10. (a) In view of the findings of the Congress and the purposes of sections 6 to 10 of this Act set forth in section 302, the Congress hereby expressly declares its intent that section 1073 of title 18, United States Code, apply to cases involving parental kidnaping and interstate or international flight to avoid prosecution under applicable State felony statutes.[**]

------

[**] U.S.C. title 18, § 1073 provides that:

"Whoever moves or travels in interstate or foreign commerce with intent either (1) to avoid prosecution, or custody or confinement after conviction, under the laws of the place from which he flees, for a crime, or an attempt to commit a crime, punishable by death or which is a felony under the laws of the place from

(b) The Attorney General of the United States, not later than 120 days after the date of the enactment of this section (and once every 6 months during the 3–year period following such 120–day period), shall submit a report to the Congress with respect to steps taken to comply with the intent of the Congress set forth in subsection (a). Each such report shall include—

(1) data relating to the number of applications for complaints under section 1073 of title 18, United States Code, in cases involving parental kidnaping;

(2) data relating to the number of complaints issued in such cases; and

(3) such other information as may assist in describing the activities of the Department of Justice in conformance with such intent.

---

which the fugitive flees, or which, in the case of New Jersey, is a high misdemeanor under the laws of said State, or (2) to avoid giving testimony in any criminal proceedings in such place in which the commission of an offense punishable by death or which is a felony under the laws of such place, or which in the case of New Jersey, is a high misdemeanor under the laws of said State, is charged, or (3) to avoid service of, or contempt proceedings for alleged disobedience of, lawful process requiring attendance and the giving of testimony or the production of documentary evidence before an agency of a State empowered by the law of such State to conduct investigations of alleged criminal activities, shall be fined not more than $5,000 or imprisoned not more than five years, or both.

"Violations of this section may be prosecuted only in the Federal judicial district in which the original crime was alleged to have been committed, or in which the person was held in custody or confinement, or in which an avoidance of service of process or a contempt referred to in clause (3) of the first paragraph of this section is alleged to have been committed, and only upon formal approval in writing by the Attorney General or an Assistant Attorney General of the United States, which function of approving prosecutions may not be delegated."

# FULL FAITH AND CREDIT FOR CHILD SUPPORT ORDERS ACT (1994)
# 28 UNITED STATES CODE ANNOTATED

*[ED.—The following section was added to 28 U.S.C.A. § 1738 by P.L. 103-383 (the Act designated above) on October 20, 1994.]*

## § 1738B. Full faith and credit for child support orders

(a) General rule.--The appropriate authorities of each State--

(1) shall enforce according to its terms a child support order made consistently with this section by a court of another State;  and

(2) shall not seek or make a modification of such an order except in accordance with subsection (e).

(b) Definitions.--In this section:

"child" means--

(A) a person under 18 years of age;  and

(B) a person 18 or more years of age with respect to whom a child support order has been issued pursuant to the laws of a State.

"child's State" means the State in which a child resides.

"child support" means a payment of money, continuing support, or arrearages or the provision of a benefit (including payment of health insurance, child care, and educational expenses) for the support of a child.

"child support order"--

(A) means a judgment, decree, or order of a court requiring the payment of child support in periodic amounts or in a lump sum;  and

(B) includes--

(i) a permanent or temporary order;  and

(ii) an initial order or a modification of an order.

"contestant" means--

(A) a person (including a parent) who--

(i) claims a right to receive child support;

(ii) is a party to a proceeding that may result in the issuance of a child support order;  or

(iii) is under a child support order;  and

(B) a State or political subdivision of a State to which the right to obtain child support has been assigned.

"court" means a court or administrative agency of a State that is authorized by State law to establish the amount of child support payable by a contestant or make a modification of a child support order.

"modification" means a change in a child support order that affects the amount, scope, or duration of the order and modifies, replaces, supersedes, or otherwise is made subsequent to the child support order.

"State" means a State of the United States, the District of Columbia, the Commonwealth of Puerto Rico, the territories and possessions of the United States, and Indian country (as defined in section 1151 of title 18).

(c) Requirements of child support orders.--A child support order made is made consistently with this section if--

(1) a court that makes the order, pursuant to the laws of the State in which the court is located--

(A) has subject matter jurisdiction to hear the matter and enter such an order;  and

(B) has personal jurisdiction over the contestants;  and

(2) reasonable notice and opportunity to be heard is given to the contestants.

(d) Continuing jurisdiction.--A court of a State that has made a child support order consistently with this section has continuing, exclusive jurisdiction over the order if the State is the child's State or the residence of any contestant unless the court of another State, acting in accordance with subsection (e), has made a modification of the order.

(e) Authority to modify orders.--A court of a State may make a modification of a child support order with respect to a child that is made by a court of another State if--

(1) the court has jurisdiction to make such a child support order;  and

(2)(A) the court of the other State no longer has continuing, exclusive jurisdiction of the child support order because that State no longer is the child's State or the residence of any contestant;  or

(B) each contestant has filed written consent to that court's making the modification and assuming continuing, exclusive jurisdiction over the order.

(f) Enforcement of prior orders.--A court of a State that no longer has continuing, exclusive jurisdiction of a child support order may enforce the order with respect to nonmodifiable obligations and unsatisfied obligations that accrued before the date on which a modification of the order is made under subsection (e).

(g) Choice of law.--

(1) In general.--In a proceeding to establish, modify, or enforce a child support order, the forum State's law shall apply except as provided in paragraphs (2) and (3).

(2) Law of State of issuance of order.--In interpreting a child support order, a court shall apply the law of the State of the court that issued the order.

(3) Period of limitation.--In an action to enforce a child support order,

a court shall apply the statute of limitation of the forum State or the State of the court that issued the order, whichever statute provides the longer period of limitation.

*[ED.—Section 2 of Public Law 103-383 included the following findings and explanation of the purpose of the preceding statutory provision:]*

## SECTION 2.  FINDINGS AND PURPOSES

"(a) Findings.--The Congress finds that--

"(1) there is a large and growing number of child support cases annually involving disputes between parents who reside in different States;

"(2) the laws by which the courts of different jurisdictions determine their authority to establish child support orders are not uniform;

"(3) those laws, along with the limits imposed by the Federal system on the authority of each State to take certain actions outside its own boundaries--

"(A) encourage noncustodial parents to relocate outside the States where their children and the custodial parents reside to avoid the jurisdiction of the courts of such States, resulting in an increase in the amount of interstate travel and communication required to establish and collect on child support orders and a burden on custodial parents that is expensive, time consuming, and disruptive of occupations and commercial activity;

"(B) contribute to the pressing problem of relatively low levels of child support payments in interstate cases and to inequities in child support payments levels that are based solely on the noncustodial parent's choice of residence;

"(C) encourage a disregard of court orders resulting in massive arrearages nationwide;

"(D) allow noncustodial parents to avoid the payment of regularly scheduled child support payments for extensive periods of time, resulting in substantial hardship for the children for whom support is due and for their custodians;  and

"(E) lead to the excessive relitigation of cases and to the establishment of conflicting orders by the courts of various jurisdictions, resulting in confusion, waste of judicial resources, disrespect for the courts, and a diminution of public confidence in the rule of law;  and

"(4) among the results of the conditions described in this subsection are--

"(A) the failure of the courts of the States to give full faith and credit to the judicial proceedings of the other States;

"(B) the deprivation of rights of liberty and property without due process of law;

"(C) burdens on commerce among the States;  and

"(D) harm to the welfare of children and their parents and other custodians.

"(b) Statement of policy.--In view of the findings made in subsection (a), it is necessary to establish national standards under which the courts of the various States shall determine their jurisdiction to issue a child support order and the effect to be given by each State to child support orders issued by the courts of other States.

"(c) Purposes.--The purposes of this Act [enacting this section and a provision set out as a note under section 1 of this title] are--

"(1) to facilitate the enforcement of child support orders among the States;

"(2) to discourage continuing interstate controversies over child support in the interest of greater financial stability and secure family relationships for the child; and

"(3) to avoid jurisdictional competition and conflict among State courts in the establishment of child support orders."

# PART III.  TREATIES AND IMPLEMENTING LEGISLATION

## HAGUE CONFERENCE ON PRIVATE INTERNATIONAL LAW: CONVENTION ON THE CIVIL ASPECTS OF INTERNATIONAL CHILD ABDUCTION
### (Fourteenth Session, October 25, 1980)

The States signatory to the present Convention, Firmly convinced that the interests of children are of paramount importance in matters relating to their custody,

Desiring to protect children internationally from the harmful effects of their wrongful removal or retention and to establish procedures to ensure their prompt return to the State of their habitual residence, as well as to secure protection for rights of access,

Have resolved to conclude a Convention to this effect, and have agreed upon the following provisions --

CHAPTER I -- SCOPE OF THE CONVENTION

Article 1

The objects of the present Convention are -- a to secure the prompt return of children wrongfully removed to or retained in any Contracting State; and b to ensure that rights of custody and of access under the law of one Contracting State are effectively respected in the other Contracting States.

Article 2

Contracting States shall take all appropriate measures to secure within their territories the implementation of the objects of the Convention. For this purpose they shall use the most expeditious procedures available.

Article 3

The removal or the retention of a child is to be considered wrongful where -- a it is in breach of rights of custody attributed to a person, an institution or any other body, either jointly or alone, under the law of the State in which the child was habitually resident immediately before the removal or retention; and b at the time of removal or retention those rights were actually exercised, either jointly or alone, or would have been so exercised but for the removal or retention. The rights of custody mentioned in sub-paragraph a above, may arise in particular by operation of law or by reason of a judicial or administrative decision, or by reason of an agreement having legal effect under the law of that State.

## Article 4

The Convention shall apply to any child who was habitually resident in a Contracting State immediately before any breach of custody or access rights. The Convention shall cease to apply when the child attains the age of 16 years.

## Article 5

For the purposes of this Convention -- a 'rights of custody' shall include rights relating to the care of the person of the child and, in particular, the right to determine the child's place of residence; b 'rights of access' shall include the right to take a child for a limited period of time to a place other than the child's habitual residence.

## CHAPTER II -- CENTRAL AUTHORITIES

## Article 6

A Contracting State shall designate a Central Authority to discharge the duties which are imposed by the Convention upon such authorities.

Federal States, States with more than one system of law or States having autonomous territorial organizations shall be free to appoint more than one Central Authority and to specify the territorial extent of their powers. Where a State has appointed more than one Central Authority, it shall designate the Central Authority to which applications may be addressed for transmission to the appropriate Central Authority within that State.

## Article 7

Central Authorities shall co-operate with each other and promote co-operation amongst the competent authorities in their respective States to secure the prompt return of children and to achieve the other objects of this Convention.

In particular, either directly or through any intermediary, they shall take all appropriate measures -- a to discover the whereabouts of a child who has been wrongfully removed or retained; b to prevent further harm to the child or prejudice to interested parties by taking or causing to be taken provisional measures; c to secure the voluntary return of the child or to bring about an amicable resolution of the issues; d to exchange, where desirable, information relating to the social background of the child; e to provide information of a general character as to the law of their State in connection with the application of the Convention; f to initiate or facilitate the institution of judicial or administrative proceedings with a view to obtaining the return of the child and, in a proper case, to make arrangements for organizing or securing the effective exercise of rights of access; g where the circumstances so require, to provide or facilitate the provision of legal aid and advice, including the participation of legal counsel and advisers; h to provide such administrative arrangements as may be necessary and appropriate to secure the safe return of the child; i to keep each other informed with respect to the operation of this Convention and, as far as possible, to eliminate any obstacles to its application.

## CHAPTER III -- RETURN OF CHILDREN

Article 8

Any person, institution or other body claiming that a child has been removed or retained in breach of custody rights may apply either to the Central Authority of the child's habitual residence or to the Central Authority of any other Contracting State for assistance in securing the return of the child.

The application shall contain -- a information concerning the identity of the applicant, of the child and of the person alleged to have removed or retained the child; b where available, the date of birth of the child; c the grounds on which the applicant's claim for return of the child is based; d all available information relating to the whereabouts of the child and the identity of the person with whom the child is presumed to be.

The application may be accompanied or supplemented by -- e an authenticated copy of any relevant decision or agreement; f a certificate or an affidavit emanating from a Central Authority, or other competent authority of the State of the child's habitual residence, or from a qualified person, concerning the relevant law of that State; g any other relevant document.

Article 9

If the Central Authority which receives an application referred to in Article 8 has reason to believe that the child is in another Contracting State, it shall directly and without delay transmit the application to the Central Authority of that Contracting State and inform the requesting Central Authority, or the applicant, as the case may be.

## Article 10

The Central Authority of the State where the child is shall take or cause to be taken all appropriate measures in order to obtain the voluntary return of the child.

## Article 11

The judicial or administrative authorities of Contracting States shall act expeditiously in proceedings for the return of children.

If the judicial or administrative authority concerned has not reached a decision within six weeks from the date of commencement of the proceedings, the applicant or the Central Authority of the requested State, on its own initiative or if asked by the Central Authority of the requesting State, shall have the right to request a statement of the reasons for the delay. If a reply is received by the Central Authority of the requested State, that Authority shall transmit the reply to the Central Authority of the requesting State, or to the applicant, as the case may be.

## Article 12

Where a child has been wrongfully removed or retained in terms of Article 3 and, at the date of the commencement of the proceedings before the judicial or administrative authority of the Contracting State where the child is, a period of less than one year has elapsed from the date of the wrongful removal or retention, the authority concerned shall order the return of the child forthwith. The judicial or administrative authority, even where the proceedings have been commenced after the expiration of the period of one year referred to in the preceding paragraph, shall also order the return of the child, unless it is demonstrated that the child is now settled in its new environment.

Where the judicial or administrative authority in the requested State has reason to believe that the child has been taken to another State, it may stay the proceedings or dismiss the application for the return of the child.

## Article 13

Notwithstanding the provisions of the preceding Article, the judicial or administrative authority of the requested State is not bound to order the return of the child if the person, institution or other body which opposes its return establishes that -- a the person, institution or other body having the care of the person of the child was not actually exercising the custody rights at the time of removal or retention, or had consented to or subsequently acquiesced in the removal or retention; or b there is a grave risk that his or her return would expose the child to physical or psychological harm or otherwise place the child in an intolerable situation. The judicial or administrative authority may also refuse to order the return of the child if it finds that the child objects to being returned and has attained an age and degree of maturity at which it is appropriate to take account of its views.

In considering the circumstances referred to in this Article, the judicial and administrative authorities shall take into account the information relating to the social background of the child provided by the Central Authority or other competent authority of the child's habitual residence.

## Article 14

In ascertaining whether there has been a wrongful removal or retention within the meaning of Article 3, the judicial or administrative authorities of the requested State may take notice directly of the law of, and of judicial or administrative decisions, formally recognized or not in the State of the habitual residence of the child, without recourse to the specific procedures for the proof of that law or for the recognition of foreign decisions which would otherwise be applicable.

## Article 15

The judicial or administrative authorities of a Contracting State may, prior to the making of an order for the return of the child, request that the applicant obtain from the authorities of the State of the habitual residence of the child a decision or other determination that the removal or retention was wrongful within the meaning of Article 3 of the Convention, where such a decision or determination may be obtained in that State. The Central Authorities of the Contracting States shall so far as practicable assist applicants to obtain such a decision or determination.

## Article 16

After receiving notice of a wrongful removal or retention of a child in the sense of Article 3, the judicial or administrative authorities of the Contracting State to which the child has been removed or in which it has been retained shall not decide on the merits of rights of custody until it has been determined that the child is not to be returned under this Convention or unless an application under this Convention is not lodged within a reasonable time following receipt of the notice.

Article 17

The sole fact that a decision relating to custody has been given in or is entitled to recognition in the requested State shall not be a ground for refusing to return a child under this Convention, but the judicial or administrative authorities of the requested State may take account of the reasons for that decision in applying this Convention.

Article 18

The provisions of this Chapter do not limit the power of a judicial or administrative authority to order the return of the child at any time.

Article 19

A decision under this Convention concerning the return of the child shall not be taken to be a determination on the merits of any custody issue.

Article 20

The return of the child under the provisions of Article 12 may be refused if this would not be permitted by the fundamental principles of the requested State relating to the protection of human rights and fundamental freedoms.

CHAPTER IV -- RIGHTS OF ACCESS

Article 21

An application to make arrangements for organizing or securing the effective exercise of rights of access may be presented to the Central Authorities of the Contracting States in the same way as an application for the return of a child.

The Central Authorities are bound by the obligations of co-operation which are set forth in Article 7 to promote the peaceful enjoyment of access rights and the fulfilment of any conditions to which the exercise of those rights may be subject. The Central Authorities shall take steps to remove, as far as possible, all obstacles to the exercise of such rights.

The Central Authorities, either directly or through intermediaries, may initiate or assist in the institution of proceedings with a view to organizing or protecting these rights and securing respect for the conditions to which the exercise of these rights may be subject.

## CHAPTER V -- GENERAL PROVISIONS

### Article 22

No security, bond or deposit, however described, shall be required to guarantee the payment of costs and expenses in the judicial or administrative proceedings falling within the scope of this Convention.

### Article 23

No legalization or similar formality may be required in the context of this Convention.

### Article 24

Any application, communication or other document sent to the Central Authority of the requested State shall be in the original language, and shall be accompanied by a translation into the official language or one of the official languages of the requested State or, where that is not feasible, a translation into French or English.

However, a Contracting State may, by making a reservation in accordance with Article 42, object to the use of either French or English, but not both, in any application, communication or other document sent to its Central Authority.

### Article 25

Nationals of the Contracting States and persons who are habitually resident within those States shall be entitled in matters concerned with the application of this Convention to legal aid and advice in any other Contracting State on the same conditions as if they themselves were nationals of and habitually resident in that State.

### Article 26

Each Central Authority shall bear its own costs in applying this

Convention.

Central Authorities and other public services of Contracting States shall not impose any charges in relation to applications submitted under this Convention. In particular, they may not require any payment from the applicant towards the costs and expenses of the proceedings or, where applicable, those arising from the participation of legal counsel or advisers. However, they may require the payment of the expenses incurred or to be incurred in implementing the return of the child.

However, a Contracting State may, by making a reservation in accordance with Article 42, declare that it shall not be bound to assume any costs referred to in the preceding paragraph resulting from the participation of legal counsel or advisers or from court proceedings, except insofar as those costs may be covered by its system of legal aid and advice.

Upon ordering the return of a child or issuing an order concerning rights of access under this Convention, the judicial or administrative authorities may, where appropriate, direct the person who removed or retained the child, or who prevented the exercise of rights of access, to pay necessary expenses incurred by or on behalf of the applicant, including travel expenses, any costs incurred or payments made for locating the child, the costs of legal representation of the applicant, and those of returning the child.

## Article 27

When it is manifest that the requirements of this Convention are not fulfilled or that the application is otherwise not well founded, a Central Authority is not bound to accept the application. In that case, the Central Authority shall forthwith inform the applicant or the Central Authority through which the application was submitted, as the case may be, of its reasons.

## Article 28

A Central Authority may require that the application be accompanied by a written authorization empowering it to act on behalf of the applicant, or to designate a representative so to act.

## Article 29

This Convention shall not preclude any person, institution or body who claims that there has been a breach of custody or access rights within the meaning of Article 3 or 21 from applying directly to the judicial or administrative authorities of a Contracting State, whether or not under the provisions of this

Convention.

## Article 30

Any application submitted to the Central Authorities or directly to the judicial or administrative authorities of a Contracting State in accordance with the terms of this Convention, together with documents and any other information appended thereto or provided by a Central Authority, shall be admissible in the courts or administrative authorities of the Contracting States.

## Article 31

In relation to a State which in matters of custody of children has two or more systems of law applicable in different territorial units -- a any reference to habitual residence in that State shall be construed as referring to habitual residence in a territorial unit of that State; b any reference to the law of the State of habitual residence shall be construed as referring to the law of the territorial unit in that State where the child habitually resides.

## Article 32
In relation to a State which in matters of custody of children has two or more systems of law applicable to different categories of persons, any reference to the law of that State shall be construed as referring to the legal system specified by the law of that State.

## Article 33

A State within which different territorial units have their own rules of law in respect of custody of children shall not be bound to apply this Convention where a State with a unified system of law would not be bound to do so.

## Article 34

This Convention shall take priority in matters within its scope over the Convention of 5 October 1961 concerning the powers of authorities and the law applicable in respect of the protection of minors, as between Parties to both Conventions. Otherwise the present Convention shall not restrict the application of an international instrument in force between the State of origin and the State addressed or other law of the State addressed for the purposes of obtaining the return of a child who has been wrongfully removed or retained or of organizing access rights.

Article 35

This Convention shall apply as between Contracting States only to wrongful removals or retentions occurring after its entry into force in those States.

Where a declaration has been made under Article 39 or 40, the reference in the preceding paragraph to a Contracting State shall be taken to refer to the territorial unit or units in relation to which this Convention applies.

Article 36

Nothing in this Convention shall prevent two or more Contracting States, in order to limit the restrictions to which the return of the child may be subject, from agreeing among themselves to derogate from any provisions of this Convention which may imply such a restriction.

CHAPTER VI -- FINAL CLAUSES

Article 37

The Convention shall be open for signature by the States which were Members of the Hague Conference on Private International Law at the time of its Fourteenth Session. It shall be ratified, accepted or approved and the instruments of ratification, acceptance or approval shall be deposited with the Ministry of Foreign Affairs of the Kingdom of the Netherlands.

Article 38

Any other State may accede to the Convention. The instrument of accession shall be deposited with the Ministry of Foreign Affairs of the Kingdom of the Netherlands.

The Convention shall enter into force for a State acceding to it on the first day of the third calendar month after the deposit of its instrument of accession.

The accession will have effect only as regards the relations between the acceding State and such Contracting States as will have declared their acceptance of the accession. Such a declaration will also have to be made by any Member State ratifying, accepting or approving the Convention after an accession. Such declaration shall be deposited at the Ministry of Foreign Affairs of the Kingdom of the Netherlands; this Ministry shall forward, through diplomatic channels, a certified copy to each of the Contracting States.

The Convention will enter into force as between the acceding State and the State that has declared its acceptance of the accession on the first day of the third calendar month after the deposit of the declaration of acceptance.

## Article 39

Any State may, at the time of signature, ratification, acceptance, approval or accession, declare that the Convention shall extend to all the territories for the international relations of which it is responsible, or to one or more of them. Such a declaration shall take effect at the time the Convention enters into force for that State.

Such declaration, as well as any subsequent extension, shall be notified to the Ministry of Foreign Affairs of the Kingdom of the Netherlands.

## Article 40

If a Contracting State has two or more territorial units in which different systems of law are applicable in relation to matters dealt with in this Convention, it may at the time of signature, ratification, acceptance, approval or accession declare that this Convention shall extend to all its territorial units or only to one or more of them and may modify this declaration by submitting another declaration at any time.

Any such declaration shall be notified to the Ministry of Foreign Affairs of the Kingdom of the Netherlands and shall state expressly the territorial units to which the Convention applies.

## Article 41

Where a Contracting State has a system of government under which executive, judicial and legislative powers are distributed between central and other authorities within that State, its signature or ratification, acceptance or approval of, or accession to this Convention, or its making of any declaration in terms of Article 40 shall carry no implication as to the internal distribution of powers within that State.

## Article 42

Any State may, not later than the time of ratification, acceptance, approval or accession, or at the time of making a declaration in terms of Article 39 or 40, make one or both of the reservations provided for in Article 24 and Article 26, third paragraph. No other reservation shall be permitted.

Any State may at any time withdraw a reservation it has made. The withdrawal shall be notified to the Ministry of Foreign Affairs of the Kingdom of the Netherlands.

The reservation shall cease to have effect on the first day of the third calendar month after the notification referred to in the preceding paragraph.

## Article 43

The Convention shall enter into force on the first day of the third calendar month after the deposit of the third instrument of ratification, acceptance, approval or accession referred to in Articles 37 and 38.

Thereafter the Convention shall enter into force -- 1 for each State ratifying, accepting, approving or acceding to it subsequently, on the first day of the third calendar month after the deposit of its instrument of ratification, acceptance, approval or accession; 2 for any territory or territorial unit to which the Convention has been extended in conformity with Article 39 or 40, on the first day of the third calendar month after the notification referred to in that Article.

## Article 44

The Convention shall remain in force for five years from the date of its entry into force in accordance with the first paragraph of Article 43 even for States which subsequently have ratified, accepted, approved it or acceded to it. If there has been no denunciation, it shall be renewed tacitly every five years.

Any denunciation shall be notified to the Ministry of Foreign Affairs of the Kingdom of the Netherlands at least six months before the expiry of the five year period. It may be limited to certain of the territories or territorial units to which the Convention applies.

The denunciation shall have effect only as regards the State which has notified it. The Convention shall remain in force for the other Contracting States.

*[ED.—Article 45, dealing with notification of members and various "housekeeping" issues, has been omitted,]*

# INTERNATIONAL CHILD ABDUCTION REMEDIES ACT
# TITLE 42, UNITED STATES CODE ANNOTATED

*[ED.—18 U.S.C.A. § 1204, making international parental kidnaping a crime, is reproduced in Part III, supra at page 151.]*

### §11601. Findings and declarations

(a) Findings

The Congress makes the following findings:

(1) The international abduction or wrongful retention of children is harmful to their well-being.

(2) Persons should not be permitted to obtain custody of children by virtue of their wrongful removal or retention.

(3) International abductions and retentions of children are increasing, and only concerted cooperation pursuant to an international agreement can effectively combat this problem.

(4) The Convention on the Civil Aspects of International Child Abduction, done at The Hague on October 25, 1980, establishes legal rights and procedures for the prompt return of children who have been wrongfully removed or retained, as well as for securing the exercise of visitation rights. Children who are wrongfully removed or retained within the meaning of the Convention are to be promptly returned unless one of the narrow exceptions set forth in the Convention applies. The Convention provides a sound treaty framework to help resolve the problem of international abduction and retention of children and will deter such wrongful removals and retentions.

(b) Declarations

The Congress makes the following declarations:

(1) It is the purpose of this chapter to establish procedures for the implementation of the Convention in the United States.

(2) The provisions of this chapter are in addition to and not in lieu of the provisions of the Convention.

(3) In enacting this chapter the Congress recognizes--

(A) the international character of the Convention; and

(B) the need for uniform international interpretation of the Convention.

(4) The Convention and this chapter empower courts in the United States to determine only rights under the Convention and not the merits of any underlying child custody claims.

## §11602. Definitions

For the purposes of this chapter--

(1) the term "applicant" means any person who, pursuant to the Convention, files an application with the United States Central Authority or a Central Authority of any other party to the Convention for the return of a child alleged to have been wrongfully removed or retained or for arrangements for organizing or securing the effective exercise of rights of access pursuant to the Convention;

(2) the term "Convention" means the Convention on the Civil Aspects of International Child Abduction, done at The Hague on October 25, 1980;

(3) the term "Parent Locator Service" means the service established by the Secretary of Health and Human Services under section 653 of this title;

(4) the term "petitioner" means any person who, in accordance with this chapter, files a petition in court seeking relief under the Convention;

(5) the term "person" includes any individual, institution, or other legal entity or body;

(6) the term "respondent" means any person against whose interests a petition is filed in court, in accordance with this chapter, which seeks relief under the Convention;

(7) the term "rights of access" means visitation rights;

(8) the term "State" means any of the several States, the District of Columbia, and any commonwealth, territory, or possession of the United States; and

(9) the term "United States Central Authority" means the agency of the Federal Government designated by the President under section 11606(a) of this title.

## §11603. Judicial remedies

(a) Jurisdiction of the courts

The courts of the States and the United States district courts shall have concurrent original jurisdiction of actions arising under the Convention.

(b) Petitions

Any person seeking to initiate judicial proceedings under the Convention for the return of a child or for arrangements for organizing or securing the effective exercise of rights of access to a child may do so by commencing a civil action by filing a petition for the relief sought in any court which has jurisdiction of such action and which is authorized to exercise its jurisdiction in the place where the child is located at the time the petition is filed.

(c) Notice

Notice of an action brought under subsection (b) of this section shall be given in accordance with the applicable law governing notice in interstate child custody proceedings.

(d) Determination of case

The court in which an action is brought under subsection (b) of this section shall decide the case in accordance with the Convention.

(e) Burdens of proof

(1) A petitioner in an action brought under subsection (b) of this section shall establish by a preponderance of the evidence--

(A) in the case of an action for the return of a child, that the child has been wrongfully removed or retained within the meaning of the Convention; and

(B) in the case of an action for arrangements for organizing or securing the effective exercise of rights of access, that the petitioner has such rights.

(2) In the case of an action for the return of a child, a respondent who opposes the return of the child has the burden of establishing--

(A) by clear and convincing evidence that one of the exceptions set forth in article 13b or 20 of the Convention applies; and

(B) by a preponderance of the evidence that any other exception set forth in article 12 or 13 of the Convention applies.

(f) Application of the Convention

For purposes of any action brought under this chapter--

(1) the term "authorities", as used in article 15 of the Convention to refer to the authorities of the state of the habitual residence of a child, includes courts and appropriate government agencies;

(2) the terms "wrongful removal or retention" and "wrongfully removed or retained", as used in the Convention, include a removal or retention of a child before the entry of a custody order regarding that child; and

(3) the term "commencement of proceedings", as used in article 12 of the Convention, means, with respect to the return of a child located in the United States, the filing of a petition in accordance with subsection (b) of this section.

(g) Full faith and credit

Full faith and credit shall be accorded by the courts of the States and the courts of the United States to the judgment of any other such court ordering or denying the return of a child, pursuant to the Convention, in an action brought under this chapter.

(h) Remedies under the Convention not exclusive

The remedies established by the Convention and this chapter shall be in addition to remedies available under other laws or international agreements.

## §11604. Provisional remedies

(a) Authority of courts

In furtherance of the objectives of article 7(b) and other provisions of the Convention, and subject to the provisions of subsection (b) of this section, any court exercising jurisdiction of an action brought under section 11603(b) of this title may take or cause to be taken measures under Federal or State law, as appropriate, to protect the well-being of the child involved or to prevent the child's further removal or concealment before the final disposition of the petition.

(b) Limitation on authority

No court exercising jurisdiction of an action brought under section 11603(b) of this title may, under subsection (a) of this section, order a child removed from a person having physical control of the child unless the applicable requirements of State law are satisfied.

## §11605. Admissibility of documents

With respect to any application to the United States Central Authority, or any petition to a court under section 11603 of this title, which seeks relief under the Convention, or any other documents or information included with such application or petition or provided after such submission which relates to the application or petition, as the case may be, no authentication of such application, petition, document, or information shall be required in order for the application, petition, document, or information to be admissible in court.

## §11606. United States Central Authority

(a) Designation

The President shall designate a Federal agency to serve as the Central Authority for the United States under the Convention.

(b) Functions

The functions of the United States Central Authority are those ascribed to the Central Authority by the Convention and this chapter.

(c) Regulatory authority

The United States Central Authority is authorized to issue such regulations as may be necessary to carry out its functions under the Convention and this chapter.

(d) Obtaining information from Parent Locator Service

The United States Central Authority may, to the extent authorized by the Social Security Act [42 U.S.C.A. § 301 et seq.], obtain information from the Parent Locator Service.

## §11606. United States Central Authority

(a) Designation

The President shall designate a Federal agency to serve as the Central Authority for the United States under the Convention.

(b) Functions

The functions of the United States Central Authority are those ascribed to the Central Authority by the Convention and this chapter.

(c) Regulatory authority

The United States Central Authority is authorized to issue such regulations as may be necessary to carry out its functions under the Convention and this chapter.

(d) Obtaining information from Parent Locator Service

The United States Central Authority may, to the extent authorized by the Social Security Act [42 U.S.C.A. § 301 et seq.], obtain information from the Parent Locator Service.

## §11607. Costs and fees

(a) Administrative costs

No department, agency, or instrumentality of the Federal Government or of any State or local government may impose on an applicant any fee in relation to the administrative processing of applications submitted under the Convention.

(b) Costs incurred in civil actions

(1) Petitioners may be required to bear the costs of legal counsel or advisors, court costs incurred in connection with their petitions, and travel costs for the return of the child involved and any accompanying persons, except as provided in paragraphs (2) and (3).

(2) Subject to paragraph (3), legal fees or court costs incurred in connection with an action brought under section 11603 of this title shall be borne by the petitioner unless they are covered by payments from Federal, State, or local legal assistance or other programs.

(3) Any court ordering the return of a child pursuant to an action brought under section 11603 of this title shall order the respondent to pay necessary expenses incurred by or on behalf of the petitioner, including court costs, legal fees, foster home or other care during the course of proceedings in the action, and transportation costs related to the return of the child, unless the respondent establishes that such order would be clearly inappropriate.

## §11608. Collection, maintenance, and dissemination of information

(a) In general

In performing its functions under the Convention, the United States Central Authority may, under such conditions as the Central Authority prescribes by regulation, but subject to subsection (c) of this section, receive from or transmit to any department, agency, or instrumentality of the Federal Government or of any State or foreign government, and receive from or transmit to any applicant, petitioner, or respondent, information necessary to locate a child or for the purpose of otherwise implementing the Convention with respect to a child, except that the United States Central Authority--

(1) may receive such information from a Federal or State department, agency, or instrumentality only pursuant to applicable Federal and State statutes; and

(2) may transmit any information received under this subsection notwithstanding any provision of law other than this chapter.

(b) Requests for information

Requests for information under this section shall be submitted in such manner and form as the United States Central Authority may prescribe by regulation and shall be accompanied or supported by such documents as the United States Central Authority may require.

(c) Responsibility of government entities

Whenever any department, agency, or instrumentality of the United States or of any State receives a request from the United States Central Authority for information authorized to be provided to such Central Authority under subsection (a) of this section, the head of such department, agency, or instrumentality shall promptly cause a search to be made of the files and records maintained by such department, agency, or instrumentality in order to determine whether the information requested is contained in any such files or records. If such search discloses the information requested, the head of such department, agency, or instrumentality shall immediately transmit such information to the United States Central Authority, except that any such information the disclosure of which--

(1) would adversely affect the national security interests of the United States or the law enforcement interests of the United States or of any State; or

(2) would be prohibited by section 9 of Title 13;

shall not be transmitted to the Central Authority. The head of such department, agency, or instrumentality shall, immediately upon completion of the requested search, notify the Central Authority of the results of the search, and whether an exception set forth in paragraph (1) or (2) applies. In the event that the United States Central Authority receives information and the appropriate Federal or State department, agency, or instrumentality thereafter notifies the Central Authority that an exception set forth in paragraph (1) or (2) applies to that information, the Central Authority may not disclose that information under subsection (a) of this section.

(d) Information available from Parent Locator Service

To the extent that information which the United States Central Authority is authorized to obtain under the provisions of subsection (c) of this section can be obtained through the Parent Locator Service, the United States Central Authority shall first seek to obtain such information from the Parent Locator Service, before requesting such information directly under the provisions of subsection (c) of this section.

(e) Recordkeeping

The United States Central Authority shall maintain appropriate records concerning its activities and the disposition of cases brought to its attention.

## §11609. Interagency coordinating group

The Secretary of State, the Secretary of Health and Human Services, and the Attorney General shall designate Federal employees and may, from time to time, designate private citizens to serve on an interagency coordinating group to monitor the operation of the Convention and to provide advice on its implementation to the United States Central Authority and other Federal agencies. This group shall meet from time to time at the request of the United States Central Authority. The agency in which the United States Central Authority is located is authorized to reimburse such private citizens for travel and other expenses incurred in participating at meetings of the interagency coordinating group at rates not to exceed those authorized under subchapter I of chapter 57 of Title 5 for employees of agencies.

§11610. Authorization of appropriations

There are authorized to be appropriated for each fiscal year such sums as may be necessary to carry out the purposes of the Convention and this chapter.

*[ED.—The United States deposited its instrument of ratification of the Hague Convention on the Civil Aspects of International Child Abduction on April 29, 1988. The Convention entered into force for the United States on July 1, 1988. On August 8, 1988. President Ronald Reagan designated the Department of State as the Central Authority of the United States for purposes of the Convention, authorizing and empowering the Secretary of State, in accordance with such regulations as he may prescribe, to perform all lawful acts necessary and proper to execute the functions of the Central Authority in a timely and efficient manner.]*

# HAGUE CONFERENCE ON PRIVATE INTERNATIONAL LAW:  CONVENTION ON PROTECTION OF CHILDREN AND COOPERATION IN RESPECT OF INTERCOUNTRY ADOPTION

The States signatory to the present Convention,

Recognizing that the child, for the full and harmonious development of his or her personality, should grow up in a family environment, in an atmosphere of happiness, love and understanding,

Recalling that each State should take, as a matter of priority, appropriate measures to enable the child to remain in the care of his or her family of origin,

Recognizing that intercountry adoption may offer the advantage of a permanent family to a child for whom a suitable family cannot be found in his or her State of origin,

Convinced of the necessity to take measures to ensure that intercountry adoptions are made in the best interests of the child and with respect for his or her fundamental rights, and to prevent the abduction. the sale of, or traffic in children,

Desiring to establish common provisions to this effect, taking into account the principles set forth in international instruments, in particular the United Nations Convention on the Rights of the Child, of 20 November 1989, and the United Nations Declaration on Social and Legal Principles relating to the Protection and Welfare of Children, with Special Reference to Foster Placement and Adoption Nationally and Internationally (General Assembly Resolution 41/85, of 3 December 1986),

Have agreed upon the following provisions -

CHAPTER I--SCOPE OF THE CONVENTION

Article I

The objects of the present Convention are -

a.     to establish safeguards to ensure that intercountry adoptions take place in the best interests of the child and with respect for his or her fundamental rights as recognized in international law;

b.        to establish a system of co-operation amongst Contracting States to ensure that those safeguards are respected and thereby prevent the abduction, the sale of, or traffic in children;

c.        to secure the recognition in Contracting States of adoptions made in accordance with the Convention.

Article 2

1.        The Convention shall apply where a child habitually resident in one Contracting State ('the State of origin') has been, is being, or is to be moved to another Contracting State ('the receiving State') either after his or her adoption in the State of origin by spouses or a person habitually resident in the receiving State, or for the purposes of such an adoption in the receiving State or in the State of origin.

2.        The Convention covers only adoptions which create a permanent parent-child relationship.

Article 3

The Convention ceases to apply if the agreements mentioned in Article 17, sub-paragraph c, have not been given before the child attains the age of eighteen years.

CHAPTER II--REQUIREMENTS FOR INTERCOUNTRY ADOPTIONS

Article 4

An adoption within the scope of the Convention shall take place only if the competent authorities of the State of origin

a.        have established that the child is adoptable;

b.        have determined, after possibilities for placement of the child within the State of origin have been given due consideration, that an intercountry adoption is in the child's best interests;

c.      have ensured that

(1)     the persons, institutions and authorities whose consent is necessary for adoption have been counselled as may be necessary and duly informed of the effects of their consent, in particular whether or not an adoption will result in the termination of the legal relationship between the child and his or her family of origin,

(2)     such persons, institutions and authorities have given their consent freely, in the required legal form, and expressed or evidenced in writing,

(3)     the consents have not been induced by payment or compensation of any kind and have not been withdrawn, and

(4)     the consent of the mother, where required, has been given only after the birth of the child; and

d.      have ensured, having regard to the age and degree of maturity of the child, that

(1)     he or she has been counselled and duly informed of the effects of the adoption and of his or her consent to the adoption, where such consent is required,

(2)     consideration has been given to the child's wishes and opinions,

(3)     the child's consent to the adoption, where such consent is required, has been given freely, in the required legal form, and expressed or evidenced in writing, and

(4)     such consent has not been induced by payment or compensation of any kind.

Article 5

An adoption within the scope of the Convention shall take place only if the competent authorities of the receiving State -

a.      have determined that the prospective adoptive parents are eligible and suited to adopt;

b.   have ensured that the prospective adoptive parents have been counselled as may be necessary; and

c.   have determined that the child is or will be authorized to enter and reside permanently in that State.

## CHAPTER III--CENTRAL AUTHORITIES AND ACCREDITED BODIES

### Article 6

1.   A Contracting State shall designate a Central Authority to discharge the duties which are imposed by the Convention upon such authorities.

2.   Federal States, States with more than one system of law or States having autonomous territorial units shall be free to appoint more than one Central Authority and to specify the territorial or personal extent of their functions. Where a State has appointed more than one Central Authority, it shall designate the Central Authority to which any communication may be addressed for transmission to the appropriate Central Authority within that State.

### Article 7

1.   Central Authorities shall co-operate with each other and promote co-operation amongst the competent authorities in their States to protect children and to achieve the other objects of the Convention.

2.   They shall take directly all appropriate measures to -

a.   provide information as to the laws of their States concerning adoption and other general information, such as statistics and standard forms:

b.   keep one another informed about the operation of the Convention and, as far as possible, eliminate any obstacles to its application.

### Article 8

Central Authorities shall take, directly or through public authorities, all appropriate measures to prevent improper financial or other gain in connection with an adoption and to deter all practices contrary to the objects of the Convention.

Article 9

Central Authorities shall take, directly or through public authorities or other bodies duly accredited in their State, all appropriate measures, in particular to -

a.      collect, preserve and exchange information about the situation of the child and the prospective adoptive parents, so far as is necessary to complete the adoption:

b.      facilitate follow and expedite proceedings with a view to obtaining the adoption;

c.      promote the development of adoption counselling and post-adoption services in their States;

d.      provide each other with general evaluation reports about experience with intercountry adoption:

e.      reply, in so far as is permitted by the law of their State, to justified requests from other Central Authorities or public authorities for information about a particular adoption situation.

Article 10

Accreditation shall only be granted to and maintained by bodies demonstrating their competence to carry out properly the tasks with which they may be entrusted.

Article 11

An accredited body shall -

a.      pursue only non-profit objectives according to such conditions and within such limits as may be established by the competent authorities of the State of accreditation;

b.      be directed and staffed by persons qualified by their ethical standards and by training or experience to work in the field of intercountry adoption; and

c.      be subject to supervision by competent authorities of that State as
        to its composition, operation and financial situation.

Article 12

A body accredited in one Contracting State may act in another Contracting State
only if the competent authorities of both States have authorized it to do so.

Article 13

The designation of the Central Authorities and, where appropriate, the extent of
their functions, as well as the names and addresses of the accredited bodies shall
be communicated by each Contracting State to the Permanent Bureau of the
Hague Conference on Private International Law.

CHAPTER IV--PROCEDURAL REQUIREMENTS IN INTERCOUNTRY
ADOPTION

Article 14

Persons habitually resident in a Contracting State, who wish to adopt a child
habitually resident in another Contracting State, shall apply to the Central
Authority in the State of their habitual residence.

Article 15

1.      If the Central Authority of the receiving State is satisfied that the
        applicants are eligible and suited to adopt, it shall prepare a report
        including information about their identity eligibility and suitability
        to adopt background, family and medical history, social
        environment, reasons for adoption, ability to undertake an
        intercountry adoption, as well as the characteristics of the children
        for whom they would be qualified to care.

2.      It shall transmit the report to the Central Authority of the State of
        origin.

Article 16

1.      If the Central Authority of the State of origin is satisfied that the
        child is adoptable, it shall -

a.      prepare a report including information about his or her identity, adoptability, background, social environment, family history, medical history including that of the child's family, and any special needs of the child;

b.      give due consideration to the child's upbringing and to his or her ethnic, religious and cultural background;

c.      ensure that consents have been obtained in accordance with Article 4; and

d.      determine. on the basis in particular of the reports relating to the child and the prospective adoptive parents, whether the envisaged placement is in the best interests of the child.

2.      It shall transmit to the Central Authority of the receiving State its report on the child, proof that the necessary consents have been obtained and the reasons for its determination on the placement, taking care not to reveal the identity of the mother and the father if, in the State of origin, these identities may not be disclosed.

Article 17

Any decision in the State of origin that a child should be entrusted to prospective adoptive parents may only be made if

a.      the Central Authority of that State has ensured that the prospective adoptive parents agree;

b.      the Central Authority of the receiving State has approved such decision, where such approval is required by the law of that State or by the Central Authority of the State of origin;

c.      the Central Authorities of both States have agreed that the adoption may proceed; and

d.      it has been determined, in accordance with Article 5, that the prospective adoptive parents are eligible and suited to adopt and that the child is or will be authorized to enter and reside permanently in the receiving State.

Article 18

The Central Authorities of both States shall take all necessary steps to obtain permission for the child to leave the State of origin and to enter and reside permanently in the receiving State.

Article 19

1.     The transfer of the child to the receiving State may only be carried out if the requirements of Article 17 have been satisfied.

2.     The Central Authorities of both States shall ensure that this transfer takes place in secure and appropriate circumstances and, if possible, in the company of the adoptive or prospective adoptive parents.

3.     If the transfer of the child does not take place, the reports referred to in Articles 15 and 16 are to be sent back to the authorities who forwarded them.

Article 20

The Central Authorities shall keep each other informed about the adoption process and the measures taken to complete it, as well as about the progress of the placement if a probationary period is required.

Article 21

1.     Where the adoption is to take place after the transfer of the child to the receiving State and it appears to the Central Authority of that State that the continued placement of the child with the prospective adoptive parents is not in the child's best interests, such Central Authority shall take the measures necessary to protect the child, in particular -

a.     to cause the child to be withdrawn from the prospective adoptive parents and to arrange temporary care;

b.     in consultation with the Central Authority of the State of origin, to arrange without delay a new placement of the child with a view to adoption or, if this is not appropriate. to arrange alternative long-term care; an adoption shall not take place until the Central Authority of the State of origin has been duly informed concerning the new prospective adoptive parents;

c.      as a last resort, to arrange the return of the child. if his or her interests so require.

2.      Having regard in particular to the age and degree of maturity of the child. he or she shall be consulted and, where appropriate, his or her consent obtained in relation to measures to be taken under this Article.

Article 22

1.      The functions of a Central Authority under this Chapter may be performed by public authorities or by bodies accredited under Chapter III, to the extent permitted by the law of its State.

2.      Any Contracting State may declare to the depositary of the Convention that the functions of the Central Authority under Articles 15 to 21 may be performed in that State, to the extent permitted by the law and subject to the supervision of the competent authorities of that State, also by bodies or persons who

a.      meet the requirements of integrity, professional competence, experience and accountability of that State; and

b.      are qualified by their ethical standards and by training or experience to work in the field of intercountry adoption.

3.      A Contracting State which makes the declaration provided for in paragraph 2 shall keep the Permanent Bureau of the Hague Conference on Private International Law informed of the names and addresses of these bodies and persons.

4.      Any Contracting State may declare to the depositary of the Convention that adoptions of children habitually resident in its territory may only take place if the functions of the Central Authorities are performed in accordance with paragraph 1.

5.      Notwithstanding any declaration made under paragraph 2. the

reports provided for in Articles 15 and 16 shall. in every case, be prepared under the responsibility of the Central Authority or other authorities or bodies in accordance with paragraph 1.

## CHAPTER V--RECOGNITION AND EFFECTS OF THE ADOPTION

Article 23

1.      An adoption certified by the competent authority of the State of the adoption as having been made in accordance with the Convention shall be recognized by operation of law in the other Contracting States. The certificate shall specify when and by whom the agreements under Article 17, sub-paragraph c, were given.

2.      Each Contracting State shall, at the time of signature, ratification. acceptance, approval or accession, notify the depositary of the Convention of the identity and the functions of the authority or the authorities which, in that State, are competent to make the certification. It shall also notify the depositary of any modification in the designation of these authorities.

Article 24

The recognition of an adoption may be refused in a Contracting State only if the adoption is manifestly contrary to its public policy, taking into account the best interests of the child.

Article 25

Any Contracting State may declare to the depositary of the Convention that it will not be bound under this Convention to recognize adoptions made in accordance with an agreement concluded by application of Article 39, paragraph 2.

Article 26

1.      The recognition of an adoption includes recognition of

a.      the legal parent-child relationship between the child and his or her adoptive parents;

b.      parental responsibility of the adoptive parents for the child;

c.      the termination of a pre-existing legal relationship between the child and his or her mother and father. if the adoption has this effect in the Contracting State where it was made.

2.      In the case of an adoption having the effect of terminating a pre-existing legal parent-child relationship the child shall enjoy in the receiving State, and in any other Contracting State where the adoption is recognized, rights equivalent to those resulting from adoptions having this effect in each such State.

3.      The preceding paragraphs shall not prejudice the application of any provision more favorable for the child, in force in the Contracting State which recognizes the adoption.

Article 27

Where an adoption granted in the State of origin does not have the effect of terminating a pre-existing legal parent-child relationship, it may, in the receiving State which recognizes the adoption under the Convention, be converted into an adoption having such an effect

a.      if the law of the receiving State so permits; and

b.      if the consents referred to in Article 4, subparagraphs c and d, have been or are given for the purpose of such an adoption.

2.      Article 23 applies to the decision converting the adoption.

CHAPTER VI--GENERAL PROVISIONS

Article 28

The Convention does not affect any law of a State of origin which requires that the adoption of a child habitually resident within that State take place in that State or which prohibits the child's placement in, or transfer to, the receiving State prior to adoption.

Article 29

There shall be no contact between the prospective adoptive parents and the child's parents or any other person who has care of the child until the requirements of Article 4, sub-paragraphs a to c, and Article 5, subparagraph a, have been met, unless the adoption takes place within a family or unless the contact is in compliance with the conditions established by the competent authority of the State of origin.

Article 30

1.      The competent authorities of a Contracting State shall ensure that information held by them concerning the child's origin, in particular information concerning the identity of his or her parents, as well as the medical history, is preserved.

2.      They shall ensure that the child or his or her representative has access to such information, under appropriate guidance, in so far as is permitted by the law of that State.

Article 31

Without prejudice to Article 30, personal data gathered or transmitted under the Convention, especially data referred to in Articles 15 and 16, shall be used only for the purposes for which they were gathered or transmitted.

Article 32

1.      No one shall derive improper financial or other gain from an activity related to an intercountry adoption.

2.      Only costs and expenses, including reasonable professional fees of persons involved in the adoption, may be charged or paid.

3.      The directors, administrators and employees of bodies involved in an adoption shall not receive remuneration which is unreasonably high in relation to services rendered.

Article 33

A competent authority which finds that any provision of the Convention has not been respected or that there is a serious risk that it may not be respected, shall immediately inform the Central Authority of its State. This Central Authority shall be responsible for ensuring that appropriate measures are taken.

Article 34

If the competent authority of the State of destination of a document so requests, a translation certified as being in conformity with the original must be furnished. Unless otherwise provided, the costs of such translation are to be borne by the prospective adoptive parents.

Article 35

The competent authorities of the Contracting States shall act expeditiously in the process of adoption.

Article 36

In relation to a State which has two or more systems of law and regard to adoption applicable in different territorial units -

a.      any reference to habitual residence in that State shall be construed as referring to habitual residence in a territorial unit of that State;

b.      any reference to the law of that State shall be construed as referring to the law in force in the relevant territorial unit;

c.      any reference to the competent authorities or to the public authorities of that State shall be construed as referring to those authorized to act in the relevant territorial unit;

d.      any reference to the accredited bodies of that State shall be construed as referring to bodies accredited int he relevant territorial unit.

Article 37

In relation to a State which with regard to adoption has two or more systems of law applicable to different categories of persons, any reference to the law of that State shall be construed as referring to the legal system specified by the law of that

State.

## Article 38

A State within which different territorial units have their own rules of law in respect of adoption shall not be bound to apply the Convention where a State with a unified system of law would not be bound to do so.

## Article 39

1.     The Convention does not affect any international instrument to which Contracting States are Parties and which contains provisions on matters governed by the Convention, unless a contrary declaration is made by the States Parties to such instrument.

2.     Any Contracting State may enter into agreements with one or more other Contracting States, with a view to improving the application of the Convention in their mutual relations. These agreements may derogate only from the provisions of Articles 14 to 16 and 18 to 21. The States which have concluded such an agreement shall transmit a copy to the depositary of the Convention.

## Article 40

No reservation to the Convention shall be permitted.

## Article 41

The Convention shall apply in every case where an application pursuant to Article 14 has been received after the Convention has entered into force in the receiving State and the State of origin.

## Article 42

The Secretary General of the Hague Conference on Private International Law shall at regular intervals convene a Special Commission in order to review the practical operation of the Convention.

CHAPTER VII--FINAL CLAUSES

Article 43

1.      The Convention shall be open for signature by the States which were Members of the Hague Conference on Private International Law at the time of its Seventeenth Session and by the other States which participated in that Session.

2.      It shall be ratified, accepted or approved and the instruments of ratification, acceptance or approval shall be deposited with the Ministry of Foreign Affairs of the Kingdom of the Netherlands, depositary of the Convention.

Article 44

1.      Any other State may accede to the Convention after it has entered into force in accordance with Article 46, paragraph 1.

2.      The instrument of accession shall be deposited with the depositary.

3.      Such accession shall have effect only as regards the relations between the acceding State and those Contracting States which have not raised an objection to its accession in the six months after the receipt of the notification referred to in sub-paragraph b of Article 48. Such an objection may also be raised by States at the time when they ratify, accept or approve the Convention after an accession. Any such objection shall be notified to the depositary.

Article 45

1.      If a State has two or more territorial units in which different systems of law are applicable in relation to matters dealt with in the Convention, it may at the time of signature, ratification, acceptance, approval or accession declare that this Convention shall extend to all its territorial units or only to one or more of them and may modify this declaration by submitting another declaration at any time.

2.      Any such declaration shall be notified to the depositary and shall state expressly the territorial units to which the Convention

applies.

3.     If a State makes no declaration under this Article, the Convention is to extend to all territorial units of that State.

## Article 46

1.     The Convention shall enter into force on the first day of the month following the expiration of three months after the deposit of the third instrument of ratification, acceptance or approval referred to in Article 43.

2.     Thereafter the Convention shall enter into force -

a.     for each State ratifying, accepting or approving it subsequently, or acceding to it, on the first day of the month following the expiration of three months after the deposit of its instrument of ratification, acceptance, approval or accession;

b.     for a territorial unit to which the Convention has been extended in conformity with Article 45, on the first day of the month following the expiration of three months after the notification referred to in that Article.

## Article 47

1.     A State Party to the Convention may denounce it by a notification in writing addressed to the depositary.

2.     The denunciation takes effect on the first day of the month following the expiration of twelve months after the notification is received by the depositary. Where a longer period for the denunciation to take effect is specified in the notification, the denunciation takes effect upon the expiration of such longer period after the notification is received by the depositary.

*[ED.—Article 48, dealing with notification of Member States and other "housekeeping" problems, has been omitted.]*

# UNITED NATIONS: CONVENTION ON THE RIGHTS OF THE CHILD (November 20, 1989)

The States Parties to the present Convention,

Considering that, in accordance with the principles proclaimed in the Charter of the United Nations, recognition of the inherent dignity and of the equal and inalienable rights of all members of the human family is the foundation of freedom, justice and peace in the world,

Bearing in mind that the peoples of the United Nations have, in the Charter, reaffirmed their faith in fundamental human rights and in the dignity and worth of the human person, and have determined to promote social progress and better standards of life in larger freedom,

Recognizing that the United Nations has, in the Universal Declaration of Human Rights and in the International Covenants on Human Rights, proclaimed and agreed that everyone is entitled to all the rights and freedoms set forth therein, without distinction of any kind, such as race, colour, sex, language, religion, political or other opinion, national or social origin, property, birth or other status,

Recognizing that, in all countries in the world, there are children living in exceptionally difficult conditions, and that such children need special consideration,

Taking due account of the importance of the traditions and cultural values of each people for the protection and harmonious development of the child,

Recognizing the importance of international co-operation for improving the living conditions of children in every country, in particular in the developing countries,

Have agreed as follows:

## PART I
### Article 1

For the purposes of the present Convention, a child means every human being below the age of eighteen years unless, under the law applicable to the child, majority is attained earlier.

### Article 2

1. States Parties shall respect and ensure the rights set forth in the present Convention to each child within their jurisdiction without discrimination of any kind, irrespective of the child's or his or her parent's or legal guardian's race,

colour, sex, language, religion, political or other opinion, national, ethnic or social origin, property, disability, birth or other status.

2. States Parties shall take all appropriate measures to ensure that the child is protected against all forms of discrimination or punishment on the basis of the status, activities, expressed opinions, or beliefs of the child's parents, legal guardians, or family members.

## Article 3

1. In all actions concerning children, whether undertaken by public or private social welfare institutions, courts of law, administrative authorities or legislative bodies, the best interests of the child shall be a primary consideration.

2. States Parties undertake to ensure the child such protection and care as is necessary for his or her well-being, taking into account the rights and duties of his or her parents, legal guardians, or other individuals legally responsible for him or her, and, to this end, shall take all appropriate legislative and administrative measures.

3. States Parties shall ensure that the institutions, services and facilities responsible for the care or protection of children shall conform with the standards established by competent authorities, particularly in the areas of safety, health, in the number and suitability of their staff, as well as competent supervision.

## Article 4

States Parties shall undertake all appropriate legislative, administrative, and other measures for the implementation of the rights recognized in the present Convention. With regard to economic, social and cultural rights, States Parties shall undertake such measures to the maximum extent of their available resources and, where needed, within the framework of international co-operation.

## Article 5

States Parties shall respect the responsibilities, rights and duties of parents or, where applicable, the members of the extended family or community as provided for by local custom, legal guardians or other persons legally responsible for the child, to provide, in a manner consistent with the evolving capacities of the child, appropriate direction and guidance in the exercise by the child of the rights recognized in the present Convention.

## Article 6

1. States Parties recognize that every child has the inherent right to life.

2. States Parties shall ensure to the maximum extent possible the survival and development of the child.

## Article 7

1. The child shall be registered immediately after birth and shall have the right from birth to a name, the right to acquire a nationality and, as far as possible, the right to know and be cared for by his or her parents.

2. States Parties shall ensure the implementation of these rights in accordance with their national law and their obligations under the relevant international instruments in this field, in particular where the child would otherwise be stateless.

## Article 8

1. States Parties undertake to respect the right of the child to preserve his or her identity, including nationality, name and family relations as recognized by law without unlawful interference.

2. Where a child is illegally deprived of some or all of the elements of his or her identity, States Parties shall provide appropriate assistance and protection, with a view to speedily re-establishing his or her identity.

## Article 9

1. States Parties shall ensure that a child shall not be separated from his or her parents against their will, except when competent authorities subject to judicial review determine, in accordance with applicable law and procedures, that such separation is necessary for the best interests of the child. Such determination may be necessary in a particular case such as one involving abuse or neglect of the child by the parents, or one where the parents are living separately and a decision must be made as to the child's place of residence.

2. In any proceedings pursuant to paragraph 1 of the present article, all interested parties shall be given an opportunity to participate in the proceedings and make their views known.

3. States Parties shall respect the right of the child who is separated from one or both parents to maintain personal relations and direct contact with both parents on a regular basis, except if it is contrary to the child's best interests.

4. Where such separation results from any action initiated by a State Party, such as the detention, imprisonment, exile, deportation or death (including death arising from any cause while the person is in the custody of the State) of one or

both parents or of the child, that State Party shall, upon request, provide the parents, the child or, if appropriate, another member of the family with the essential information concerning the whereabouts of the absent member(s) of the family unless the provision of the information would be detrimental to the well-being of the child. States Parties shall further ensure that the submission of such a request shall of itself entail no adverse consequences for the person(s) concerned.

## Article 10

1. In accordance with the obligation of States Parties under article 9, paragraph 1, applications by a child or his or her parents to enter or leave a State Party for the purpose of family reunification shall be dealt with by States Parties in a positive, humane and expeditious manner. States Parties shall further ensure that the submission of such a request shall entail no adverse consequences for the applicants and for the members of their family.

2. A child whose parents reside in different States shall have the right to maintain on a regular basis, save in exceptional circumstances personal relations and direct contacts with both parents. Towards that end and in accordance with the obligation of States Parties under article 9, paragraph 2, States Parties shall respect the right of the child and his or her parents to leave any country, including their own, and to enter their own country. The right to leave any country shall be subject only to such restrictions as are prescribed by law and which are necessary to protect the national security, public order (ordre public), public health or morals or the rights and freedoms of others and are consistent with the other rights recognized in the present Convention.

## Article 11

1. States Parties shall take measures to combat the illicit transfer and non-return of children abroad.

2. To this end, States Parties shall promote the conclusion of bilateral or multilateral agreements or accession to existing agreements.

## Article 12

1. States Parties shall assure to the child who is capable of forming his or her own views the right to express those views freely in all matters affecting the child, the views of the child being given due weight in accordance with the age and maturity of the child.

2. For this purpose, the child shall in particular be provided the opportunity

to be heard in any judicial and administrative proceedings affecting the child, either directly, or through a representative or an appropriate body, in a manner consistent with the procedural rules of national law.

## Article 13

1. The child shall have the right to freedom of expression; this right shall include freedom to seek, receive and impart information and ideas of all kinds, regardless of frontiers, either orally, in writing or in print, in the form of art, or through any other media of the child's choice.

2. The exercise of this right may be subject to certain restrictions, but these shall only be such as are provided by law and are necessary:

(a) For respect of the rights or reputations of others; or

(b) For the protection of national security or of public order (ordre public), or of public health or morals.

## Article 14

1. States Parties shall respect the right of the child to freedom of thought, conscience and religion.

2. States Parties shall respect the rights and duties of the parents and, when applicable, legal guardians, to provide direction to the child in the exercise of his or her right in a manner consistent with the evolving capacities of the child.

3. Freedom to manifest one's religion or beliefs may be subject only to such limitations as are prescribed by law and are necessary to protect public safety, order, health or morals, or the fundamental rights and freedoms of others.

## Article 15

1. States Parties recognize the rights of the child to freedom of association and to freedom of peaceful assembly.

2. No restrictions may be placed on the exercise of these rights other than those imposed in conformity with the law and which are necessary in a democratic society in the interests of national security or public safety, public order (ordre public), the protection of public health or morals or the protection of the rights and freedoms of others.

## Article 16

1. No child shall be subjected to arbitrary or unlawful interference with his or her privacy, family, home or correspondence, nor to unlawful attacks on his or her honour and reputation.

2. The child has the right to the protection of the law against such interference or attacks.

## Article 17

States Parties recognize the important function performed by the mass media and shall ensure that the child has access to information and material from a diversity of national and international sources, especially those aimed at the promotion of his or her social, spiritual and moral well-being and physical and mental health. To this end, States Parties shall:

(a) Encourage the mass media to disseminate information and material of social and cultural benefit to the child and in accordance with the spirit of article 29;

(b) Encourage international co-operation in the production, exchange and dissemination of such information and material from a diversity of cultural, national and international sources;

(c) Encourage the production and dissemination of children's books;

(d) Encourage the mass media to have particular regard to the linguistic needs of the child who belongs to a minority group or who is indigenous;

(e) Encourage the development of appropriate guidelines for the protection of the child from information and material injurious to his or her well-being, bearing in mind the provisions of articles 13 and 18.

## Article 18

1. States Parties shall use their best efforts to ensure recognition of the principle that both parents have common responsibilities for the upbringing and development of the child. Parents or, as the case may be, legal guardians, have the primary responsibility for the upbringing and development of the child. The best interests of the child will be their basic concern.

2. For the purpose of guaranteeing and promoting the rights set forth in the present Convention, States Parties shall render appropriate assistance to parents and legal guardians in the performance of their child-rearing responsibilities and shall ensure the development of institutions, facilities and services for the care of children.

3. States Parties shall take all appropriate measures to ensure that children of working parents have the right to benefit from child-care services and facilities for which they are eligible.

## Article 19

1. States Parties shall take all appropriate legislative, administrative, social

and educational measures to protect the child from all forms of physical or mental violence, injury or abuse, neglect or negligent treatment, maltreatment or exploitation, including sexual abuse, while in the care of parent(s), legal guardian(s) or any other person who has the care of the child.

2. Such protective measures should, as appropriate, include effective procedures for the establishment of social programmes to provide necessary support for the child and for those who have the care of the child, as well as for other forms of prevention and for identification, reporting, referral, investigation, treatment and follow-up of instances of child maltreatment described heretofore, and, as appropriate, for judicial involvement.

## Article 20

1. A child temporarily or permanently deprived of his or her family environment, or in whose own best interests cannot be allowed to remain in that environment, shall be entitled to special protection and assistance provided by the State.

2. States Parties shall in accordance with their national laws ensure alternative care for such a child.

3. Such care could include, inter alia, foster placement, kafalah of Islamic law, adoption or if necessary placement in suitable institutions for the care of children. When considering solutions, due regard shall be paid to the desirability of continuity in a child's upbringing and to the child's ethnic, religious, cultural and linguistic background.

## Article 21

States Parties that recognize and/or permit the system of adoption shall ensure that the best interests of the child shall be the paramount consideration and they shall:

(a) Ensure that the adoption of a child is authorized only by competent authorities who determine, in accordance with applicable law and procedures and on the basis of all pertinent and reliable information, that the adoption is permissible in view of the child's status concerning parents, relatives and legal guardians and that, if required, the persons concerned have given their informed consent to the adoption on the basis of such counselling as may be necessary;

(b) Recognize that inter-country adoption may be considered as an alternative means of child's care, if the child cannot be placed in a foster or an adoptive family or cannot in any suitable manner be cared for in the child's country of origin;

(c) Ensure that the child concerned by inter-country adoption enjoys safeguards and standards equivalent to those existing in the case of national adoption,

(d) Take all appropriate measures to ensure that, in inter-country adoption, the placement does not result in improper financial gain for those involved in it;

(e) Promote, where appropriate, the objectives of the present article by concluding bilateral or multilateral arrangements or agreements, and endeavour, within this framework, to ensure that the placement of the child in another country is carried out by competent authorities or organs.

## Article 22

1. States Parties shall take appropriate measures to ensure that a child who is seeking refugee status or who is considered a refugee in accordance with applicable international or domestic law and procedures shall, whether unaccompanied or accompanied by his or her parents or by any other person, receive appropriate protection and humanitarian assistance in the enjoyment of applicable rights set

## Article 23

1. States Parties recognize that a mentally or physically disabled child should enjoy a full and decent life, in conditions which ensure dignity, promote self-reliance and facilitate the child's active participation in the community.

2. States Parties recognize the right of the disabled child to special care and shall encourage and ensure the extension, subject to available resources, to the eligible child and those responsible for his or her care, of assistance for which application is made and which is appropriate to the child's condition and to the circumstances of the parents or others caring for the child.

3. Recognizing the special needs of a disabled child, assistance extended in accordance with paragraph 2 of the present article shall be provided free of charge, whenever possible, taking into account the financial resources of the parents or others caring for the child, and shall be designed to ensure that the disabled child has effective access to and receives education, training, health care services, rehabilitation services, preparation for employment and recreation opportunities in a manner conducive to the child's achieving the fullest possible social integration and individual development, including his or her cultural and spiritual development.

4. States Parties shall promote, in the spirit of international co-operation, the exchange of appropriate information in the field of preventive health care and of medical, psychological and functional treatment of disabled children, including dissemination of and access to information concerning methods of rehabilitation,

education and vocational services, with the aim of enabling States Parties to improve their capabilities and skills and to widen their experience in these areas. In this regard, particular account shall be taken of the needs of developing countries.

## Article 24

1. States Parties recognize the right of the child to the enjoyment of the highest attainable standard of health and to facilities for the treatment of illness and rehabilitation of health. States Parties shall strive to ensure that no child is deprived of his or her right of access to such health care services. forth in the present Convention and in other international human rights or humanitarian instruments to which the said States are Parties.

2. For this purpose, States Parties shall provide, as they consider appropriate, co-operation in any efforts by the United Nations and other competent intergovernmental organizations or non-governmental organizations co- operating with the United Nations to protect and assist such a child and to trace the parents or other members of the family of any refugee child in order to obtain information necessary for reunification with his or her family. In cases where no parents or other members of the family can be found, the child shall be accorded the same protection as any other child permanently or temporarily deprived of his or her family environment for any reason, as set forth in the present Convention.

2. States Parties shall pursue full implementation of this right and, in particular, shall take appropriate measures:

(a) To diminish infant and child mortality;

(b) To ensure the provision of necessary medical assistance and health care to all children with emphasis on the development of primary health care;

(c) To combat disease and malnutrition, including within the framework of primary health care, through, inter alia, the application of readily available technology and through the provision of adequate nutritious foods and clean drinking-water, taking into consideration the dangers and risks of environmental pollution;

(d) To ensure appropriate pre-natal and post-natal health care for mothers;

(e) To ensure that all segments of society, in particular parents and children, are informed, have access to education and are supported in the use of basic knowledge of child health and nutrition, the advantages of breast- feeding, hygiene and environmental sanitation and the prevention of accidents;

(f) To develop preventive health care, guidance for parents and family planning education and services.

3. States Parties shall take all effective and appropriate measures with a view to abolishing traditional practices prejudicial to the health of children.

4. States Parties undertake to promote and encourage international co-operation with a view to achieving progressively the full realization of the right recognized in the present article. In this regard, particular account shall be taken of the needs of developing countries.

## Article 25

States Parties recognize the right of a child who has been placed by the competent authorities for the purposes of care, protection or treatment of his or her physical or mental health, to a periodic review of the treatment provided to the child and all other circumstances relevant to his or her placement.

## Article 26

1. States Parties shall recognize for every child the right to benefit from social security, including social insurance, and shall take the necessary measures to achieve the full realization of this right in accordance with their national law.

2. The benefits should, where appropriate, be granted, taking into account the resources and the circumstances of the child and persons having responsibility for the maintenance of the child, as well as any other consideration relevant to an application for benefits made by or on behalf of the child.

## Article 27

1. States Parties recognize the right of every child to a standard of living adequate for the child's physical, mental, spiritual, moral and social development.

2. The parent(s) or others responsible for the child have the primary responsibility to secure, within their abilities and financial capacities, the conditions of living necessary for the child's development.

3. States Parties, in accordance with national conditions and within their means, shall take appropriate measures to assist parents and others responsible for the child to implement this right and shall in case of need provide material assistance and support programmes, particularly with regard to nutrition, clothing and housing.

4. States Parties shall take all appropriate measures to secure the recovery of maintenance for the child from the parents or other persons having financial responsibility for the child, both within the State Party and from abroad. In particular, where the person having financial responsibility for the child lives in a State different from that of the child, States Parties shall promote the accession to international agreements or the conclusion of such agreements, as well as the making of other appropriate arrangements.

## Article 28

1. States Parties recognize the right of the child to education, and with a view to achieving this right progressively and on the basis of equal opportunity, they shall, in particular:

(a) Make primary education compulsory and available free to all;

(b) Encourage the development of different forms of secondary education, including general and vocational education, make them available and accessible to every child, and take appropriate measures such as the introduction of free education and offering financial assistance in case of need;

(c) Make higher education accessible to all on the basis of capacity by every appropriate means;

(d) Make educational and vocational information and guidance available and accessible to all children;

(e) Take measures to encourage regular attendance at schools and the reduction of drop-out rates.

2. States Parties shall take all appropriate measures to ensure that school discipline is administered in a manner consistent with the child's human dignity and in conformity with the present Convention.

3. States Parties shall promote and encourage international co-operation in matters relating to education, in particular with a view to contributing to the elimination of ignorance and illiteracy throughout the world and facilitating access to scientific and technical knowledge and modern teaching methods. In this regard, particular account shall be taken of the needs of developing countries.

## Article 29

1. States Parties agree that the education of the child shall be directed to:

(a) The development of the child's personality, talents and mental and physical abilities to their fullest potential;

(b) The development of respect for human rights and fundamental freedoms, and for the principles enshrined in the Charter of the United Nations;

(c) The development of respect for the child's parents, his or her own cultural identity, language and values, for the national values of the country in which the child is living, the country from which he or she may originate, and for civilizations different from his or her own;

(d) The preparation of the child for responsible life in a free society, in the spirit of understanding, peace, tolerance, equality of sexes, and friendship among all peoples, ethnic, national and religious groups and persons of indigenous origin;

(e) The development of respect for the natural environment.

2. No part of the present article or article 28 shall be construed so as to

interfere with the liberty of individuals and bodies to establish and direct educational institutions, subject always to the observance of the principles set forth in paragraph 1 of the present article and to the requirements that the education given in such institutions shall conform to such minimum standards as may be laid down by the State.

## Article 30

In those States in which ethnic, religious or linguistic minorities or persons of indigenous origin exist, a child belonging to such a minority or who is indigenous shall not be denied the right, in community with other members of his or her group, to enjoy his or her own culture, to profess and practise his or her own religion, or to use his or her own language.

## Article 31

1. States Parties recognize the right of the child to rest and leisure, to engage in play and recreational activities appropriate to the age of the child and to participate freely in cultural life and the arts.

2. States Parties shall respect and promote the right of the child to participate fully in cultural and artistic life and shall encourage the provision of appropriate and equal opportunities for cultural, artistic, recreational and leisure activity.

## Article 32

1. States Parties recognize the right of the child to be protected from economic exploitation and from performing any work that is likely to be hazardous or to interfere with the child's education, or to be harmful to the child's health or physical, mental, spiritual, moral or social development.

2. States Parties shall take legislative, administrative, social and educational measures to ensure the implementation of the present article. To this end, and having regard to the relevant provisions of other international instruments, States Parties shall in particular:

(a) Provide for a minimum age or minimum ages for admission to employment;

(b) Provide for appropriate regulation of the hours and conditions of employment;

(c) Provide for appropriate penalties or other sanctions to ensure the effective enforcement of the present article.

## Article 33

States Parties shall take all appropriate measures, including legislative, administrative, social and educational measures, to protect children from the illicit use of narcotic drugs and psychotropic substances as defined in the relevant international treaties, and to prevent the use of children in the illicit production and trafficking of such substances.

## Article 34

States Parties undertake to protect the child from all forms of sexual exploitation and sexual abuse. For these purposes, States Parties shall in particular take all appropriate national, bilateral and multilateral measures to prevent:

(a) The inducement or coercion of a child to engage in any unlawful sexual activity;

(b) The exploitative use of children in prostitution or other unlawful sexual practices;

(c) The exploitative use of children in pornographic performances and materials.

## Article 35

States Parties shall take all appropriate national, bilateral and multilateral measures to prevent the abduction of, the sale of or traffic in children for any purpose or in any form.

## Article 36

States Parties shall protect the child against all other forms of exploitation prejudicial to any aspects of the child's welfare.

## Article 37

States Parties shall ensure that:

(a) No child shall be subjected to torture or other cruel, inhuman or degrading treatment or punishment. Neither capital punishment nor life imprisonment without possibility of release shall be imposed for offences committed by persons below eighteen years of age;

(b) No child shall be deprived of his or her liberty unlawfully or arbitrarily. The arrest, detention or imprisonment of a child shall be in conformity with the law and shall be used only as a measure of last resort and for the shortest appropriate period of time;

(c) Every child deprived of liberty shall be treated with humanity and respect for the inherent dignity of the human person, and in a manner which takes into account the needs of persons of his or her age. In particular, every child deprived of liberty shall be separated from adults unless it is considered in the child's best interest not to do so and shall have the right to maintain contact with his or her family through correspondence and visits, save in exceptional circumstances;

(d) Every child deprived of his or her liberty shall have the right to prompt access to legal and other appropriate assistance, as well as the right to challenge the legality of the deprivation of his or her liberty before a court or other competent, independent and impartial authority, and to a prompt decision on any such action.

## Article 38

1. States Parties undertake to respect and to ensure respect for rules of international humanitarian law applicable to them in armed conflicts which are relevant to the child.

2. States Parties shall take all feasible measures to ensure that persons who have not attained the age of fifteen years do not take a direct part in hostilities.

3. States Parties shall refrain from recruiting any person who has not attained the age of fifteen years into their armed forces. In recruiting among those persons who have attained the age of fifteen years but who have not attained the age of eighteen years, States Parties shall endeavour to give priority to those who are oldest.

4. In accordance with their obligations under international humanitarian law to protect the civilian population in armed conflicts, States Parties shall take all feasible measures to ensure protection and care of children who are affected by an armed conflict.

## Article 39

States Parties shall take all appropriate measures to promote physical and psychological recovery and social reintegration of a child victim of: any form of neglect, exploitation, or abuse; torture or any other form of cruel, inhuman or degrading treatment or punishment; or armed conflicts. Such recovery and reintegration shall take place in an environment which fosters the health, self-respect and dignity of the child.

## Article 40

1. States Parties recognize the right of every child alleged as, accused of, or recognized as having infringed the penal law to be treated in a manner consistent with the promotion of the child's sense of dignity and worth, which reinforces the child's respect for the human rights and fundamental freedoms of others and which takes into account the child's age and the desirability of promoting the child's reintegration and the child's assuming a constructive role in society.

2. To this end, and having regard to the relevant provisions of international instruments, States Parties shall, in particular, ensure that:

(a) No child shall be alleged as, be accused of, or recognized as having infringed the penal law by reason of acts or omissions that were not prohibited by national or international law at the time they were committed;

(b) Every child alleged as or accused of having infringed the penal law has at least the following guarantees: (i) To be presumed innocent until proven guilty according to law; (ii) To be informed promptly and directly of the charges against him or her, and, if appropriate, through his or her parents or legal guardians, and to have legal or other appropriate assistance in the preparation and presentation of his or her defence; (iii) To have the matter determined without delay by a competent, independent and impartial authority or judicial body in a fair hearing according to law, in the presence of legal or other appropriate assistance and, unless it is considered not to be in the best interest of the child, in particular, taking into account his or her age or situation, his or her parents or legal guardians; (iv) Not to be compelled to give testimony or to confess guilt; to examine or have examined adverse witnesses and to obtain the participation and examination of witnesses on his or her behalf under conditions of equality; (v) If considered to have infringed the penal law, to have this decision and any measures imposed in consequence thereof reviewed by a higher competent, independent and impartial authority or judicial body according to law; (vi) To have the free assistance of an interpreter if the child cannot understand or speak the language used; (vii) To have his or her privacy fully respected at all stages of the proceedings.

3. States Parties shall seek to promote the establishment of laws, procedures, authorities and institutions specifically applicable to children alleged as, accused of, or recognized as having infringed the penal law, and, in particular:

(a) The establishment of a minimum age below which children shall be presumed not to have the capacity to infringe the penal law;

(b) Whenever appropriate and desirable, measures for dealing with such children without resorting to judicial proceedings, providing that human rights and legal safeguards are fully respected.

4. A variety of dispositions, such as care, guidance and supervision orders;

counselling; probation; foster care; education and vocational training programmes and other alternatives to institutional care shall be available to ensure that children are dealt with in a manner appropriate to their well-being and proportionate both to their circumstances and the offence.

## Article 41

Nothing in the present Convention shall affect any provisions which are more conducive to the realization of the rights of the child and which may be contained in:

(a) The law of a State Party; or

(b) International law in force for that State.

## PART II
## Article 42

States Parties undertake to make the principles and provisions of the Convention widely known, by appropriate and active means, to adults and children alike.

## Article 43

1. For the purpose of examining the progress made by States Parties in achieving the realization of the obligations undertaken in the present Convention, there shall be established a Committee on the Rights of the Child, which shall carry out the functions hereinafter provided.

2. The Committee shall consist of ten experts of high moral standing and recognized competence in the field covered by this Convention. The members of the Committee shall be elected by States Parties from among their nationals and shall serve in their personal capacity, consideration being given to equitable geographical distribution, as well as to the principal legal systems.

3. The members of the Committee shall be elected by secret ballot from a list of persons nominated by States Parties. Each State Party may nominate one person from among its own nationals.

4. The initial election to the Committee shall be held no later than six months after the date of the entry into force of the present Convention and thereafter every second year. At least four months before the date of each election, the Secretary-General of the United Nations shall address a letter to States Parties inviting them to submit their nominations within two months. The Secretary-General shall subsequently prepare a list in alphabetical order of all persons thus nominated, indicating States Parties which have nominated them, and

shall submit it to the States Parties to the present Convention.

5. The elections shall be held at meetings of States Parties convened by the Secretary-General at United Nations Headquarters. At those meetings, for which two thirds of States Parties shall constitute a quorum, the persons elected to the Committee shall be those who obtain the largest number of votes and an absolute majority of the votes of the representatives of States Parties present and voting.

6. The members of the Committee shall be elected for a term of four years. They shall be eligible for re-election if renominated. The term of five of the members elected at the first election shall expire at the end of two years; immediately after the first election, the names of these five members shall be chosen by lot by the Chairman of the meeting.

7. If a member of the Committee dies or resigns or declares that for any other cause he or she can no longer perform the duties of the Committee, the State Party which nominated the member shall appoint another expert from among its nationals to serve for the remainder of the term, subject to the approval of the Committee.

8. The Committee shall establish its own rules of procedure.

9. The Committee shall elect its officers for a period of two years.

10. The meetings of the Committee shall normally be held at United Nations Headquarters or at any other convenient place as determined by the Committee. The Committee shall normally meet annually. The duration of the meetings of the Committee shall be determined, and reviewed, it necessary, by a meeting of the States Parties to the present Convention, subject to the approval of the General Assembly.

11. The Secretary-General of the United Nations shall provide the necessary staff and facilities for the effective performance of the functions of the Committee under the present Convention.

12. With the approval of the General Assembly, the members of the Committee established under the present Convention shall receive emoluments from United Nations resources on such terms and conditions as the Assembly may decide.

## Article 44

1. States Parties undertake to submit to the Committee, through the Secretary-General of the United Nations, reports on the measures they have adopted which give effect to the rights recognized herein and on the progress made on the enjoyment of those rights:

(a) Within two years of the entry into force of the Convention for the State Party concerned;

(b) Thereafter every five years.

2. Reports made under the present article shall indicate factors and difficulties, if any, affecting the degree of fulfilment of the obligations under the present Convention. Reports shall also contain sufficient information to provide the Committee with a comprehensive understanding of the implementation of the Convention in the country concerned.

3. A State Party which has submitted a comprehensive initial report to the Committee need not, in its subsequent reports submitted in accordance with paragraph 1 (b) of the present article, repeat basic information previously provided.

4. The Committee may request from States Parties further information relevant to the implementation of the Convention.

5. The Committee shall submit to the General Assembly, through the Economic and Social Council, every two years, reports on its activities.

6. States Parties shall make their reports widely available to the public in their own countries.

## Article 45

In order to foster the effective implementation of the Convention and to encourage international co-operation in the field covered by the Convention:

(a) The specialized agencies, the United Nations Children's Fund, and other United Nations organs shall be entitled to be represented at the consideration of the implementation of such provisions of the present Convention as fall within the scope of their mandate. The Committee may invite the specialized agencies, the United Nations Children's Fund and other competent bodies as it may consider appropriate to provide expert advice on the implementation of the Convention in areas falling within the scope of their respective mandates. The Committee may invite the specialized agencies, the United Nations Children's Fund, and other United Nations organs to submit reports on the implementation of the Convention in areas falling within the scope of their activities;

(b) The Committee shall transmit, as it may consider appropriate, to the specialized agencies, the United Nations Children's Fund and other competent bodies, any reports from States Parties that contain a request, or indicate a need, for technical advice or assistance, along with the Committee's observations and suggestions, if any, on these requests or indications;

(c) The Committee may recommend to the General Assembly to request the Secretary-General to undertake on its behalf studies on specific issues relating to the rights of the child;

(d) The Committee may make suggestions and general recommendations based on information received pursuant to articles 44 and 45 of the present Convention. Such suggestions and general recommendations shall be transmitted to any State Party concerned and reported to the General Assembly, together with comments, if any, from States Parties.

PART III
Article 46

The present Convention shall be open for signature by all States.

Article 47

The present Convention is subject to ratification. Instruments of ratification shall be deposited with the Secretary-General of the United Nations.

Article 48

The present Convention shall remain open for accession by any State. The instruments of accession shall be deposited with the Secretary-General of the United Nations.

Article 49

1. The present Convention shall enter into force on the thirtieth day following the date of deposit with the Secretary-General of the United Nations of the twentieth instrument of ratification or accession.

2. For each State ratifying or acceding to the Convention after the deposit of the twentieth instrument of ratification or accession, the Convention shall enter into force on the thirtieth day after the deposit by such State of its instrument of ratification or accession.

Article 50

1. Any State Party may propose an amendment and file it with the Secretary-General of the United Nations. The Secretary-General shall thereupon communicate the proposed amendment to States Parties, with a request that they indicate whether they favour a conference of States Parties for the purpose of considering and voting upon the proposals. In the event that, within four months from the date of such communication, at least one third of the States Parties favour such a conference, the Secretary-General shall convene the conference under the auspices of the United Nations. Any amendment adopted by a majority of States Parties present and voting at the conference shall be submitted to the General Assembly for approval.

2. An amendment adopted in accordance with paragraph 1 of the present article shall enter into force when it has been approved by the General Assembly of the United Nations and accepted by a two-thirds majority of States Parties.

3. When an amendment enters into force, it shall be binding on those States Parties which have accepted it, other States Parties still being bound by the provisions of the present Convention and any earlier amendments which they have accepted.

## Article 51

1. The Secretary-General of the United Nations shall receive and circulate to all States the text of reservations made by States at the time of ratification or accession.

2. A reservation incompatible with the object and purpose of the present Convention shall not be permitted.

3. Reservations may be withdrawn at any time by notification to that effect addressed to the Secretary-General of the United Nations, who shall then inform all States. Such notification shall take effect on the date on which it is received by the Secretary-General.

## Article 52

A State Party may denounce the present Convention by written notification to the Secretary-General of the United Nations. Denunciation becomes effective one year after the date of receipt of the notification by the Secretary-General.

## Article 53

The Secretary-General of the United Nations is designated as the depositary of the present Convention.

## Article 54

The original of the present Convention, of which the Arabic, Chinese, English, French, Russian and Spanish texts are equally authentic, shall be deposited with the Secretary-General of the United Nations.

In witness thereof the undersigned plenipotentiaries, being duly authorized thereto by their respective Governments, have signed the present Convention.

## IV. STATE LAWS

## A. Abuse, neglect and children in need of services

## INDIANA CODE, TITLE 31
## CHILDREN IN NEED OF SERVICES

### 31-6-4-3 Child in need of services

Sec. 3. (a) A child is a child in need of services if before the child's eighteenth birthday:

(1) the child's physical or mental condition is seriously impaired or seriously endangered as a result of the inability, refusal, or neglect of the child's parent, guardian, or custodian to supply the child with necessary food, clothing, shelter, medical care, education, or supervision;

(2) the child's physical or mental health is seriously endangered due to injury by the act or omission of the child's parent, guardian, or custodian;

(3) the child is the victim of a sex offense under IC 35-42-4-1, IC 35-42-4-2, IC 35-42-4-3, IC 35-42-4-4, IC 35-42-4-7, IC 35-45-4-1, IC 35-45-4-2, or IC 35-46-1-3;

(4) the child's parent, guardian, or custodian allows the child to participate in an obscene performance (as defined by IC 35-49-2-2 or IC 35-49-3-2);

(5) the child's parent, guardian, or custodian allows the child to commit a sex offense prohibited by IC 35-45-4;

(6) the child substantially endangers the child's own health or the health of another;

(7) the child's parent, guardian, or custodian fails to participate in a disciplinary proceeding in connection with the student's improper behavior, as provided for by IC 20-8.1-5-7, where the behavior of the student has been repeatedly disruptive in the school; or

(8) the child is a missing child (as defined in IC 10-1-7-2);
and needs care, treatment, or rehabilitation that the child is not receiving, and that is unlikely to be provided or accepted without the coercive intervention of the court.

(b) An omission under subdivision (a)(2) is an occurrence in which the parent, guardian, or custodian allowed that person's child to receive any injury that the parent, guardian, or custodian had a reasonable opportunity to prevent or mitigate.

(c) A custodian under subsection (a) includes any person responsible for the child's welfare who is employed by a public or private residential school or foster care facility.

(d) When a parent, guardian, or custodian fails to provide specific medical treatment for a child because of the legitimate and genuine practice of the parent's, guardian's, or custodian's religious beliefs, a rebuttable presumption arises that the child is not a child in need of services because of such failure. However, this presumption does not prevent a juvenile court from ordering, when the health of a child requires, medical services from a physician licensed to practice medicine in Indiana. This presumption does not apply to situations in which the life or health of a child is in serious danger.

(e) Nothing in this chapter limits the right of a person to use reasonable corporal punishment when disciplining a child if the person is the parent, guardian, or custodian of the child. In addition, nothing in this chapter limits the lawful practice or teaching of religious beliefs.

(f) A child in need of services under subsection (a) includes a child with a disability who is deprived of nutrition that is necessary to sustain life, or who is deprived of medical or surgical intervention that is necessary to remedy or ameliorate a life threatening medical condition, if the nutrition or medical or surgical intervention is generally provided to similarly situated children with or without disabilities.

(g) A child with a disability under subsection (f) is an individual under eighteen (18) years of age who has a disability (as defined in IC 22-9-1- 3(q)).

## 31-6-4-3.1 Child in need of services; alcohol, controlled substances, or legend drugs

Sec. 3.1. (a) Except as provided in subsections (b) and (c), a child is a child in need of services if:

(1) the child is born with:

(A) fetal alcohol syndrome; or

(B) any amount, including a trace amount, of a controlled substance or a legend drug in the child's body; or

(2) the child:

(A) has an injury;

(B) has abnormal physical or psychological development; or

(C) is at a substantial risk of a life threatening condition;

that arises or is substantially aggravated because the child's mother used alcohol, a controlled substance, or a legend drug during pregnancy;

and needs care, treatment, or rehabilitation that the child is not receiving, or that is unlikely to be provided or accepted without the coercive intervention of the court.

(b) A child is not a child in need of services under subsection (a) if:

(1) a drug detected in the body of the child under subsection (a)(1) or the condition described in subsection (a)(2) was caused by a legend drug; and

(2) during pregnancy the child's mother:

(A) possessed a valid prescription for the legend drug;

(B) was not in violation of IC 16-42-19 (the Indiana legend drug act); and

(C) made a good faith attempt to use the legend drug according to the prescription instructions.

(c) A child is not a child in need of services under subsection (a) if:

(1) a drug detected in the body of the child under subsection (a)(1) or the condition described in subsection (a)(2) was caused by a controlled substance; and

(2) during pregnancy the child's mother:

(A) possessed a valid prescription for the controlled substance; and

(B) made a good faith attempt to use the controlled substance according to the prescription instructions.

# MICHIGAN COMPILED LAWS ANNOTATED (West 1994)
## CHILD PROTECTION LAW
### (Reporting Abuse and Neglect)

**722.623. Required reports of child abuse or neglect; disposition**

Sec. 3. (1) A physician, coroner, dentist, registered dental hygienist, medical examiner, nurse, a person licensed to provide emergency medical care, audiologist, psychologist, marriage and family therapist, licensed professional counselor, certified social worker, social worker, social work technician, school administrator, school counselor or teacher, law enforcement officer, or regulated child care provider who has reasonable cause to suspect child abuse or neglect shall make immediately, by telephone or otherwise, an oral report, or cause an oral report to be made, of the suspected child abuse or neglect to the department. Within 72 hours after making the oral report, the reporting person shall file a written report as required in this act. If the reporting person is a member of the staff of a hospital, agency, or school, the reporting person shall notify the person in charge of the hospital, agency, or school of his or her finding and that the report has been made, and shall make a copy of the written report available to the person in charge. One report from a hospital, agency, or school shall be considered adequate to meet the reporting requirement. A member of the staff of a hospital, agency, or school shall not be dismissed or otherwise penalized for making a report required by this act or for cooperating in an investigation.

(2) The written report shall contain the name of the child and a description of the abuse or neglect. If possible, the report shall contain the names and addresses of the child's parents, the child's guardian, the persons with whom the child resides, and the child's age. The report shall contain other information available to the reporting person which might establish the cause of the abuse or neglect, and the manner in which the abuse or neglect occurred.

(3) The department shall inform the reporting person of the required contents of the written report at the time the oral report is made by the reporting person.

(4) The written report required in this section shall be mailed or otherwise transmitted to the county department of social services of the county in which the child suspected of being abused or neglected is found.

(5) Upon receipt of a written report of suspected child abuse or neglect, the department may provide copies to the prosecuting attorney and the probate court of the counties in which the child suspected of being abused or neglected resides and is found.

(6) If the report or subsequent investigation indicates a violation of sections 136b and 145c or sections 520b to 520g of the Michigan penal code

[Mich. Comp. Laws §§ 750.136b, 750.145c and 750.520b to 750.520g], or if the report or subsequent investigation indicates that the suspected abuse was not committed by a person responsible for the child's health or welfare, and the department believes that the report has basis in fact, the department shall transmit a copy of the written report and the results of any investigation to the prosecuting attorney of the counties in which the child resides and is found.

(7) If a local law enforcement agency receives a written report of suspected child abuse or neglect, whether from the reporting person or the department, the report or subsequent investigation indicates that the abuse or neglect was committed by a person responsible for the child's health or welfare, and the local law enforcement agency believes that the report has basis in fact, the local law enforcement agency shall provide a copy of the written report and the results of any investigation to the county department of social services of the county in which the abused or neglected child is found. Nothing in this subsection or subsection (6) shall be construed to relieve the department of its responsibility to investigate reports of suspected child abuse or neglect under this act.

(8) For purposes of this act, the pregnancy of a child less than 12 years of age or the presence of a venereal disease in a child who is over 1 month of age but less than 12 years of age shall be reasonable cause to suspect child abuse and neglect have occurred.

## 722.624. Reports by those not required to report

Sec. 4. In addition to those persons required to report child abuse or neglect under section 3 [Section 722.623], any person, including a child, who has reasonable cause to suspect child abuse or neglect may report the matter to the department or a law enforcement agency.

## 722.625. Reporting persons, identity, immunity from liability, good faith

Sec. 5. Except for records available in section 7(1)(a) and (b) [Section 722.627(1)(a) and (b)], the identity of a reporting person shall be confidential subject to disclosure only with the consent of that person or by judicial process. A person acting in good faith who makes a report, cooperates in an investigation, or assists in any other requirement of this act is immune from civil or criminal liability that might otherwise be incurred by that action. A person making a report or assisting in any other requirement of this act is presumed to have acted in good faith. This immunity from civil or criminal liability extends only to acts done pursuant to this act and does not extend to a negligent act that causes personal injury or death or to the malpractice of a physician which results in personal injury or death.

**722.626. Detention, examination, and medical evaluation of child**

Sec. 6. (1) If a child suspected of being abused or neglected is admitted to a hospital or brought to a hospital for outpatient services and the attending physician determines that the release of the child would endanger the child's health or welfare, the attending physician shall notify the person in charge and the department. The person in charge may detain the child in temporary protective custody until the next regular business day of the probate court, at which time the probate court shall order the child detained in the hospital or in some other suitable place pending a preliminary hearing as required by . . . section 712A.14 of the Michigan Compiled Laws, or order the child released to the child's parent, guardian, or custodian.

(2) When a child suspected of being an abused or neglected child is seen by a physician, the physician shall make the necessary examinations, which may include physical examinations, x-rays, photographs, laboratory studies, and other pertinent studies. The physician's written report to the department shall contain summaries of the evaluation, including medical test results.

(3) If a report is made by a person other than a physician, or if the physician's report is not complete, the department may request a court order for a medical evaluation of the child. The department shall have a medical evaluation made without a court order if the child's health is seriously endangered and a court order cannot be obtained.

**722.627. Central registry system; documents and photographs, confidentiality; reports, amending or expunging**

Sec. 7. (1) The department shall maintain a central registry to carry out the intent of this act. A written report, document, or photograph filed with the department pursuant to this act is a confidential record available only to 1 or more of the following:

(a) A legally mandated public or private child protective agency investigating a report of known or suspected child abuse or neglect.

(b) A police or other law enforcement agency investigating a report of known or suspected child abuse or neglect.

(c) A physician who is treating a child whom the physician reasonably suspects may be abused or neglected.

(d) A person legally authorized to place a child in protective custody when the person is confronted with a child whom the person reasonably suspects may be abused or neglected and the confidential record is necessary to determine whether to place the child in protective custody.

(e) A person, agency, or organization, including a multidisciplinary case consultation team, authorized to diagnose, care for, treat, or supervise a child or family who is the subject of a report or record under this act, or who is responsible for the child's health or welfare.

(f) A person named in the report or record, if the identity of the reporting person is protected pursuant to section 5 [Section 722.625].

(g) A court that determines the information is necessary to decide an issue before the court.

(h) A grand jury that determines the information is necessary in the conduct of the grand jury's official business.

(i) A person, agency, or organization engaged in a bona fide research or evaluation project, except information identifying a person named in the report or record shall not be made available unless the department has obtained that person's written consent. The person, agency, or organization shall not conduct a personal interview with a family without the family's prior consent and shall not disclose information that would identify the child or the child's family or other identifying information.

(j) A person appointed as legal counsel pursuant to section 10 [Section 722.630].

(k) A child placing agency licensed under Act No. 116 of the Public Acts of 1973, being sections 722.111 to 722.128 of the Michigan Compiled Laws, for the purpose of investigating an applicant for adoption, a foster care applicant or licensee or an employee of a foster care applicant or licensee, an adult member of an applicant's or licensee's household, or other persons in a foster care or adoptive home who are directly responsible for the care and welfare of children, to determine suitability of a home for adoption or foster care. The child placing agency shall disclose the information to a foster care applicant or licensee under Act No. 116 of the Public Acts of 1973, or to an applicant for adoption.

(l) Juvenile court staff authorized by the court to investigate foster care applicants and licensees, employees of foster care applicants and licensees, adult members of the applicant's or licensee's household, and other persons in the home who are directly responsible for the care and welfare of children, for the purpose of determining the suitability of the home for foster care. The court shall disclose this information to the applicant or licensee.

(m) Subject to section 7a [Section 722.627a], a standing or select committee or appropriations subcommittee of either house of the legislature having jurisdiction over protective services matters for children.

(n)      The children's ombudsman appointed under the children's ombudsman act [Mich. Comp. Laws §§ 722.921 to 722.935].

(2) A person or entity to whom a report, document, or photograph is made available shall make the report, document, or photograph available only to a person or entity described in subsection (1). This subsection shall not be construed to require a court proceeding to be closed that otherwise would be open to the public

(3)  If a report of suspected child abuse or neglect is substantiated, the department shall maintain a record in the central registry and, within 30 days after the substantiation, shall notify in writing each individual who is named in the record as a perpetrator of the child abuse or neglect.  The notice shall set forth the individual's right to request expunction of the record and the right to a hearing if the department refuses the request.  The notice shall not identify the person reporting the suspected child abuse or neglect.

(4) A person who is the subject of a report or record made pursuant to this act may request the department to amend an inaccurate report or record from the central registry and local office file.  A person who is the subject of a report or record made pursuant to this act may request the department to expunge from the central registry a report or record in which no relevant and accurate evidence of abuse or neglect is found to exist.  A report or record filed in a local office file shall not be subject to expunction except as the department shall authorize, when considered in the best interest of the child.

(5)  If the department refuses a request for amendment or expunction, or fails to act within 30 days after receiving the request, the person shall be granted a hearing to determine by a preponderance of the evidence whether the report or record in whole or in part should be amended or expunged from the central registry on the grounds that the report or record is not relevant or accurate evidence of abuse or neglect.  The hearing shall be before a hearing officer appointed by the department and shall be conducted pursuant to the administrative procedures act [Mich.  Comp.  Laws §§ 24.201 to 24.328].

(6)  If the investigation of a report conducted pursuant to this act fails to disclose evidence of abuse or neglect, the information identifying the subject of the report shall be expunged from the central registry.  If evidence of abuse or neglect exists, the information identifying the subject of the report shall be expunged when the child alleged to be abused or neglected reaches the age of 18, or 10 years after the report is received by the department, whichever occurs later.

(7)  In releasing information under this act, the department shall not include a report compiled by a police agency or other law enforcement agency related to an investigation of suspected child abuse or neglect.  This subsection does not prevent the department from including reports of convictions of crimes related to child abuse and neglect.

### 722.627a. Availability of information to select committee;  confidentiality

Sec. 7a. (1) The department shall make information contained in the central registry and reports and records made pursuant to this act available to a standing or select committee or appropriations subcommittee of either house of the legislature having jurisdiction over protective services matters for children subject to all of the following:

(a) The department shall not provide confidential information protected by section 7 [Section 722.627] to the committee unless the committee members appointed and serving agree by roll call vote that the information is essential for the protection of Michigan children or for legislative oversight of the protective services program and that the confidential information will only be considered at a closed session of the committee. The affirmative vote required by this subdivision shall be by not less than the super majority required by section 7 of the open meetings act [§ 15.267 of the Michigan Compiled Laws], and may serve as the vote required under that section for holding a closed session.

(b) In addition to compliance with [§§ 15.261 to 15.275 of the Michigan Compiled Laws], a closed session held under this section shall comply with all of the following:

(i) Tape recording, camera, or other electronic equipment for documenting the proceedings shall not be permitted in the closed session.

(ii) Attendance at the closed session shall be limited to committee members, other members of the legislature and legislative staff at the discretion of the chairperson, and staff members from the department designated by the director.

(2) A person who discloses or causes to be disclosed confidential information to which the person has gained access at a meeting held under this section is guilty of a misdemeanor. A person who keeps a confidential record or file, or a copy of a confidential record or file, at the conclusion of a closed session held under this section, which record or file is obtained at that meeting, is guilty of a misdemeanor.

## 722.628. Investigations

Sec. 8. (1) Within 24 hours after receiving a report made pursuant to this act, the department shall refer the report to the prosecuting attorney if the report meets the requirements of section 3(6) [Section 722.623(6)] or shall commence an investigation of the child suspected of being abused or neglected. Within 24 hours after receiving a report whether from the reporting person or from the department under section 3(6), the local law enforcement agency shall refer the report to the department if the report meets the requirements of section 3(7) [Section 722.623(7)] or shall commence an investigation of the child suspected of being abused or neglected. If the child suspected of being abused is not in the physical custody of the parent or legal guardian and informing the parent or legal guardian would not endanger the child's health or welfare, the agency or the department shall inform the child's parent or legal guardian of the investigation as soon as the agency or the department discovers the identity of the child's parent or legal guardian.

(2) In the course of its investigation, the department shall determine if the

child is abused or neglected. The department shall cooperate with law enforcement officials, courts of competent jurisdiction, and appropriate state agencies providing human services in relation to preventing, identifying, and treating child abuse and neglect; shall provide, enlist, and coordinate the necessary services, directly or through the purchase of services from other agencies and professions; and shall take necessary action to prevent further abuses, to safeguard and enhance the welfare of the child, and to preserve family life where possible.

(3) In conducting its investigation, the department shall seek the assistance of and cooperate with law enforcement officials within 24 hours after becoming aware that 1 or more of the following conditions exists:

(a) Abuse or neglect is the suspected cause of a child's death.

(b) The child is the victim of suspected sexual abuse or sexual exploitation.

(c) Abuse or neglect resulting in severe physical injury to the child requires medical treatment or hospitalization. For purposes of this subdivision, "severe physical injury" means brain damage, skull or bone fracture, subdural hemorrhage or hematoma, dislocation, sprains, internal injuries, poisoning, burns, scalds, severe cuts, or any other physical injury that seriously impairs the health or physical well-being of a child.

(d) Law enforcement intervention is necessary for the protection of the child, a department employee, or another person involved in the investigation.

(e) The alleged perpetrator of the child's injury is not a person responsible for the child's health or welfare.

(4) Law enforcement officials shall cooperate with the department in conducting investigations pursuant to subsections (1) and (3) and shall comply with sections 5 and 7 [Sections 722.625 and 722.627].

(5) Involvement of law enforcement officials pursuant to this section shall not relieve or prevent the department from proceeding with its investigation or treatment if there is reasonable cause to suspect that the child abuse or neglect was committed by a person responsible for the child's health or welfare.

(6) In each county, the prosecuting attorney and the department shall develop and establish procedures for involving law enforcement officials as provided in this section.

(7) If there is reasonable cause to suspect that a child in the care of or under the control of a public or private agency, institution, or facility is an abused or neglected child, the agency, institution, or facility shall be investigated by an agency administratively independent of the agency, institution, or facility being investigated. If the investigation produces evidence of a violation of section 145c or sections 520b to 520g [§§ 750.145c and 750.520b to 750.520g of the Michigan Compiled Laws], the investigating agency shall transmit a copy of the results of the investigation to the prosecuting attorney of the county in which the agency,

institution, or facility is located. The prosecuting attorney may proceed under [sections 750.135 to 750.145c and 750.520b to 750.520g of the Michigan Compiled Laws] when a violation of these sections has occurred.

(8) Schools and other institutions shall cooperate with the department during an investigation of a report of child abuse or neglect. Cooperation includes allowing access to the child without parental consent if access is necessary to complete the investigation or to prevent abuse or neglect of the child. However, the person responsible for the child's health or welfare shall be notified of the department's contact with the child at the time or as soon afterward as the person can be reached and no child shall be subjected to a search at a school which requires the child to remove his or her clothing to expose his buttocks or genitalia or her breasts, buttocks or genitalia unless the department has obtained an order from a court of competent jurisdiction permitting such a search. If the access occurs within a hospital, the investigation shall be conducted so as not to interfere with the medical treatment of the child or other patients.

(9) Upon completion of the investigation by the local law enforcement agency or the department, the law enforcement agency or department may inform the person who made the report as to the disposition of the report.

## 722.629. Professional services; continuing education; information for general public

Sec. 9. (1) The department, in discharging its responsibilities under this act, shall provide, directly or through the purchase of services from other agencies and professions, multidisciplinary services such as those of a pediatrician, psychologist, psychiatrist, public health nurse, social worker, or attorney through the establishment of regionally based or strategically located teams. The department shall prepare a biennial report to the legislature containing information on the activities of the teams created pursuant to this subsection and including recommendations by the teams and the department regarding child abuse and neglect when committed by persons responsible for the child's health or welfare.

(2) The department shall assure a continuing education program for department, probate court, and private agency personnel. The program shall include responsibilities, obligations, and powers under this act and the diagnosis and treatment of child abuse and neglect when committed by persons responsible for the child's health or welfare.

(3) The department shall provide for the dissemination of information to the general public with respect to the problem of child abuse and neglect in this state and the facilities, prevention, and treatment methods available to combat child abuse and neglect when committed by persons responsible for the child's health or welfare.

**722.631. Attorney-client privilege**

Sec. 11. Any legally recognized privileged communication except that between attorney and client is abrogated and shall neither constitute grounds for excusing a report otherwise required to be made nor for excluding evidence in a civil child protective proceeding resulting from a report made pursuant to this act.

**722.632. Reports to law enforcement officials or probate court**

Sec. 12. This act shall not prohibit a person who has reasonable cause to suspect child abuse or neglect from making a report to the appropriate law enforcement officials or probate court.

**722.633. Failure to report; dissemination of information; failure to expunge record; false report**

Sec. 13. (1) A person who is required by this act to report an instance of suspected child abuse or neglect and who fails to do so is civilly liable for the damages proximately caused by the failure.

(2) A person who is required by this act to report an instance of suspected child abuse or neglect and who knowingly fails to do so is guilty of a misdemeanor.

(3) Except as provided in section 7 [Section 722.627(3)], a person who disseminates, or who permits or encourages the dissemination of, information contained in the central registry and in reports and records made pursuant to this act is guilty of a misdemeanor and is civilly liable for the damages proximately caused by the dissemination.

(4) A person who willfully maintains a report or record required to be expunged under section 7(3) [Section 722.627(3)] is guilty of a misdemeanor.

(5) A person who knowingly and maliciously makes a false report of child abuse or neglect under this act is guilty of a misdemeanor.

## B.  Assisted conception and surrogacy

# CODE OF VIRGINIA, TITLE 20
# STATUS OF CHILDREN OF ASSISTED CONCEPTION

*[ED.—The following statute is based on the Uniform Status of Children of Assisted Conception Act.  However, it is substantially more detailed and contains additional limitations and penalties.]*

### § 20-156  Definitions.

As used in this chapter unless the context requires a different meaning:

"Assisted conception" means a pregnancy resulting from any intervening medical technology, other than the pregnancy of a woman resulting from the insemination of her ovum using her husband's sperm, whether in vivo or in vitro, which completely or partially replaces sexual intercourse as the means of conception.  Such intervening medical technology includes, but is not limited to, conventional medical and surgical treatment as well as noncoital reproductive technology such as artificial insemination by donor, cryopreservation of gametes and embryos, in vitro fertilization, uterine embryo lavage, embryo transfer, gamete intrafallopian tube transfer, and low tubal ovum transfer.

"Compensation" means payment of any valuable consideration for services in excess of reasonable medical and ancillary costs.

"Cryopreservation" means freezing and storing of gametes and embryos for possible future use in assisted conception.

"Donor" means an individual, other than a surrogate, unrelated by marriage to the recipient who contributes the sperm or egg used in assisted conception.

"Gamete" means either a sperm or an ovum.

"Genetic parent" means an individual who contributes a gamete resulting in a conception.

"Gestational mother" means the woman who gives birth to a child, regardless of her genetic relationship to the child.

"Embryo" means the organism resulting from the union of a sperm and an ovum from first cell division until approximately the end of the second month of gestation.

"Embryo transfer" means the placing of a viable embryo into the uterus of a gestational mother.

"Infertile" means the inability to conceive after one year of unprotected sexual intercourse.

"Intended parents" means a man and a woman, married to each other, who enter into an agreement with a surrogate under the terms of which they will be the parents of any child born to the surrogate through assisted conception regardless of the genetic relationships between the intended parents, the surrogate, and the child.

"In vitro" means any process that can be observed in an artificial environment such as a test tube or tissue culture plate.

"In vitro fertilization" means the fertilization of ova by sperm in an artificial environment.

"In vivo" means any process occurring within the living body.

"Ovum" means the female gamete or reproductive cell prior to fertilization.

"Reasonable medical and ancillary costs" means the costs of the performance of assisted conception, the costs of prenatal maternal health care, the costs of maternal and child health care for a reasonable post partum period, the reasonable costs for medications and maternity clothes, and any additional and reasonable costs for housing and other living expenses attributable to the pregnancy.

"Sperm" means the male gametes or reproductive cells which impregnate the ova.

"Surrogacy contract" means an agreement between intended parents, a surrogate, and her husband, if any, in which the surrogate agrees to be impregnated through the use of assisted conception, to carry any resulting fetus, and to relinquish to the intended parents the custody of and parental rights to any resulting child.

"Surrogate" means any adult woman who agrees to bear a child carried for intended parents.

## § 20-157  Virginia law to control.

The provisions of this chapter shall control, without exception, in any action brought in the courts of this Commonwealth to enforce or adjudicate any rights or responsibilities arising under this chapter.

## § 20-158 Parentage of child resulting from assisted conception.

A. Determination of parentage, generally. -- Except as provided in subsections B, C, D, and E of this section, the parentage of any child resulting from the performance of assisted conception shall be determined as follows:

1. The gestational mother of a child is the child's mother.

2. The husband of the gestational mother of a child is the child's father, notwithstanding any declaration of invalidity or annulment of the marriage obtained after the performance of assisted conception, unless he commences an action in which the mother and child are parties within two years after he discovers or, in the exercise of due diligence, reasonably should have discovered the child's birth and in which it is determined that he did not consent to the performance of assisted conception.

3. A donor is not the parent of a child conceived through assisted conception.

B. Death of spouse. -- Any child resulting from the insemination of a wife's ovum using her husband's sperm, with his consent, is the child of the husband and wife notwithstanding that, during the ten-month period immediately preceding the birth, either party died.

However, any person who dies before in utero implantation of an embryo resulting from the union of his sperm or her ovum with another gamete, whether or not the other gamete is that of the person's spouse, is not the parent of any resulting child unless (i) implantation occurs before notice of the death can reasonably be communicated to the physician performing the procedure or (ii) the person consents to be a parent in writing executed before the implantation.

C. Divorce. -- Any child resulting from insemination of a wife's ovum using her husband's sperm, with his consent, is the child of the husband and wife notwithstanding that either party filed for a divorce or annulment during the ten-month period immediately preceding the birth. Any person who is a party to an action for divorce or annulment commenced by filing before in utero implantation of an embryo resulting from the union of his sperm or her ovum with another gamete, whether or not the other gamete is that of the person's spouse, is not the parent of any resulting child unless (i) implantation occurs before notice of the filing can reasonably be communicated to the physician performing the procedure or (ii) the person consents in writing to be a parent, whether the writing was executed before or after the implantation.

D. Birth pursuant to court approved surrogacy contract. -- After approval of a surrogacy contract by the court and entry of an order as provided in subsection D of § 20-160, the intended parents are the parents of any resulting child. However, if the court vacates the order approving the agreement pursuant to subsection B of § 20-161, the surrogate is the mother of the resulting child and her husband is the father. The intended parents may only obtain parental rights through adoption as provided in Chapter 11 (§ 63.1-220 et seq.) of Title 63.1.

E. Birth pursuant to surrogacy contract not approved by court. — In the case of a surrogacy contract that has not been approved by a court as provided in § 20-160, the parentage of any resulting child shall be determined as follows:

1. The gestational mother is the child's mother unless the intended mother is a genetic parent, in which case the intended mother is the mother.

2. If either of the intended parents is a genetic parent of the resulting child, the intended father is the child's father. However, if (i) the surrogate is married, (ii) her husband is a party to the surrogacy contract, and (iii) the surrogate exercises her right to retain custody and parental rights to the resulting child pursuant to § 20-162, then the surrogate and her husband are the parents.

3. If neither of the intended parents is a genetic parent of the resulting child, the surrogate is the mother and her husband is the child's father if he is a party to the contract. The intended parents may only obtain parental rights through adoption as provided in Chapter 11 (§ 63.1-220 et seq.) of Title 63.1.

4. After the signing and filing of the surrogate consent and report form in conformance with the requirements of subsection A of § 20-162, the intended parents are the parents of the child and the surrogate and her husband, if any, shall not be the parents of the child.

### § 20-159 Surrogacy contracts permissible.

A. A surrogate, her husband, if any, and prospective intended parents may enter into a written agreement whereby the surrogate may relinquish all her rights and duties as parent of a child conceived through assisted conception, and the intended parents may become the parents of the child as provided in subsection D or E of § 20-158.

B. Surrogacy contracts shall be approved by the court as provided in § 20-160. However, any surrogacy contract that has not been approved by the court shall be governed by the provisions of §§ 20-156 through 20-159 and §§ 20-162 through 20-165 including the provisions for reformation in conformance with this chapter as provided in § 20-162.

### § 20-160 Petition and hearing for court approval of surrogacy contract; requirements; orders.

A. Prior to the performance of assisted conception, the intended parents, the surrogate, and her husband shall join in a petition to the circuit court of the county or city in which at least one of the parties resides. The surrogacy contract shall be signed by all the parties and acknowledged before an officer or other person authorized by law to take acknowledgments.

A copy of the contract shall be attached to the petition. The court shall appoint a guardian ad litem to represent the interests of any resulting child and shall appoint counsel to represent the surrogate. The court shall order a home study by a local department of social services or welfare or a licensed child-placing agency, to be completed prior to the hearing on the petition.

All hearings and proceedings conducted under this section shall be held in camera, and all court records shall be confidential and subject to inspection only under the standards applicable to adoptions as provided in § 63.1-235. The court conducting the proceedings shall have exclusive and continuing jurisdiction of all matters arising under the surrogacy contract until all provisions of the contract are fulfilled.

B. The court shall hold a hearing on the petition. The court shall enter an order approving the surrogacy contract and authorizing the performance of assisted conception for a period of twelve months after the date of the order, and may discharge the guardian ad litem and attorney for the surrogate upon finding that:

1. The court has jurisdiction in accordance with § 20-157;

2. A local department of social services or welfare or a licensed child-placing agency has conducted a home study of the intended parents, the surrogate, and her husband, and has filed a report of this home study with the court;

3. The intended parents, the surrogate, and her husband meet the standards of fitness applicable to adoptive parents;

4. All the parties have voluntarily entered into the surrogacy contract and understand its terms and the nature, meaning, and effect of the proceeding and understand that any agreement between them for payment of compensation is void and unenforceable;

5. The agreement contains adequate provisions to guarantee the payment of reasonable medical and ancillary costs either in the form of insurance, cash, escrow, bonds, or other arrangements satisfactory to the parties, including allocation of responsibility for such costs in the event of termination of the pregnancy, termination of the contract pursuant to s 20-161, or breach of the contract by any party;

6. The surrogate is married and has had at least one pregnancy, and has experienced at least one live birth, and bearing another child does not pose an unreasonable risk to her physical or mental health or to that of any resulting child. This finding shall be supported by medical evidence;

7. Prior to signing the surrogacy contract, the intended parents, the surrogate, and her husband have submitted to physical examinations and psychological evaluations by practitioners licensed to perform such services pursuant to Title 54.1, and the court and all parties have been given access to the records of the physical examinations and psychological evaluations;

8. The intended mother is infertile, is unable to bear a child, or is unable to do so without unreasonable risk to the unborn child or to the physical or mental

health of the intended mother or the child. This finding shall be supported by medical evidence;

9. At least one of the intended parents is expected to be the genetic parent of any child resulting from the agreement;

10. The husband of the surrogate is a party to the surrogacy agreement;

11. All parties have received counseling concerning the effects of the surrogacy by a qualified health care professional or social worker, and a report containing conclusions about the capacity of the parties to enter into and fulfill the agreement has been filed with the court; and

12. The agreement would not be substantially detrimental to the interests of any of the affected persons.

C. Unless otherwise provided in the surrogacy contract, all court costs, counsel fees, and other costs and expenses associated with the hearing, including the costs of the home study, shall be assessed against the intended parents.

D. Within seven days of the birth of any resulting child, the intended parents shall file a written notice with the court that the child was born to the surrogate within 300 days after the last performance of assisted conception. Upon the filing of this notice and a finding that at least one of the intended parents is the genetic parent of the resulting child as substantiated by medical evidence, the court shall enter an order directing the State Registrar of Vital Records to issue a new birth certificate naming the intended parents as the parents of the child pursuant to § 32.1-261.

If evidence cannot be produced that at least one of the intended parents is the genetic parent of the resulting child, the court shall not enter an order directing the issuance of a new birth certificate naming the intended parents as the parents of the child, and the surrogate and her husband shall be the parents of the child.

## § 20-161  Termination of court-approved surrogacy contract.

A. Subsequent to an order entered pursuant to subsection B of § 20-160, but before the surrogate becomes pregnant through the use of assisted conception, the court for cause, or the surrogate, her husband, or the intended parents may terminate the agreement by giving written notice of termination to all other parties and by filing notice of the termination with the court. Upon receipt of the notice, the court shall vacate the order entered under subsection B of § 20-160.

B. Within 180 days after the last performance of any assisted conception, a surrogate who is also a genetic parent may terminate the agreement by filing written notice with the court. The court shall vacate the order entered pursuant to subsection B of § 20-160 upon finding, after notice to the parties to the agreement and a hearing, that the surrogate has voluntarily terminated the agreement and that she understands the effects of the termination.

Unless otherwise provided in the contract as approved, the surrogate shall incur no liability to the intended parents for exercising her rights of termination pursuant to this section.

## § 20-162 Contracts not approved by the court; requirements.

A. In the case of any surrogacy agreement for which prior court approval has not been obtained pursuant to s 20-160, the provisions of this section and §§ 20-156 through 20-159 and §§ 20-163 through 20-165 shall apply. Any provision in a surrogacy contract that attempts to reduce the rights or responsibilities of the intended parents, surrogate, or her husband, if any, or the rights of any resulting child shall be reformed to include the requirements set forth in this chapter. A provision in the contract providing for compensation to be paid to the surrogate is void and unenforceable. Such surrogacy contracts shall be enforceable and shall be construed only as follows:

1. The surrogate, her husband, if any, and the intended parents shall be parties to any such surrogacy contract.

2. The contract shall be in writing, signed by all the parties, and acknowledged before an officer or other person authorized by law to take acknowledgments.

3. Upon expiration of twenty-five days following birth of any resulting child, the surrogate may relinquish her parental rights to the intended parents, if at least one of the intended parents is the genetic parent of the child, by signing a surrogate consent and report form naming the intended parents as the parents of the child. The form shall be obtained from the State Registrar of Vital Records and shall be signed and acknowledged before an officer or other person authorized by law to take acknowledgments. The form, a copy of the contract, and a certificate from the physician who performed the assisted conception stating the genetic relationships between the child, the surrogate, and the intended parents shall be filed with the State Registrar within sixty days after the birth.

4. Upon the filing of the surrogate consent and report form and the required attachments within sixty days of the birth, a new birth certificate shall be established by the State Registrar for the child naming the intended parents as the parents of the child as provided in s 32.1-261 if the physician's certificate provides medical evidence that at least one of the intended parents is the genetic parent of the child.

B. Any contract governed by the provisions of this section shall include or, in the event such provisions are not explicitly covered in the contract or are included but are inconsistent with this section, shall be deemed to include the following provisions:

1. The intended parents shall be the parents of any resulting child only when the surrogate relinquishes her parental rights as provided in subdivision A 3 of this section and a new birth certificate is established as provided in

subdivision A 4 of this section and § 32.1-261;

      2. Incorporation of this chapter and a statement by each of the parties that they have read and understood the contract, they know and understand their rights and responsibilities under Virginia law, and the contract was entered into knowingly and voluntarily; and

      3. A guarantee by the intended parents for payment of reasonable medical and ancillary costs either in the form of insurance, cash, escrow, bonds, or other arrangements satisfactory to the parties, including allocation of responsibility for such costs in the event of termination of the pregnancy, termination of the contract, or breach of the contract by any party.

      C. Under any contract that does not include an allocation of responsibility for reasonable medical and ancillary costs in the event of termination of the pregnancy, termination of the contract, or breach of the contract by any party, the following provisions shall control:

      1. If the intended parents and the surrogate and her husband, if any, and if he is a party to the contract, consent in writing to termination of the contract, the intended parents are responsible for all reasonable medical and ancillary costs for a period of six weeks following the termination.

      2. If the surrogate voluntarily terminates the contract during the pregnancy, without consent of the intended parents, the intended parents shall be responsible for one-half of the reasonable medical and ancillary costs incurred prior to the termination.

      3. If, after the birth of any resulting child, the surrogate fails to relinquish parental rights to the intended parents pursuant to the contract, the intended parents shall be responsible for one-half of the reasonable medical and ancillary costs incurred prior to the birth.

### § 20-164  Relation of parent and child.

      A child whose status as a child is declared or negated by this chapter is the child only of his parent or parents as determined under this chapter, Title 64.1, and, when applicable, Chapter 3.1 (§ 20-49.1 et seq.) of this title for all purposes including, but not limited to, (i) intestate succession; (ii) probate law exemptions, allowances, or other protections for children in a parent's estate; and (iii) determining eligibility of the child or its descendants to share in a donative transfer from any person as an individual or as a member of a class determined by reference to the relationship. However, a child born more than ten months after the death of a parent shall not be recognized as such parent's child for the purposes of subdivisions (i), (ii) and (iii) of this section.

### § 20-165  Surrogate brokers prohibited; penalty; liability of surrogate brokers.

A. It shall be unlawful for any person, firm, corporation, partnership, or other entity to accept compensation for recruiting or procuring surrogates or to otherwise arrange or induce intended parents and surrogates to enter into surrogacy contracts in this Commonwealth. A violation of this section shall be punishable as a Class 1 misdemeanor.

B. Any person who acts as a surrogate broker in violation of this section shall, in addition, be liable to all the parties to the purported surrogacy contract in a total amount equal to three times the amount of compensation to have been paid to the broker pursuant to the contract. One-half of the damages under this subsection shall be due the surrogate and her husband, if any, and if he is a party to the contract, and one-half shall be due the intended parents.

An action under this section shall be brought within five years of the date of the contract.

C. The provisions of this section shall not apply to the services of an attorney in giving legal advice or in preparing a surrogacy contract.

## C. Consent for medical care

### ARKANSAS CODE 20-9-602 (Supp. 1995)

#### § 20-9-602. Consent generally

It is recognized and established that, in addition to such other persons as may be so authorized and empowered, any one (1) of the following persons is authorized and empowered to consent, either orally or otherwise, to any surgical or medical treatment or procedures not prohibited by law which may be suggested, recommended, prescribed, or directed by a licensed physician:

(1) Any adult, for himself;

(2) Any parent, whether an adult or a minor, for his minor child or for his adult child of unsound mind whether the child is of the parent's blood, is an adopted child, is a stepchild, or is a foster child; provided, however, the father of an illegitimate child cannot consent for the child solely on the basis of parenthood;

(3) Any married person, whether an adult or a minor, for himself;

(4) Any female, regardless of age or marital status, for herself when given in connection with pregnancy or childbirth, except the unnatural interruption of a pregnancy;

(5) Any person standing in loco parentis whether formally serving or not, and any guardian, conservator, or custodian, for his ward or other charge under disability;

(6) Any emancipated minor, for himself;

(7) Any unemancipated minor of sufficient intelligence to understand and appreciate the consequences of the proposed surgical or medical treatment or procedures, for himself;

(8) Any adult, for his minor sibling or his adult sibling of unsound mind;

(9) During the absence of a parent so authorized and empowered, any maternal grandparent and, if the father is so authorized and empowered, any paternal grandparent, for his minor grandchild or for his adult grandchild of unsound mind;

(10) Any married person, for a spouse of unsound mind;

(11) Any adult child, for his mother or father of unsound mind;

(12) Any minor incarcerated in the Department of Correction or the Department of Community Punishment.

# CALIFORNIA FAMILY CODE West 1995)
# CONSENT BY PERSON HAVING CARE OF MINOR
# OR BY COURT

## § 6910. Medical treatment of minor;  adult entrusted with consensual power

The parent or guardian of a minor may authorize in writing an adult into whose care a minor has been entrusted to consent to medical care or dental care, or both, for the minor.

## § 6911. Consent by court;  conditions

(a) Upon application by a minor, the court may summarily grant consent for medical care or dental care or both for the minor if the court determines all of the following:

(1) The minor is 16 years of age or older and resides in this state.

(2) The consent of a parent or guardian is necessary to permit the medical care or dental care or both, and the minor has no parent or guardian available to give the consent.

(b) No fee may be charged for proceedings under this section.

## § 6920. Capacity of minor to consent

Subject to the limitations provided in this chapter, notwithstanding any other provision of law, a minor may consent to the matters provided in this chapter, and the consent of the minor's parent or guardian is not necessary.

## § 6921. Effect of minority upon consent

A consent given by a minor under this chapter is not subject to disaffirmance because of minority.

## § 6922. Conditions for consent of minor;  liability of parents or guardians; notification of minor's parents or guardians

(a) A minor may consent to the minor's medical care or dental care if all of the following conditions are satisfied:

(1) The minor is 15 years of age or older.

(2) The minor is living separate and apart from the minor's parents or guardian, whether with or without the consent of a parent or guardian and regardless of the duration of the separate residence.

(3) The minor is managing the minor's own financial affairs, regardless of the source of the minor's income.

(b) The parents or guardian are not liable for medical care or dental care provided pursuant to this section.

(c) A physician and surgeon or dentist may, with or without the consent of the minor patient, advise the minor's parent or guardian of the treatment given or needed if the physician and surgeon or dentist has reason to know, on the basis of the information given by the minor, the whereabouts of the parent or guardian.

### § 6924. Mental health treatment or counseling services; involvement of parents or guardians; liability of parents or guardians

(a) As used in this section:

(1) "Mental health treatment or counseling services" means the provision of mental health treatment or counseling on an outpatient basis by any of the following:

(A) A governmental agency.

(B) A person or agency having a contract with a governmental agency to provide the services.

(C) An agency that receives funding from community united funds.

(D) A runaway house or crisis resolution center.

(E) A professional person, as defined in paragraph (2).

(2) "Professional person" means any of the following:

(A) A person designated as a mental health professional in Sections 622 to 626, inclusive, of Article 8 of Subchapter 3 of Chapter 1 of Title 9 of the California Code of Regulations.

(B) A marriage, family and child counselor as defined in Chapter 13 (commencing with Section 4980) of Division 2 of the Business and Professions Code.

(C) A licensed educational psychologist as defined in Article 5 (commencing with Section 4986) of Chapter 13 of Division 2 of the Business and Professions Code.

(D) A credentialed school psychologist as described in Section 49424 of the Education Code.

(E) A clinical psychologist as defined in Section 1316.5 of the Health and Safety Code.

(F) The chief administrator of an agency referred to in paragraph (1) or (3).

(3) "Residential shelter services" means any of the following:

(A) The provision of residential and other support services to minors on a temporary or emergency basis in a facility that services only minors by a governmental agency, a person or agency having a contract with a governmental agency to provide these services, an agency that receives funding from community funds, or a licensed community care facility or crisis resolution center.

(B) The provision of other support services on a temporary or emergency basis by any professional person as defined in paragraph (2).

(b) A minor who is 12 years of age or older may consent to mental health treatment or counseling on an outpatient basis, or to residential shelter services, if both of the following requirements are satisfied:

(1) The minor, in the opinion of the attending professional person, is mature enough to participate intelligently in the outpatient services or residential shelter services.

(2) The minor (A) would present a danger of serious physical or mental harm to self or to others without the mental health treatment or counseling or residential shelter services, or (B) is the alleged victim of incest or child abuse.

(c) A professional person offering residential shelter services, whether as an individual or as a representative of an entity specified in paragraph (3) of subdivision (a), shall make his or her best efforts to notify the parent or guardian of the provision of services.

(d) The mental health treatment or counseling of a minor authorized by this section shall include involvement of the minor's parent or guardian unless, in the opinion of the professional person who is treating or counseling the minor, the involvement would be inappropriate. The professional person who is treating or counseling the minor shall state in the client record whether and when the person attempted to contact the minor's parent or guardian, and whether the attempt to contact was successful or unsuccessful, or the reason why, in the professional person's opinion, it would be inappropriate to contact the minor's parent or guardian.

(e) The minor's parents or guardian are not liable for payment for mental health treatment or counseling services provided pursuant to this section unless the parent or guardian participates in the mental health treatment or counseling, and then only for services rendered with the participation of the parent or guardian. The minor's parents or guardian are not liable for payment for any residential shelter services provided pursuant to this section unless the parent or guardian consented to the provision of those services.

(f) This section does not authorize a minor to receive convulsive therapy or psychosurgery as defined in subdivisions (f) and (g) of Section 5325 of the Welfare and Institutions Code, or psychotropic drugs without the consent of the minor's parent or guardian.

## § 6925. Prevention or treatment of pregnancy

(a) A minor may consent to medical care related to the prevention or treatment of pregnancy.

(b) This section does not authorize a minor:

(1) To be sterilized without the consent of the minor's parent or guardian.

(2) To receive an abortion without the consent of a parent or guardian other than as provided in Section 25958 of the Health and Safety Code.

## § 6926. Diagnosis or treatment of infectious, contagious, or communicable diseases; liability of parents or guardians

(a) A minor who is 12 years of age or older and who may have come into contact with an infectious, contagious, or communicable disease may consent to medical care related to the diagnosis or treatment of the disease, if the disease or condition is one that is required by law or regulation adopted pursuant to law to be reported to the local health officer, or is a related sexually transmitted disease, as may be determined by the State Director of Health Services.

(b) The minor's parents or guardian are not liable for payment for medical care provided pursuant to this section.

## § 6927. Diagnosis or treatment for rape

A minor who is 12 years of age or older and who is alleged to have been raped may consent to medical care related to the diagnosis or treatment of the condition and the collection of medical evidence with regard to the alleged rape.

## § 6928. Diagnosis or treatment for sexual assault

(a) "Sexually assaulted" as used in this section includes, but is not limited to, conduct coming within Section 261, 286, or 288a of the Penal Code.

(b) A minor who is alleged to have been sexually assaulted may consent to medical care related to the diagnosis and treatment of the condition, and the collection of medical evidence with regard to the alleged sexual assault.

(c) The professional person providing medical treatment shall attempt to contact the minor's parent or guardian and shall note in the minor's treatment record the date and time the professional person attempted to contact the parent or guardian and whether the attempt was successful or unsuccessful. This subdivision does not apply if the professional person reasonably believes that the minor's parent or guardian committed the sexual assault on the minor.

## § 6929. Diagnosis or treatment for alcohol or drug abuse; liability of parents or guardians

(a) As used in this section:

(1) "Counseling" means the provision of counseling services by a provider under a contract with the state or a county to provide alcohol or drug abuse counseling services pursuant to Part 2 (commencing with Section 5600) of Division 5 of the Welfare and Institutions Code or pursuant to Division 10.5 (commencing with Section 11750) of the Health and Safety Code.

(2) "Drug or alcohol" includes, but is not limited to, any substance listed in any of the following:

(A) Section 380 or 381 of the Penal Code.

(B) Division 10 (commencing with Section 11000) of the Health and

Safety Code.

(C) Subdivision (f) of Section 647 of the Penal Code.

(3) "Professional person" means a physician and surgeon, registered nurse, psychologist, clinical social worker, or marriage, family, and child counselor.

(b) A minor who is 12 years of age or older may consent to medical care and counseling relating to the diagnosis and treatment of a drug or alcohol related problem.

(c) The treatment plan of a minor authorized by this section shall include the involvement of the minor's parent or guardian, if appropriate, as determined by the professional person or treatment facility treating the minor. The professional person providing medical care or counseling to a minor shall state in the minor's treatment record whether and when the professional person attempted to contact the minor's parent or guardian, and whether the attempt to contact the parent or guardian was successful or unsuccessful, or the reason why, in the opinion of the professional person, it would not be appropriate to contact the minor's parent or guardian.

(d) The minor's parents or guardian are not liable for payment for any care provided to a minor pursuant to this section, except that if the minor's parent or guardian participates in a counseling program pursuant to this section, the parent or guardian is liable for the cost of the services provided to the minor and the parent or guardian.

(e) This section does not authorize a minor to receive methadone treatment without the consent of the minor's parent or guardian.

## D.  Domestic violence

# MASSACHUSETTS GENERAL LAWS ANNOTATED
# TITLE III.  DOMESTIC RELATIONS
# CHAPTER 209A.  ABUSE PREVENTION

### § 1. Definitions

As used in this chapter the following words shall have the following meanings:

"Abuse", the occurrence of one or more of the following acts between family or household members:

(a) attempting to cause or causing physical harm;

(b) placing another in fear of imminent serious physical harm;

(c) causing another to engage involuntarily in sexual relations by force, threat or duress.

"Court", the superior, probate and family, district or Boston municipal court departments of the trial court, except when the petitioner is in a dating relationship when "Court" shall mean district, probate, or Boston municipal courts.

"Family or household members", persons who:

(a) are or were married to one another;

(b) are or were residing together in the same household;

(c) are or were related by blood or marriage;

(d) having a child in common regardless or*** whether they have ever married or lived together;  or

(e) are or have been in a substantive dating or engagement relationship, which shall be adjudged by district, probate or Boston municipal courts consideration of the following factors:

(1) the length of time of the relationship;  (2) the type of relationship;  (3) the frequency of interaction between the parties;  and (4) if the relationship has been terminated by either person, the length of time elapsed since the termination of the relationship.

"Law officer", any officer authorized to serve criminal process.

"Vacate order", court order to leave and remain away from a premises and surrendering forthwith any keys to said premises to the plaintiff.  The defendant shall not damage any of the plaintiff's belongings or those of any other occupant and shall not shut off or cause to be shut off any utilities or mail delivery to the plaintiff.  In the case where the premises designated in the vacate order is a

***  So in enrolled bill;  probably should read "of".

residence, so long as the plaintiff is living at said residence, the defendant shall not interfere in any way with the plaintiff's right to possess such residence, except by order or judgment of a court of competent jurisdiction pursuant to appropriate civil eviction proceedings, a petition to partition real estate, or a proceeding to divide marital property. A vacate order may include in its scope a household, a multiple family dwelling and the plaintiff's workplace. When issuing an order to vacate the plaintiff's workplace, the presiding justice must consider whether the plaintiff and defendant work in the same location or for the same employer.

## § 2. Venue

Proceedings under this chapter shall be filed, heard and determined in the superior court department or the Boston municipal court department or respective divisions of the probate and family or district court departments having venue over the plaintiff's residence. If the plaintiff has left a residence or household to avoid abuse, such plaintiff shall have the option of commencing an action in the court having venue over such prior residence or household, or in the court having venue over the present residence or household.

## § 3. Remedies; period of relief

A person suffering from abuse from an adult or minor family or household member may file a complaint in the court requesting protection from such abuse, including, but not limited to, the following orders:

(a) ordering the defendant to refrain from abusing the plaintiff, whether the defendant is an adult or minor;

(b) ordering the defendant to refrain from contacting the plaintiff, unless authorized by the court, whether the defendant is an adult or minor;

(c) ordering the defendant to vacate forthwith and remain away from the household, multiple family dwelling, and workplace. Notwithstanding the provisions of section thirty-four B of chapter two hundred and eight, an order to vacate shall be for a fixed period of time, not to exceed one year, at the expiration of which time the court may extend any such order upon motion of the plaintiff, with notice to the defendant, for such additional time as it deems necessary to protect the plaintiff from abuse;

(d) awarding the plaintiff temporary custody of a minor child;

(e) ordering the defendant to pay temporary support for the plaintiff or any child in the plaintiff's custody or both, when the defendant has a legal obligation to support such a person. In determining the amount to be paid, the court shall apply the standards established in the child support guidelines;

(f) ordering the defendant to pay the person abused monetary compensation for the losses suffered as a direct result of such abuse. Compensatory losses shall include, but not be limited to, loss of earnings or support, costs for restoring utilities, out-of-pocket losses for injuries sustained, replacement costs for locks or personal property removed or destroyed, medical and moving expenses and reasonable attorney's fees;

(g) ordering the plaintiff's address to be impounded as provided in section nine;

(h) ordering the defendant to refrain from abusing or contacting the plaintiff's child, or child in plaintiff's care or custody, unless authorized by the court;

(i) the judge may recommend to the defendant that the defendant attend a recognized batterer's treatment program.

No filing fee shall be charged for the filing of the complaint. Neither the plaintiff nor the plaintiff's attorney shall be charged for certified copies of any orders entered by the court, or any copies of the file reasonably required for future court action or as a result of the loss or destruction of plaintiff's copies.

Any relief granted by the court shall be for a fixed period of time not to exceed one year. Every order shall on its face state the time and date the order is to expire and shall include the date and time that the matter will again be heard. If the plaintiff appears at the court at the date and time the order is to expire, the court shall determine whether or not to extend the order for any additional time reasonably necessary to protect the plaintiff or to enter a permanent order. When the expiration date stated on the order is on a weekend day or holiday, or a date when the court is closed to business, the order shall not expire until the next date that the court is open to business. The plaintiff may appear on such next court business day at the time designated by the order to request that the order be extended. The court may also extend the order upon motion of the plaintiff, for such additional time as it deems necessary to protect from abuse the plaintiff or any child in the plaintiff's care or custody. The fact that abuse has not occurred during the pendency of an order shall not, in itself, constitute sufficient ground for denying or failing to extend the order, of allowing an order to expire or be vacated, or for refusing to issue a new order.

The court may modify its order at any subsequent time upon motion by either party. When the plaintiff's address is impounded and the defendant has filed a motion to modify the court's order, the court shall be responsible for notifying the plaintiff. In no event shall the court disclose any impounded address.

No order under this chapter shall in any manner affect title to real property.

No court shall compel parties to mediate any aspect of their case. Although the court may refer the case to the family service office of the probation department or victim/witness advocates for information gathering purposes, the court shall not compel the parties to meet together in such information gathering sessions.

A court shall not deny any complaint filed under this chapter solely because it was not filed within a particular time period after the last alleged incident of abuse.

A court may issue a mutual restraining order or mutual no-contact order pursuant to any abuse prevention action only if the court has made specific written findings of fact. The court shall then provide a detailed order, sufficiently specific to apprise any law officer as to which party has violated the order, if the parties are in or appear to be in violation of the order.

Any action commenced under the provisions of this chapter shall not preclude any other civil or criminal remedies. A party filing a complaint under this chapter shall be required to disclose any prior or pending actions involving the parties for divorce, annulment, paternity, custody or support, guardianship, separate support or legal separation, or abuse prevention.

If there is a prior or pending custody support order from the probate and family court department of the trial court, an order issued in the superior, district or Boston municipal court departments of the trial court pursuant to this chapter may include any relief available pursuant to this chapter except orders for custody or support.

If the parties to a proceeding under this chapter are parties in a subsequent proceeding in the probate and family court department for divorce, annulment, paternity, custody or support, guardianship or separate support, any custody or support order or judgment issued in the subsequent proceeding shall supersede any prior custody or support order under this chapter.

## § 3A. Nature of proceedings and availability of other criminal proceedings; information required to be given to complainant upon filing

Upon the filing of a complaint under this chapter, a complainant shall be informed that the proceedings hereunder are civil in nature and that violations of orders issued hereunder are criminal in nature. Further, a complainant shall be given information prepared by the appropriate district attorney's office that other criminal proceedings may be available and such complainant shall be instructed by such district attorney's office relative to the procedures required to initiate criminal proceedings including, but not limited to, a complaint for a violation of section forty-three of chapter two hundred and sixty-five. Whenever possible, a complainant shall be provided with such information in the complainant's native language.

## § 3B. Order for suspension and surrender of firearms license or firearms identification card; surrender of firearms; petition for review; hearing

Upon issuance of a temporary or emergency order under section four or five of this chapter, the court shall, if the plaintiff demonstrates a substantial likelihood of immediate danger of abuse, order the immediate suspension and surrender of any license to carry firearms and or firearms identification card which the defendant may hold and order the defendant to surrender all firearms, rifles, shotguns, machine guns and ammunition which he then possesses in accordance with the provisions of this chapter and any license to carry firearms or firearms identification cards which the defendant may hold shall be surrendered to the appropriate law enforcement officials in accordance with the provisions of this chapter. Notice of such suspension and ordered surrender shall be appended to the copy of abuse prevention order served on the defendant pursuant to section seven. Law enforcement officials, upon the service of said orders, shall immediately take possession of all firearms, rifles, shotguns, machine guns, ammunition, any license to carry firearms and any firearms identification cards in the control, ownership, or possession of said defendant. Any violation of such orders shall be punishable by a fine of not more than five thousand dollars, or by imprisonment for not more than two and one-half years in a house of correction, or by both such fine and imprisonment.

Any defendant aggrieved by an order of surrender or suspension as described in the first sentence of this section may petition the court which issued such suspension or surrender order for a review of such action and such petition shall be heard no later than ten court business days after the receipt of the notice of the petition by the court. If said license to carry firearms or firearms identification card has been suspended upon the issuance of an order issued pursuant to section four or five, said petition may be heard contemporaneously with the hearing specified in the second sentence of the second paragraph of section four. Upon the filing of an affidavit by the defendant that a firearm, rifle, shotgun, machine gun or ammunition is required in the performance of the defendant's employment, and upon a request for an expedited hearing, the court shall order said hearing within two business days of receipt of such affidavit and request but only on the issue of surrender and suspension pursuant to this section.

## § 3C. Continuation or modification of order for suspension or surrender

Upon the continuation and/or modification of an order issued pursuant to section four of this chapter or upon a petition for review described in section 3B of this chapter, the court shall also order or continue to order the immediate suspension and surrender of the defendant's license to carry firearms and firearms identification card and the surrender of all firearms, rifles, shotguns, machine guns and ammunition which he then possesses if the court makes a determination that the return of said license to carry, firearms identification card or firearms, rifles, shotguns, machine guns and ammunition presents a likelihood of abuse to the plaintiff. A suspension and surrender order issued pursuant to this section shall continue so long as the restraining order to which it relates is in effect.

## § 4. Temporary orders; notice; hearing

Upon the filing of a complaint under this chapter, the court may enter such temporary orders as it deems necessary to protect a plaintiff from abuse, including relief as provided in section three. Such relief shall not be contingent upon the filing of a complaint for divorce, separate support, or paternity action.

If the plaintiff demonstrates a substantial likelihood of immediate danger of abuse, the court may enter such temporary relief orders without notice as it deems necessary to protect the plaintiff from abuse and shall immediately thereafter notify the defendant that the temporary orders have been issued. The court shall give the defendant an opportunity to be heard on the question of continuing the temporary order and of granting other relief as requested by the plaintiff no later than ten court business days after such orders are entered.

Notice shall be made by the appropriate law enforcement agency as provided in section seven.

If the defendant does not appear at such subsequent hearing, the temporary orders shall continue in effect without further order of the court.

## § 5. Granting of relief when court closed; certification

When the court is closed for business, any justice of the superior, probate and family, district or Boston municipal court departments may grant relief to the plaintiff as provided under section four if the plaintiff demonstrates a substantial likelihood of immediate danger of abuse. In the discretion of the justice, such relief may be granted and communicated by telephone to an officer or employee of an appropriate law enforcement agency, who shall record such order on a form of order promulgated for such use by the chief administrative justice and shall deliver a copy of such order on the next court day to the clerk-magistrate of the court having venue and jurisdiction over the matter. If relief has been granted without the filing of a complaint pursuant to this section of this chapter, then the plaintiff shall appear in court on the next available business day to file said complaint. Notice to the plaintiff and defendant and an opportunity for the defendant to be heard shall be given as provided in said section four.

Any order issued under this section and any documentation in support thereof shall be certified on the next court day by the clerk-magistrate or register of the court issuing such order to the court having venue and jurisdiction over the matter. Such certification to the court shall have the effect of commencing proceedings under this chapter and invoking the other provisions of this chapter but shall not be deemed necessary for an emergency order issued under this section to take effect.

## § 6. Powers of police

Whenever any law officer has reason to believe that a family or household member has been abused or is in danger of being abused, such officer shall use all reasonable means to prevent further abuse. The officer shall take, but not be limited to the following action:

(1) remain on the scene of where said abuse occurred or was in danger of occurring as long as the officer has reason to believe that at least one of the parties involved would be in immediate physical danger without the presence of a law officer. This shall include, but not be limited to remaining in the dwelling for a reasonable period of time;

(2) assist the abused person in obtaining medical treatment necessitated by an assault, which may include driving the victim to the emergency room of the nearest hospital, or arranging for appropriate transportation to a health care facility, notwithstanding any law to the contrary;

(3) assist the abused person in locating and getting to a safe place; including but not limited to a designated meeting place for a shelter or a family member's or friend's residence. The officer shall consider the victim's preference in this regard and what is reasonable under all the circumstances;

(4) give such person immediate and adequate notice of his or her rights. Such notice shall consist of handing said person a copy of the statement which follows below and reading the same to said person. Where said person's native language is not English, the statement shall be then provided in said person's native language whenever possible.

"You have the right to appear at the Superior, Probate and Family, District or Boston Municipal Court, if you reside within the appropriate jurisdiction, and file a complaint requesting any of the following applicable orders: (a) an order restraining your attacker from abusing you; (b) an order directing your attacker to leave your household, building or workplace; (c) an order awarding you custody of a minor child; (d) an order directing your attacker to pay support for you or any minor child in your custody, if the attacker has a legal obligation of support; and (e) an order directing your attacker to pay you for losses suffered as a result of abuse, including medical and moving expenses, loss of earnings or support, costs for restoring utilities and replacing locks, reasonable attorney's fees and other out-of-pocket losses for injuries and property damage sustained.

For an emergency on weekends, holidays, or weeknights the police will refer you to a justice of the superior, probate and family, district, or Boston municipal court departments.

You have the right to go to the appropriate district court or the Boston municipal court and seek a criminal complaint for threats, assault and battery, assault with a deadly weapon, assault with intent to kill or other related offenses.

If you are in need of medical treatment, you have the right to request that an officer present drive you to the nearest hospital or otherwise assist you in obtaining medical treatment.

If you believe that police protection is needed for your physical safety, you have the right to request that the officer present remain at the scene until you and your children can leave or until your safety is otherwise ensured. You may also request that the officer assist you in locating and taking you to a safe place, including but not limited to a designated meeting place for a shelter or a family member's or a friend's residence, or a similar place of safety.

You may request a copy of the police incident report at no cost from the police department."

The officer shall leave a copy of the foregoing statement with such person before leaving the scene or premises.

(5) assist such person by activating the emergency judicial system when the court is closed for business;

(6) inform the victim that the abuser will be eligible for bail and may be promptly released; and

(7) arrest any person a law officer witnesses or has probable cause to believe has violated a temporary or permanent vacate, restraining, or no-contact order or judgment issued pursuant to section eighteen, thirty-four B or thirty-four C of chapter two hundred and eight, section thirty-two of chapter two hundred and nine, section three, four or five of this chapter, or sections fifteen or twenty of chapter two hundred and nine C. When there are no vacate, restraining, or no-contact orders or judgments in effect, arrest shall be the preferred response whenever an officer witnesses or has probable cause to believe that a person:

(a) has committed a felony;

(b) has committed a misdemeanor involving abuse as defined in section one of this chapter;

(c) has committed an assault and battery in violation of section thirteen A of chapter two hundred and sixty-five.

The safety of the victim and any involved children shall be paramount in any decision to arrest. Any officer arresting both parties must submit a detailed, written report in addition to an incident report, setting forth the grounds for dual arrest.

No law officer investigating an incident of domestic violence shall threaten, suggest, or otherwise indicate the arrest of all parties for the purpose of discouraging requests for law enforcement intervention by any party.

No law officer shall be held liable in any civil action regarding personal injury or injury to property brought by any party to a domestic violence incident for an arrest based on probable cause when such officer acted reasonably and in good faith and in compliance with this chapter and the statewide policy as established by the secretary of public safety.

Whenever any law officer investigates an incident of domestic violence, the officer shall immediately file a written incident report in accordance with the standards of the officer's law enforcement agency and, wherever possible, in the form of the National Incident-Based Reporting System, as defined by the Federal Bureau of Investigation. The latter information may be submitted voluntarily by the local police on a monthly basis to the crime reporting unit of the criminal history systems board.

The victim shall be provided a copy of the full incident report at no cost upon request to the appropriate law enforcement department.

When a judge or other person authorized to take bail bails any person arrested under the provisions of this chapter, he shall make reasonable efforts to inform the victim of such release prior to or at the time of said release.

When any person charged with or arrested for a crime involving abuse under this chapter is released from custody, the court or the emergency response judge shall issue, upon the request of the victim, a written no-contact order prohibiting the person charged or arrested from having any contact with the victim and shall use all reasonable means to notify the victim immediately of release from custody. The victim shall be given at no cost a certified copy of the no-contact order.

## § 7. Abuse prevention orders; domestic violence record search; service of order; enforcement; violations

When considering a complaint filed under this chapter, a judge shall cause a search to be made of the records contained within the statewide domestic violence record keeping system maintained by the office of the commissioner of probation and shall review the resulting data to determine whether the named defendant has a civil or criminal record involving domestic or other violence. Upon receipt of information that an outstanding warrant exists against the named defendant, a judge shall order that the appropriate law enforcement officials be notified and shall order that any information regarding the defendant's most recent whereabouts shall be forwarded to such officials. In all instances where an outstanding warrant exists, a judge shall make a finding, based upon all of the circumstances, as to whether an imminent threat of bodily injury exists to the petitioner. In all instances where such an imminent threat of bodily injury is found to exist, the judge shall notify the appropriate law enforcement officials of such finding and such officials shall take all necessary actions to execute any such outstanding warrant as soon as is practicable.

Whenever the court orders under sections eighteen, thirty-four B, and thirty-four C of chapter two hundred and eight, section thirty-two of chapter two hundred and nine, sections three, four and five of this chapter, or sections fifteen and twenty of chapter two hundred and nine C, the defendant to vacate, refrain from abusing the plaintiff or to have no contact with the plaintiff or the plaintiff's minor child, the register or clerk-magistrate shall transmit two certified copies of each such order and one copy of the complaint and summons forthwith to the appropriate law enforcement agency which, unless otherwise ordered by the court, shall serve one copy of each order upon the defendant, together with a copy of the complaint, order and summons and notice of any suspension or surrender ordered pursuant to section three B of this chapter. The law enforcement agency shall promptly make its return of service to the court.

Law enforcement officers shall use every reasonable means to enforce such abuse prevention orders. Law enforcement agencies shall establish procedures adequate to insure that an officer on the scene of an alleged violation of such order may be informed of the existence and terms of such order. The court shall notify the appropriate law enforcement agency in writing whenever any such order is vacated and shall direct the agency to destroy all record of such vacated order and such agency shall comply with that directive.

Each abuse prevention order issued shall contain the following statement: VIOLATION OF THIS ORDER IS A CRIMINAL OFFENSE.

Any violation of such order shall be punishable by a fine of not more than five thousand dollars, or by imprisonment for not more than two and one-half years in a house of correction, or by both such fine and imprisonment. Where the defendant has no prior record of any crime of violence and where the court believes, after evaluation by a certified or provisionally certified batterer's treatment program, that the defendant is amenable to treatment, the court may, in addition to any other penalty, order appropriate treatment as specified in this section. If a defendant ordered to undergo treatment has received a suspended sentence, the original sentence shall be reimposed if the defendant fails to participate in said program as required by the terms of his probation.

When a defendant has been ordered to participate in a treatment program pursuant to this section, the defendant shall be required to regularly attend a certified or provisionally certified batterer's treatment program. To the extent permitted by professional requirements of confidentiality, said program shall communicate with local battered women's programs for the purpose of protecting the victim's safety. Additionally, it shall specify the defendant's attendance requirements and keep the probation department informed of whether the defendant is in compliance.

In addition to, but not in lieu of, such orders for treatment, if the defendant has a substance abuse problem, the court may order appropriate treatment for such problem. All ordered treatment shall last until the end of the probationary period or until the treatment program decides to discharge the defendant, whichever comes first. When the defendant is not in compliance with the terms of probation, the court shall hold a revocation of probation hearing. To the extent possible, the defendant shall be responsible for paying all costs for court ordered treatment.

In each instance where there is a violation of an abuse prevention order, the court may order the defendant to pay the plaintiff for all damages including, but not limited to, cost for shelter or emergency housing, loss of earnings or support, out-of-pocket losses for injuries sustained or property damaged, medical expenses, moving expenses, cost for obtaining an unlisted telephone number, and reasonable attorney's fees.

Any such violation may be enforced in the superior, the district or Boston municipal court departments. Criminal remedies provided herein are not exclusive and do not preclude any other available civil or criminal remedies. The superior, probate and family, district and Boston municipal court departments may each enforce by civil contempt procedure a violation of its own court order.

The provisions of section eight of chapter one hundred and thirty-six shall not apply to any order, complaint or summons issued pursuant to this section.

## § 8. Address of plaintiff; exclusion from court documents; confidentiality of records

Upon the request of the plaintiff, the court shall impound the plaintiff's address by excluding same from the complaint and from all other court documents which are available for public inspection, and shall ensure that the address is kept confidential from the defendant and defendant's attorney.

The records of cases arising out of an action brought under the provisions of this chapter where the plaintiff or defendant is a minor shall be withheld from public inspection except by order of the court; provided, that such records shall be open, at all reasonable times, to the inspection of the minor, said minor's parent, guardian, attorney, and to the plaintiff and the plaintiff's attorney, or any of them.

## § 9. Form of complaint; promulgation

The administrative justices of the superior court, probate and family court, district court, and the Boston municipal court departments shall jointly promulgate a form of complaint for use under this chapter which shall be in such form and language to permit a plaintiff to prepare and file such complaint pro se.

## § 10. Assessments against persons referred to certified batterers' treatment program as condition of probation

The court shall impose an assessment of three hundred dollars against any person who has been referred to a certified batterers' treatment program as a condition of probation. Said assessment shall be in addition to the cost of the treatment program. In the discretion of the court, said assessment may be reduced or waived when the court finds that the person is indigent or that payment of the assessment would cause the person, or the dependents of such person, severe financial hardship. Assessments made pursuant to this section shall be in addition to any other fines, assessments, or restitution imposed in any disposition. All funds collected by the court pursuant to this section shall be transmitted monthly to the state treasurer, who shall deposit said funds in the General Fund.

# PART IV.  CRIMES, PUNISHMENTS AND PROCEEDINGS IN CRIMINAL CASES

## TITLE II.  PROCEEDINGS IN CRIMINAL CASES

### § 58A. Conditions for release of persons accused of certain offenses involving physical force or abuse;  hearing;  order;  review

(1) The commonwealth may move, based on dangerousness, for an order of pretrial detention or release on conditions for a felony offense that has as an element of the offense the use, attempted use, or threatened use of physical force against the person of another, or any other felony that by its nature involves a substantial risk that physical force against the person of another may result, including . . . a violation of an order pursuant to . . . section three, four or five of chapter two hundred and nine A, or section fifteen or twenty of chapter two hundred and nine C, or arrested and charged with a misdemeanor or felony involving abuse as defined in section one of said chapter two hundred and nine A while an order of protection issued under said chapter two hundred and nine A was in effect against said person . . . .

(2) Upon the appearance before a superior court or district court judge of an individual charged with an offense listed in subsection (1) and upon the motion of the commonwealth, the judicial officer shall hold a hearing pursuant to subsection (5) issue an order that, pending trial, the individual shall either be released on personal recognizance without surety;  released on conditions of release as set forth herein;  or detained under subsection (3).

If the judicial officer determines that personal recognizance will not reasonably assure the appearance of the person as required or will endanger the safety of any other person or the community, such judicial officer shall order the pretrial release of the person--

(A) subject to the condition that the person not commit a federal, state or local crime during the period of release;  and

(B) subject to the least restrictive further condition, or combination or conditions, that such judicial officer determines will reasonably assure the appearance of the person as required and the safety of any other person and the community that the person--

(i) remain in the custody of a designated person, who agrees to assume supervision and to report any violation of a release condition to the court, if the designated person is able reasonably to assure the judicial officer that the person will appear as required and will not pose a danger to the safety of any other person or the community;

(ii) maintain employment, or, if unemployed, actively seek employment;

(iii) maintain or commence an educational program;

(iv) abide by specified restrictions on personal associations, place of abode or travel;

(v) avoid all contact with an alleged victim of the crime and with potential witness who may testify concerning the offense;

(vi) report on a regular basis to a designated law enforcement agency, pretrial service agency, or other agency;

(vii) comply with a specified curfew;

(viii) refrain from possessing a firearm, destructive device, or other dangerous weapon;

(ix) refrain from excessive use of alcohol, or any use of a narcotic drug or other controlled substance, without a prescription by a licensed medical practitioner;

(x) undergo available medical, psychological, or psychiatric treatment, including treatment for drug or alcohol dependency and remain in a specified institution if required for that purpose;

(xi) execute an agreement to forfeit upon failing to appear as required, property of a sufficient unencumbered value, including money, as is reasonably necessary to assure the appearance of the person as required, and shall provide the court with proof of ownership and the value of the property along with information regarding existing encumbrances as the judicial office may require;

(xii) execute a bail bond with solvent sureties; who will execute an agreement to forfeit in such amount as is reasonably necessary to assure appearance of the person as required and shall provide the court with information regarding the value of the assets and liabilities of the surety if other than an approved surety and the nature and extent of encumbrances against the surety's property; such surety shall have a net worth which shall have sufficient unencumbered value to pay the amount of the bail bond;

(xiii) return to custody for specified hours following release for employment, schooling, or other limited purposes; and

(xiv) satisfy any other condition that is reasonably necessary to assure the appearance of the person as required and to assure the safety of any other person and the community.

The judicial officer may not impose a financial condition that results in the pretrial detention of the person.

The judicial officer may at any time amend the order to impose additional or different conditions of release.

(3) If, after a hearing pursuant to the provisions of subsection (5), the district or superior court justice finds by clear and convincing evidence that no conditions of release will reasonably assure the safety of any other person or the community, said justice shall order the detention of the prisoner prior to trial. A prisoner detained under this subsection shall be brought to a trial as soon as reasonably possible, but in absence of good cause, the prisoner so held shall not be detained for a period exceeding ninety days excluding any period of delay as defined in Massachusetts Rules of Criminal Procedure Rule 36(b)(2). A justice may not impose a financial condition under this section that results in the pretrial detention of the prisoner. Nothing in this section shall be interpreted as limiting the imposition of a financial condition upon the prisoner to reasonably assure his appearance before the courts.

(4) When a prisoner is held under arrest for an offense listed in subsection (1) and upon a motion by the commonwealth, the judge shall hold a hearing to determine whether conditions of release will reasonably assure the safety of any other person or the community.

The hearing shall be held immediately upon the prisoner's first appearance before the court unless that prisoner, or the attorney for the commonwealth, seeks a continuance. Except for good cause, a continuance on motion of the prisoner may not exceed seven days, and a continuance on motion of the attorney for the commonwealth may not exceed three business days. During a continuance, the individual shall be detained upon a showing that there existed probable cause to arrest the prisoner. At the hearing, such prisoner shall have the right to be represented by counsel, and, if financially unable to retain adequate representation, to have counsel appointed. The prisoner shall be afforded an opportunity to testify, to present witnesses, to cross-examine witnesses who appear at the hearing, and to present information. The rules concerning admissibility of evidence in criminal trials shall not apply to the presentation and consideration of information at the hearing. The facts the judge uses to support findings pursuant to subsection (3), that no conditions will reasonably assure the safety of any other person or the community, shall be supported by clear and convincing evidence. In a detention order issued pursuant to the provisions of said subsection (3) the judge shall (a) include written findings of fact and a written statement of the reasons for the detention;  (b) direct that the prisoner be committed to custody or confinement in a corrections facility separate, to the extent practicable, from persons awaiting or serving sentence or being held in custody pending appeal;  and (c) direct that the prisoner be afforded reasonable opportunity for private consultation with his counsel. The prisoner may be detained pending completion of the hearing. The hearing may be reopened before or after a determination by the justice, at any time before trial if the justice finds that information exists that was not known at the time of the hearing and that has a material bearing on the issue and whether there are conditions of release that will reasonably assure the safety of any other person and the community.

(5) In his determination as to whether there are conditions of release that will reasonably assure the safety of any other individual or the community, said justice, shall, on the basis of any information which he can reasonably obtain, take into account the nature and seriousness of the danger posed to any person or the community that would result by the prisoner's release, the nature and circumstances of the offense charged, the potential penalty the prisoner faces, the prisoner's family ties, employment record and history of mental illness, his reputation, the risk that the prisoner will obstruct or attempt to obstruct justice or threaten, injure or intimidate or attempt to threaten, injure or intimidate a prospective witness or juror, his record of convictions, if any, any illegal drug distribution or present drug dependency, whether the prisoner is on bail pending adjudication of a prior charge, whether the acts alleged involve abuse as defined in section one of chapter two hundred and nine A, or violation of a temporary or permanent order issued pursuant to section eighteen or thirty-four B of chapter two hundred and eight, section thirty-two of chapter two hundred and nine, sections three, four or five of chapter two hundred and nine A, or sections fifteen or twenty of chapter two hundred and nine C, whether the prisoner has any history of orders issued against him pursuant to the aforesaid sections, whether he is on probation, parole or other release pending completion of sentence for any conviction and whether he is on release pending sentence or appeal for any conviction.

(6) Nothing in this section shall be construed as modifying or limiting the presumption of innocence.

(7) A prisoner aggrieved by the denial of a district court justice to admit him to bail on his personal recognizance with or without surety may petition the superior court for a review of the order of the recognizance and the justice of the district court shall thereupon immediately notify such person of his right to file a petition for review in the superior court. When a petition for review is filed in the district court or with the detaining authority subsequent to petitioner's district court appearance, the clerk of the district court or the detaining authority, as the case may be, shall immediately notify by telephone, the clerk and probation officer of the district court, the district attorney for the district in which the district court is located, the prosecuting officer, the petitioner's counsel, if any, and the clerk of courts of the county to which the petition is to be transmitted. The clerk of the district court, upon the filing of a petition for review, either in the district court or with the detaining authority, shall forthwith transmit the petition for review, a copy of the complaint and the record of the court, including the appearance of the attorney, if any is entered, and a summary of the court's reasons

for denying the release of the defendant on his personal recognizance with or without surety to the superior court for the county in which the district court is located, if a justice thereof is then sitting, or to the superior court of the nearest county in which a justice is then sitting; the probation officer of the district court shall transmit forthwith to the probation officer of the superior court, copies of all records of the probation office of said district court pertaining to the petitioner, including the petitioner's record of prior convictions, if any, as currently verified by inquiry of the commissioner of probation. The district court or the detaining authority, as the case may be, shall cause any petitioner in its custody to be brought before the said superior court within two business days of the petition having been filed. The district court is authorized to order any officer authorized to execute criminal process to transfer the petition and any papers herein above described from the district court or the detaining authority to the superior court, and to coordinate the transfer of the petitioner and the papers by such officer. The petition for review shall constitute authority in the person or officer having custody of the petitioner to transport the petitioner to said superior court without the issuance of any writ or other legal process; provided, however, that any district or superior court is authorized to issue a writ of habeas corpus for the appearance forthwith of the petitioner before the superior court.

The superior court shall in accordance with the standards set forth in section fifty-eight A, hear the petition for review under section fifty-eight A as speedily as practicable and in any event within five business days of the filing of the petition. The justice of the superior court hearing the review may consider the record below which the commonwealth and the prisoner may supplement. The justice of the superior court may, after a hearing on the petition for review, order that the petitioner be released on bail on his personal recognizance without surety, or, in his discretion, to reasonably assure the effective administration of justice, make any other order of bail or recognizance or remand the petitioner in accordance with the terms of the process by which he was ordered committed by the district court.

## § 58B. Revocation of release and detention order following violation of release conditions

A prisoner who has been released after a hearing pursuant to section fifty-eight A and who has violated a condition of his release, shall be subject to a revocation of release and an order of detention. The judicial officer shall enter an order of revocation and detention if after a hearing the judicial officer finds (1) that there is probable cause to believe that the prisoner has committed a federal or state crime while on release, or clear and convincing evidence that the prisoner has violated any other condition of release; and (2) the judicial officer finds that there are no conditions of release that will reasonably assure the prisoner will not pose a danger to the safety of any other person or the community;  or the prisoner is unlikely to abide by any condition or combination of conditions of release.

If there is probable cause to believe that, while on release, the prisoner committed a federal felony or an offense described in clause (1), a rebuttable presumption arises that no condition or combination of conditions will assure that the prisoner will not pose a danger to the safety of any other prisoner or the community.  If the judicial officer finds that there are conditions of release that will assure that the prisoner will not pose a danger to the safety of any other person or the community, and that the prisoner will abide by such conditions, the judicial officer shall treat the person in accordance with the provisions of this section and may amend the conditions of release accordingly.  Upon the prisoner's first appearance before the judicial officer in the court which will conduct proceedings for revocation of an order of release under this section, the hearing concerning revocation shall be held immediately unless that prisoner or the attorney for the commonwealth seeks a continuance.  During a continuance the person shall be detained without bail unless the judicial officer finds that there are conditions of release that will reasonably assure that the prisoner will not pose a danger to the safety of any other person or the community and that the prisoner will abide by conditions of release.  If the prisoner is detained without bail, except for good cause, a continuance on motion of the person shall not exceed seven days, a continuance on motion of the attorney for the commonwealth or probation shall not exceed three business days.  A prisoner detained under this subsection, shall be brought to trial as soon as reasonably possible, but in the absence of good cause, a prisoner so held shall not be detained for a period exceeding ninety days excluding any period of delay as defined in Massachusetts Rules of Criminal Procedure Rule 36(b)(2).

## E.  Emancipation

# CALIFORNIA FAMILY CODE (West)
# EMANCIPATION OF MINORS LAW

### § 7000. Short title
This part may be cited as the Emancipation of Minors Law.

### § 7001. Purpose of part
It is the purpose of this part to provide a clear statement defining emancipation and its consequences and to permit an emancipated minor to obtain a court declaration of the minor's status.  This part is not intended to affect the status of minors who may become emancipated under the decisional case law that was in effect before the enactment of Chapter 1059 of the Statutes of 1978.

### § 7002. Emancipated minor;  description
A person under the age of 18 years is an emancipated minor if any of the following conditions is satisfied:

(a) The person has entered into a valid marriage, whether or not the marriage has been dissolved.

(b) The person is on active duty with the armed forces of the United States.

(c) The person has received a declaration of emancipation pursuant to Section 7122.

### § 7050. Purposes for which emancipated minors are considered an adult

An emancipated minor shall be considered as being an adult for the following purposes:

(a) The minor's right to support by the minor's parents.

(b) The right of the minor's parents to the minor's earnings and to control the minor.

(c) The application of Sections 300 and 601 of the Welfare and Institutions Code.

(d) Ending all vicarious or imputed liability of the minor's parents or guardian for the minor's torts.  Nothing in this section affects any liability of a parent, guardian, spouse, or employer imposed by the Vehicle Code, or any vicarious liability that arises from an agency relationship.

(e) The minor's capacity to do any of the following:

(1) Consent to medical, dental, or psychiatric care, without parental consent, knowledge, or liability.

2) Enter into a binding contract or give a delegation of power.

(3) Buy, sell, lease, encumber, exchange, or transfer an interest in real or personal property, including, but not limited to, shares of stock in a domestic or foreign corporation or a membership in a nonprofit corporation.

(4) Sue or be sued in the minor's own name.

(5) Compromise, settle, arbitrate, or otherwise adjust a claim, action, or proceeding by or against the minor.

(6) Make or revoke a will.

(7) Make a gift, outright or in trust.

(8) Convey or release contingent or expectant interests in property, including marital property rights and any right of survivorship incident to joint tenancy, and consent to a transfer, encumbrance, or gift of marital property.

(9) Exercise or release the minor's powers as donee of a power of appointment unless the creating instrument otherwise provides.

(10) Create for the minor's own benefit or for the benefit of others a revocable or irrevocable trust.

(11) Revoke a revocable trust.

(12) Elect to take under or against a will.

(13) Renounce or disclaim any interest acquired by testate or intestate succession or by inter vivos transfer, including exercise of the right to surrender the right to revoke a revocable trust.

(14) Make an election referred to in Section 13502 of, or an election and agreement referred to in Section 13503 of, the Probate Code.

(15) Establish the minor's own residence.

(16) Apply for a work permit pursuant to Section 49110 of the Education Code without the request of the minor's parents.

(17) Enroll in a school or college.

## § 7051. Insurance contracts

An insurance contract entered into by an emancipated minor has the same effect as if it were entered into by an adult and, with respect to that contract, the minor has the same rights, duties, and liabilities as an adult.

## § 7052. Powers of emancipated minor with respect to shares of stock and similar property

With respect to shares of stock in a domestic or foreign corporation held by an emancipated minor, a membership in a nonprofit corporation held by an emancipated minor, or other property held by an emancipated minor, the minor may do all of the following:

(a) Vote in person, and give proxies to exercise any voting rights, with respect to the shares, membership, or property.

(b) Waive notice of any meeting or give consent to the holding of any meeting.

(c) Authorize, ratify, approve, or confirm any action that could be taken by shareholders, members, or property owners.

## § 7110. Legislative intent; minimum expense; forms

It is the intent of the Legislature that proceedings under this part be as simple and inexpensive as possible. To that end, the Judicial Council is requested to prepare and distribute to the clerks of the superior courts appropriate forms for the proceedings that are suitable for use by minors acting as their own counsel.

## § 7111. Issuance of declaration of emancipation; effect on public social service benefits

The issuance of a declaration of emancipation does not entitle the minor to any benefits under Division 9 (commencing with Section 10000) of the Welfare and Institutions Code which would not otherwise accrue to an emancipated minor.

## § 7120. Petitions for declaration of emancipation; contents

(a) A minor may petition the superior court of the county in which the minor resides or is temporarily domiciled for a declaration of emancipation.

(b) The petition shall set forth with specificity all of the following facts:

(1) The minor is at least 14 years of age.

(2) The minor willingly lives separate and apart from the minor's parents or guardian with the consent or acquiescence of the minor's parents or guardian.

(3) The minor is managing his or her own financial affairs. As evidence of this, the minor shall complete and attach a declaration of income and expenses as provided in Section 1285.50 of the California Rules of Court.

(4) The source of the minor's income is not derived from any activity declared to be a crime by the laws of this state or the laws of the United States.

## § 7121. Notice of declaration proceedings

(a) Before the petition for a declaration of emancipation is heard, notice the court determines is reasonable shall be given to the minor's parents, guardian, or other person entitled to the custody of the minor, or proof shall be made to the court that their addresses are unknown or that for other reasons the notice cannot be given.

(b) The clerk of the court shall also notify the district attorney of the county where the matter is to be heard of the proceeding. If the minor is a ward or dependent child of the court, notice shall be given to the probation department.

(c) The notice shall include a form whereby the minor's parents, guardian, or other person entitled to the custody of the minor may give their written consent to the petitioner's emancipation. The notice shall include a warning that a court may void or rescind the declaration of emancipation and the parents may become liable for support and medical insurance coverage pursuant to Chapter 2 (commencing with Section 4000) of Part 2 of Division 9 of this code and Sections 11350, 11350.1, 11475.1, and 11490 of the Welfare and Institutions Code.

## § 7122. Findings of court; issuance of declaration of emancipation

(a) The court shall sustain the petition if it finds that the minor is a person described by Section 7120 and that emancipation would not be contrary to the minor's best interest.

(b) If the petition is sustained, the court shall forthwith issue a declaration of emancipation, which shall be filed by the county clerk.

(c) A declaration is conclusive evidence that the minor is emancipated.

## § 7123. Grant or denial of petition; filing of petition for writ of mandate

(a) If the petition is denied, the minor has a right to file a petition for a writ of mandate.

(b) If the petition is sustained, the parents or guardian have a right to file a petition for a writ of mandate if they have appeared in the proceeding and opposed the granting of the petition.

## § 7130. Grounds for voiding or rescinding declaration

(a) A declaration of emancipation obtained by fraud or by the withholding of material information is voidable.

(b) A declaration of emancipation of a minor who is indigent and has no means of support is subject to rescission.

## § 7131. Filing of petitions to void declarations

A petition to void a declaration of emancipation on the ground that the declaration was obtained by fraud or by the withholding of material information may be filed by any person or by any public or private agency. The petition shall be filed in the court that made the declaration.

## § 7132. Filing of petitions to rescind declarations

(a) A petition to rescind a declaration of emancipation on the ground that the minor is indigent and has no means of support may be filed by the minor declared emancipated, by the minor's conservator, or by the district attorney of the county in which the minor resides. The petition shall be filed in the county in which the minor or the conservator resides.

(b) The minor may be considered indigent if the minor's only source of income is from public assistance benefits. The court shall consider the impact of the rescission of the declaration of emancipation on the minor and shall find the rescission of the declaration of emancipation will not be contrary to the best interest of the minor before granting the order to rescind.

### § 7132. Filing of petitions to rescind declarations

(a) A petition to rescind a declaration of emancipation on the ground that the minor is indigent and has no means of support may be filed by the minor declared emancipated, by the minor's conservator, or by the district attorney of the county in which the minor resides. The petition shall be filed in the county in which the minor or the conservator resides.

(b) The minor may be considered indigent if the minor's only source of income is from public assistance benefits. The court shall consider the impact of the rescission of the declaration of emancipation on the minor and shall find the rescission of the declaration of emancipation will not be contrary to the best interest of the minor before granting the order to rescind.

### § 7133. Notice of petition to void or rescind declaration

(a) Before a petition under this article is heard, notice the court determines is reasonable shall be given to the minor's parents or guardian, or proof shall be made to the court that their addresses are unknown or that for other reasons the notice cannot be given.

(b) The notice to parents shall state that if the declaration of emancipation is voided or rescinded, the parents may be liable to provide support and medical insurance coverage for the child pursuant to Chapter 2 (commencing with Section 4000) of Part 2 of Division 9 of this code and Sections 11350, 11350.1, 11475.1, and 11490 of the Welfare and Institutions Code.

(c) No liability accrues to a parent or guardian not given actual notice, as a result of voiding or rescinding the declaration of emancipation, until that parent or guardian is given actual notice.

### § 7135. Effect upon contractual and property obligations

Voiding or rescission of the declaration of emancipation does not alter any contractual obligation or right or any property right or interest that arose during the period that the declaration was in effect.

### § 7140. Entry of identifying information into department of motor vehicles records systems; statement of emancipation upon identification card

On application of a minor declared emancipated under this chapter, the Department of Motor Vehicles shall enter identifying information in its law enforcement computer network, and the fact of emancipation shall be stated on the department's identification card issued to the emancipated minor.

### § 7141. Reliance on representation of emancipation;  effect

A person who, in good faith, has examined a minor's identification card and relies on a minor's representation that the minor is emancipated, has the same rights and obligations as if the minor were in fact emancipated at the time of the representation.

### § 7142. Liability of public entities or employees
No public entity or employee is liable for any loss or injury resulting directly or indirectly from false or inaccurate information contained in the Department of Motor Vehicles records system or identification cards as provided in this part.

### § 7143. Notification of motor vehicles department upon voiding or rescission of declaration of emancipation;  invalidation of identification cards
If a declaration of emancipation is voided or rescinded, notice shall be sent immediately to the Department of Motor Vehicles which shall remove the information relating to emancipation in its law enforcement computer network. Any identification card issued stating emancipation shall be invalidated.

## F. Rights of parents

# CALIFORNIA FAMILY CODE (West)
# DIVISION 12. PARENT AND CHILD RELATIONSHIP
# PART 1. RIGHTS OF PARENTS

### § 7500. Services and earnings of child
(a) The mother of an unemancipated minor child, and the father, if presumed to be the father under Section 7611, are equally entitled to the services and earnings of the child.

(b) If one parent is dead, is unable or refuses to take custody, or has abandoned the child, the other parent is entitled to the services and earnings of the child.

### § 7501. Residence of children; determination by parents; restrictions
A parent entitled to the custody of a child has a right to change the residence of the child, subject to the power of the court to restrain a removal that would prejudice the rights or welfare of the child.

### § 7502. Property of child; control
The parent, as such, has no control over the property of the child.

### § 7503. Payment of earnings to minor
The employer of a minor shall pay the earnings of the minor to the minor until the parent or guardian entitled to the earnings gives the employer notice that the parent or guardian claims the earnings.

### § 7504. Relinquishment of parental rights; abandonment
The parent, whether solvent or insolvent, may relinquish to the child the right of controlling the child and receiving the child's earnings. Abandonment by the parent is presumptive evidence of that relinquishment.

### § 7505. Parental authority; termination
The authority of a parent ceases on any of the following:
(a) The appointment, by a court, of a guardian of the person of the child.
(b) The marriage of the child.
(c) The child attaining the age of majority.

### § 7506. Support of adult child; compensation
Where a child, after attaining the age of majority, continues to serve and

to be supported by the parent, neither party is entitled to compensation, in the absence of an agreement for the compensation.

## § 7507. Abuse of parental authority;  remedy

The abuse of parental authority is the subject of judicial cognizance in a civil action brought by the child, or by the child's relative within the third degree, or by the supervisors of the county where the child resides;  and when the abuse is established, the child may be freed from the dominion of the parent, and the duty of support and education enforced.